SAFARI GUIDE

A COMPREHENSIVE GUIDE TO PLANNING YOUR HUNTING SAFARI

BY

RICHARD A. CONRAD

Safari Press Inc.

Conrad, Richard A.

First edition

Safari Press Inc.

2001, Long Beach, California

ISBN 1-57157-208-2

Library of Congress Catalog Card Number: 99-69160

10 9 8 7 6 5 4 3 2

Readers wishing to receive the Safari Press catalog, featuring many fine books on big-game hunting, wingshooting, and sporting firearms, should write to Safari Press Inc., P.O. Box 3095, Long Beach, CA 90803, USA. Tel: (714) 894-9080 or visit our Web site at www.safaripress.com.

DEDICATION

To the memory of Jim Corbett, author of *Man-eaters of Kumaon*. Of all hunting literature, none better exemplifies the attributes of a hunter and sportsman than the self-portrait revealed in Corbett's work. He embodied every important quality I admire, including intelligence, courage, compassion for both man and beast, respect and affection for the animals he hunted, remarkable skills as a naturalist and hunter, and skill with his weapons. He is a model of conduct to which all modern hunters should aspire, and to whom I owe a great debt of gratitude for helping me find my way as a hunter.

TABLE OF CONTENTS

ACKNOWLEDGMENTS

I consider myself lucky to have acquired the experience and understanding that made writing this book possible. As the son of a Romanian immigrant who grew up in a large European city, the prospect of my owning guns and participating in America's bounty of hunting and fishing were slim. Fortunately, my father met my mother while they were both in college. Her parents were Kansas farmers. My maternal grandfather's interest in guns and shooting ultimately played a significant role in introducing my father to these subjects, which became lifelong interests for him. My first "gun" was carved out of wood by my granddad when I was about four years old while my father was away in Europe, this time as a soldier in the U.S. Army.

Since my father had little experience with guns or hunting, he and I helped each other over the years to learn about these things. From my first BB gun, which I could use only under Dad's supervision, to more sophisticated firearms later, he was always supportive of my interests. He helped me pursue shooting, hunting, and fishing sports, and we shared many experiences that I shall never forget and will always value.

As a farm girl, my mother had a seemingly inexhaustible knowledge of animals, both wild and domestic. She introduced me to such diverse activities as angling for catfish with a cane pole and worm to identifying various animals on our family's outings. When I was old enough that my parents thought I could hunt on my own, Mom offered assistance far beyond the call of maternal duty. My companions and I will never forget her almost unbelievable generosity, which included driving long distances in the family station wagon—loaded with decoys and guns as well as sleepy teenage boys—at 4 A.M. just to take us to our duck-hunting grounds. She returned hours later to bring us home. In every undertaking of my life, including the writing of this book, she has always given me her unwavering support.

Bill Stacy, my old friend and colleague, has for almost thirty years provided me with his enthusiastic and unwavering support, as well as shared hunting and equestrian experiences with me, which are as memorable as any I have undertaken. Bill loaned me the money to buy my first chronograph that led to my first published work—a magazine article written initially on a yellow legal pad on an Alaskan ferry while returning from a visit one night with Bill. I want to formally thank him now for all his support over the years.

Joe Arico, an extraordinary businessman, my longtime friend, and a man of remarkable generosity, provided timely personal and financial support that made it possible for me to write this book. Without his assistance the book would have certainly taken much longer to produce, and might not have been written at all.

My brother, Steve Conrad, by his uncommon generosity and patience, gave me a refuge during a difficult period of my life so that I had a place to write the book in relative comfort.

Finally, I want to acknowledge my debt to all those men and women with whom I have shared a tale, a campfire, an outdoor experience, or a friendship that contributed to my store of knowledge and my understanding of guns and animals—my enduring interest that has made me a hunter for life.

PREFACE: COMING HOME TO AFRICA

My first sight of Africa was a rosy-pink dawn, seen through a small window of a Boeing 747 flown by Lufthansa from around thirty thousand feet as we flew over East Africa. I'd had trouble sleeping on the flight from Frankfurt and was exhausted. I doubt I'd had three hours' sleep in the last three days, and I was far past the age when I could carry on as usual without adequate sleep. I had dozed off for a few minutes and awoke to see the east African sky blushing out the left side of the aircraft. It's a moment I'll never forget, the beginning of an adventure I'd anticipated for over forty years. Though some will find it hard to believe, it was at that point that I began planning my *next* trip to Africa, even before I had taken one breath of Southern Hemisphere air!

As I already mentioned, this was my first trip to Africa. Why then "coming home"? I have used that term to help the reader understand the profound sense of belonging, of love for a place, of familiarity, which I felt at that time and for many weeks afterward. It is no exaggeration to say that for the few weeks I spent in Africa I felt more "at home" than I generally did in my own country. A lifetime of reading about Africa, imagining what it would be like to go there, had provided me with a background for experiencing it. My experience is similar to someone returning to the town where he grew up after an absence of many years. Though my visit to Africa was for only a short time, in many ways my heart is still there.

I suspect not many people will understand my feelings for Africa. Let me try to help you understand my perspective. My professional associates at home—even my family, with few exceptions—shared today's fashionable antihunting attitudes, so it was impossible to share my deep commitment to the sport or my experiences with them in a satisfying or meaningful way. But for the next several weeks on my first trip to Africa, I would be in the company of hunters and their families and friends. This alone made it a unique experience. The focus of most of our conversations was on animals, guns, African history, and hunting—the sort of things that frequently occupy my mind in leisure moments. I had many questions about the flora and fauna, the countries' history and future, and about the native people—black and white—and received answers to many of my questions either from my hosts or my own observations.

Ever since I was a child, I have sought the solitude of the outdoors and a relationship with wildlife as my principal way of relating to my environment. While individual people have been important to me, I have always preferred the sight of a herd of deer, for example, to a herd of people. As I have got older, my tendency to withdraw from the hordes of encroaching humans has become only stronger. I now understand this is a fundamental biological fact about old males of most mammalian species. That's pretty good company in my book. We curmudgeons have our own values and priorities, solitude among them.

Some people probably get a wonderful feeling of belonging and contentment when standing, say, in Central Park in New York City during a rock concert. For those who haven't experienced this park, it stands in stark contrast to the surrounding concrete and asphalt of the city. The park looks like a jungle, and I have spent many pleasant hours there while attending concerts and otherwise. But the place never felt like I was at home. I have always preferred to view a sea of water or forest or plain rather than a sea of people.

For a while I even worked in the concrete canyons of Wall Street, but I can't recall ever longing to be part of the herds of people choking the streets at lunchtime or at the beginning and ending of each workday.

I get a similar feeling of being in my element that a committed city dweller does in crowded Central Park, I suspect, when I'm looking out over uninhabited thornbush country or Alaska tundra, watching a herd of caribou or impala doing what they have done for tens of thousands of years. I have always felt I belonged in such a setting in a way I rarely felt in more civilized surroundings. And I miss the sights and sounds of Africa practically every day of my life.

The casual hunter may have difficulty relating to such feelings, but one who did not was John Hunter, who wrote that Africa is "in all but my birth my native land." At the end of his book *Hunter*, he described his experience after returning from a rather disappointing trip home to Scotland. The feelings he expressed on his return were similar to what I experienced every evening I spent in Africa, watching the sun set, sipping on a sundowner of one sort or another. He and his wife, Hilda, had just returned to their home outside Nairobi, Kenya, after an absence of several months. He described the scene this way: "The sky was thick with stars and the scent of the night-blooming flowers was heavy in the air. Hilda and I raised our glasses and drank a toast to Africa. We had come home."

INTRODUCTION

This is a book about hunting today in Africa. While an African safari has long been thought of, and once was, an activity available only to the wealthy sportsman, the situation today is different. It is now possible for an American citizen of average means to go on an African safari, which for many will be the most unforgettable experience of their lives. For those who have been fortunate enough to make many such trips in their lives, I say "welcome." But this book is not written primarily for you. I am writing the book for people like me, who work for a living and who have often dreamed of such a trip but have believed it could never be a reality for them. After reading this book, I hope you will have changed your mind.

My motivation for writing *Safari Guide* (aside from the possibility of great wealth and a place in literary history) was that I needed such a reference when planning my own safaris, but none was available. Since necessity is the mother of invention, I decided to write a reference book myself. Even if too late to help me in planning my first safari, I hope this book will benefit others in planning theirs.

Since ominous predictions have been made throughout the nineteenth and twentieth centuries about the declining numbers of African game animals, it will come as a surprise to many that legal sport hunting is still allowed in Africa. The reality is that sport hunting is not only *allowed* in many countries, but also *necessary* if many game animals are to survive in southern Africa.

Though it will probably surprise many who get their news about such matters from the mass media, some game species are actually increasing in Africa today. Furthermore, there are today too many of certain animals relative to the habitat available, elephants being the most obvious.

Although this book is ostensibly about hunting in Africa, in reality it is about much more. It reflects and represents half a century of study, of learning and honing skills, of dreaming, of true longing, and of the considerable effort and sacrifices to finally make it happen. It reflects many aspects of my own personality and life, for better or worse. It is probably accurate to say that in my mind I had a love affair with Africa and African hunting since early adolescence, which was finally consummated in 1991 when I was in my fifties.

There is much for the heart and mind for a hunter traveling to Africa. Although I thought of my travel primarily as a hunting trip, and it certainly was a successful one by my standards, in the end I was surprised that the hunting was not the most memorable aspect. The high points of the adventure turned out not to involve charging Big Five animals or even taking grand trophies. The moments that return most often to my mind and that, I believe, reflect the deeper significance of the experience, involved not hunting per se but the Africans I met and the animals and scenery I saw—a flock of small birds, three warthogs drinking from a water trough, four frightened impala trying to get a drink from a drying riverbed, a sunset, a mouse.

By the beginning of the twentieth century the effects of several wars, the establishment of agriculture and animal husbandry by European settlers, and the acquisition of firearms by native populations had resulted, directly or indirectly, in the extinction of a few species of game and a dramatic reduction in the numbers of virtually all the rest. Farmers killed antelope for meat and used the hides for export. They also killed large predators to protect their stock, in much the same way, and for the same reasons, that buffalo, elk, grizzly bear, coyote, wolves, and other game species and predators were killed in North America.* Thus, prior to the birth of the safari industry, large numbers of the wildlife originally present in southern Africa when Europeans arrived had already been killed off.

*See Brander, *Hunting and Shooting.*

The history of safari hunting in Africa as it's known today is relatively short, coinciding closely with the twentieth century. It seems ironic that widespread safari sport hunting should commence at a time when game populations were the lowest ever. That it did appears to have been the result of several factors, including improvements in transportation and weapons, and continued immigration of sportsmen from Europe. The classic safari, with tented camps on East African plains, white hunters, fez-topped waiters, and all the amenities of high living, probably came into its own shortly after the turn of the century. It seems likely that the building of the railway line from Mombasa, Kenya, to the interior about the beginning of the century, combined with the introduction of the motorcar around 1910, greatly increased the availability of African hunting. These transportation developments would have very serious consequences for the wildlife of Africa and the pursuit of them for sport.

Peter Hathaway Capstick, the consummate scholar on the history of African hunting, suggested the first recorded safari might have taken place as early as 1837. At that time, William Cornwallis Harris made a long hunting trip for sporting purposes, rather than simply for exploration or commercial venture, into southern Africa. Capstick reported that Harris's book describing the hunt was the first written about African sport hunting. Other important and inspirational works for hunters all over the world were books by Gordon Cumming and F. C. Selous. One of the distinguishing characteristics of all three works was that they described hunting undertaken for sport, rather than as incidental to exploration.

Capstick suggests that the 1909 safari by President Theodore Roosevelt and his son Kermit was probably the most influential in getting others interested in African hunting. The safari was described by Roosevelt in his book *African Game Trails*, first published in 1910.

Roosevelt's safari, undertaken in part to acquire animals for the Smithsonian Museum, required five hundred porters to carry his kit and the materials necessary to preserve and carry the trophies he and Kermit acquired. Capstick speculated that at the time there may have been only one safari company in Africa. Roosevelt used the new .30-06 Springfield on this safari, certainly among the first to do so. Today it is perhaps the most popular small bore in use in Africa, as it has been in the United States for most of the century.

But technical developments were soon to make "foot" safaris like Roosevelt's historical curiosities, having a significant effect on Africa in general and safari hunting in particular. These developments were the introduction of the motorcar, the airplane, and modern sporting rifles, all of which occurred in the late nineteenth and early twentieth centuries.

In 1920 there were reportedly just over ten thousand cars imported into South Africa, but by 1930 the number was over twenty-one thousand. By 1926 a motorcar could travel from Capetown, South Africa, to Nairobi, Kenya, on the Great Northern Trunk Road, a distance of some four thousand miles. As early as 1930 it was possible for one authoritative source to report that "two English ladies" drove a car from Capetown to Cairo, a distance of some eight thousand miles passing through several countries, in a remarkably short time. The same source reported that a "light motor car" beat the train from Elizabethville in the Congo to Johannesburg in northern South Africa, a trip of eighteen hundred miles. About the same time another chap driving "a light, low-priced car" accomplished a tour of the entire Union of South Africa, some twenty-nine hundred miles, at an average speed (have mercy!) of twenty-one miles per hour.

For motor travel information one could turn to the Royal East African Automobile Association (REAAA), headquartered in Nairobi. By the end of 1935 there were reckoned to be over eleven thousand motorcars in use in the East African countries of Uganda, Kenya, and Tanganyika (today Tanzania).

In contrast, consider that in 1871 it took F. C. Selous, the famous ivory hunter and author, two months to go from Port Elizabeth, on the southern coast of South Africa, to the "diamond fields," which I believe were at Kimberley in South Africa. Clearly, it was a new era for travel in Africa.

Another significant development was that commercial aviation was soon well established in southern Africa. In 1927 the Aero Club of East Africa, affiliated with a similar organization in Britain, was established, headquartered in Nairobi. By 1935 it had 222 members, including thirty-nine qualified pilots. By 1929 an air taxi service, Wilson Airways, was operating out of Nairobi. In 1935 the company flew nearly a half-million miles carrying nearly three thousand passengers. In that same year, the first big-game expedition by air was organized in Cape Town. By 1937 airmail service was available between sub-Saharan Africa and the rest of the world, and there were plans for passenger flights from Europe to Africa.

As a result of these developments in transportation, the long, difficult, and expensive safaris by ox-pulled wagons or on foot using porters quickly became a thing of the past as aircraft, Land Rovers, and lorries (trucks) replaced them. This development made it easier to make a safari, and it appears more people did.

Another interesting, and probably related, development at about the same time was the introduction of breechloading, smokeless powder rifles, which were more efficient and manageable than the ponderous shoulder cannons used by early hunters. Some of the best known and most widely used of the classic calibers for large African and Indian game were introduced during this period. Examples are the .404 Jeffery and .318 Westley Richards (1910), the .416 Rigby, the .333 Rimless Nitro Express (1911), and the justly famous .375 Holland & Holland Magnum (1912). These were not necessarily the first of their types, but the proliferation of these medium calibers, which were certainly easier to carry and shoot than those generally available before, must have encouraged some to try their hand at big-game hunting.

Perhaps of even greater importance for the future of African hunting was the widespread adoption for sporting purposes of the ultrasmall-bore military rifles developed around the turn of the century, including the .303 British, the 6.5mm Mannlicher, and the .30-06 Springfield. These rifles could be handled adequately by practically anyone and were found to be effective on game from dik-dik to elephant.

People who probably could not realistically shoot the monstrous muzzleloading rifles employed by early explorers could go afield with one of these small-caliber rifles with comparative ease. The little 6.5mm Mannlicher (sometimes called the .256, which is its bore diameter) in various forms was popular even among experienced hunters. It worked just fine, they reported, on everything, including elephant. Today it is considered the right weapon for a recoil-sensitive boy or woman.

Both world wars interrupted the growing safari industry, but it rebounded after each one, each time during an era of increasing technological sophistication in weapons and means of transportation. Since World War II there have been important developments all over Africa that have affected the continent's people, wildlife, and sport hunting. Particularly important was the independence of certain African countries after the exit of colonial powers, still keenly felt almost everywhere in Africa today.

There is today concern about preserving Africa's wildlife. But the concern is by no means new. Establishing preserves to prevent overhunting has been practiced in South Africa since at least 1677. Laws and preserves to protect wildlife increased under British rule after 1806, when they became the dominant colonial power in southern Africa. Game laws to protect hunted species have existed in Africa for three hundred years. Licenses to hunt have been used to control harvests and provide revenue for virtually all of the twentieth century.

Nonhunters seem to believe that classifying an animal as game and establishing a hunting season for it is somehow like sentencing it to death. But just the opposite is true. Classifying an animal as game, establishing closed seasons and bag limits, and charging for hunting licenses are ways governments protect species in danger of being overhunted. Regular closed seasons for hunted species have been the rule in many parts of southern Africa for at least two hundred fifty years.

When governments are not concerned with preserving viable populations of animals, or when a species is too destructive of the life and property of local natives, governments have typically classed the offenders as "vermin" and encouraged their elimination. These measures have included placing bounties on them and hiring professional cropping personnel to kill animals by the tens of thousands. This classification as vermin is the opposite of "game" animal. At various times, much African big game has been considered vermin, including buffalo, elephant, and rhino. Many thousands of the latter along with other nondangerous game were killed so areas could be cleared of tsetse flies to encourage human population expansion in East Africa.

There is no doubt that the sheer numbers of most game animals in Africa at the end of the twentieth century are reduced from those at its beginning. But it is also clear from the historical record that this decline had nothing to do with sport hunting. The most dramatic reduction occurred during the nineteenth century before sport hunting had even become established in Africa.

Conflicts with increasing human populations, and in some cases commercial hunting for money, rather than regulated sport hunting, are the reasons game numbers have been brought down to the levels we see today. Commercial, though illegal, hunting had even threatened the complete extermination of the black rhino long before the current poaching epidemic began. Extermination of rhino, along with many other species—undertaken so areas could be made safe for native population expansion—resulted in their being largely absent from southern Africa even early in the twentieth century. By 1937 the animal was considered scarce south of the Zambezi River, which forms much of the northern border of Zimbabwe.

Even during the nineteenth century, rhino were killed to supply Asian demand for their horns, which supposedly contained medicinal and aphrodisiac properties. During the twentieth century this practice has continued, though the poachers now carried automatic weapons instead of muzzleloaders. In spite of claims by postcolonial governments to be protecting the rhino, many government officials have been found to be cooperating with poachers. No one with any idea of what sport hunting is about would consider a band of thugs armed with machine guns shooting rhino for their horn to be sport hunters.

When the book is finally written on the decline of African wildlife, it is certain to show that a combination of killing off wildlife in order to clear land for farming or human habitation along with commercial hunting has been the primary cause for the decline. Sport hunting is likely to emerge as one of the few forces that tended to preserve wildlife rather than to eliminate it.

There are many books about Africa. The continent has long been a source of fascination to the adventurous, and its many facets have been examined in a variety of ways. To those in the hunting community, Africa has been the promised land for over one hundred years. This is because it offers a greatest variety of game birds and animals than any other place—where dangerous animals have not been entirely killed off to protect encroaching civilization—and because of the relatively primitive state of development of virtually all southern African countries. Even today, travel there provides a glimpse into history and a window on the evolution and commingling of cultures.

For these reasons, and no doubt others, hunters and other adventurous people have treasured accounts of the exploits of early Europeans who lived, explored, and hunted in Africa. The names of these hunters are familiar to all serious students of African hunting. They include Baker, Selous, Finaughty, "Karamojo" Bell, Blixen, Hunter, Burger, and Capstick. I like to think this book bears at least a family resemblance to those written by these hunters, but not because my own experiences approach either the extent or historical significance of theirs. Rather, I like to think that I share with them a love for the animals and people of Africa. This book will differ from other first-person accounts by African hunters in a significant way, for I am writing from the perspective of a modern-day, average Joe hunter.

Early twentieth-century hunters lived in a time when few could seriously imagine that the African animals they saw in such great herds could be in danger of extinction. Certainly few foresaw the devastation of game the combination of improvements in firearms and uncontrolled shooting and population expansion would cause.

During roughly the last fifty years of the nineteenth century and the first half of the twentieth, hunting was considered natural to most Americans and the upper classes in Europe. It was generally considered a noble and laudable activity whose moral standing was not seriously questioned. Acceptance—even glorification—of hunting has been a characteristic of civilized man for thousands of years.*

Unhappily, both the abundance of game animals and attitudes toward hunters changed dramatically during the late twentieth century. Factors that contributed to this attitude were the decreasing numbers of the white and black rhinoceros and, in some regions, the African elephant. Widespread ignorance and misunderstanding of the modern, regulated sport hunter's role in

*See José Ortega y Gasset, *Meditations on Hunting*, p. 7

and contribution to the preservation of African wildlife have led many to condemn hunting and hunters. In most cases, this attribution of blame is both misplaced and dangerous, since it obscures the real threats to African wildlife.

Political events, including the enormous effects of independence from colonial powers, have increased the pressures on habitat and wildlife. These pressures, in combination with weapons developed during the great world wars and now used by poachers, threaten the very existence of some of the larger African animals. While there are many hopeful signs that extinction can be avoided for most species, it seems certain that the huge herds of free-roaming antelope, elephant, and buffalo, and the lions and other predators that depend on them for food could someday be gone forever, at least outside of preserves.

There is a moral dimension to hunting today that formerly would have been the concern of relatively few. Now every hunter must consider himself or herself an important agent in the conservation of wildlife and its habitat and an example to the nonhunting majority. This includes our conduct in the field as well as support of organizations that are focused on wildlife conservation. We can be sure our actions will be carefully watched, and the judgment of the nonhunting public will almost certainly determine, rightly or wrongly, if our sport survives at all through the twenty-first century and beyond.

Having said this, let me emphasize that this book is not intended to be a treatise on either conservation or the morality of sport hunting. Rather, I will attempt to provide not only entertainment but also a perspective on African hunting, some of which is highly personal. In the course of doing so, I hope to also provide basic information that every hunter needs to intelligently plan a hunt in modern-day southern Africa.

PART I
SAFARI BASICS

AN OVERVIEW

Planning a hunting safari to Africa is not fundamentally different from planning a hunt for elk or antelope in the United States. There are some differences, of course, in the game to be hunted, particularly the range in size and number of game animals available on a single hunt. In North America one typically hunts for one species, or a "mixed bag" of two or three animals. In Africa one can expect to hunt for a dozen animals on a single trip, and the number could easily be twice that many.

The scale of an African safari—whether measured by cost, time, distance traveled, number of people working for you, or the size of the bag expected—can far exceed an annual junket for North American game. Fortunately, though, the rewards of such a trip will likely be greater. Going to Africa requires traveling halfway around the world to a strange country and hunting exotic game, and most who have done it believe the rewards are worth the effort.

Another important difference is the need for international air travel with firearms, which is similar to travel within the USA with more restrictions and even occasional roadblocks. Unforeseen problems that arise when transporting firearms across international borders can spoil the entire experience, so it's necessary to know the procedures before you arrive at the airport. But the process of preparation won't be totally unfamiliar to anyone who has traveled internationally by air or has traveled interstate on a hunting trip. Many issues are the same. The ones that are different are explained later in the book.

One surprising fact I discovered when booking my own safaris was how difficult it was to determine what hunts were being offered. Since I was new at it, I started from scratch looking in the "Where to Go" sections of outdoor magazines and following leads found in articles about Africa in the same publications. That method is not very satisfactory, as one discovers only the tiniest tip of the iceberg. I don't know how many major safari booking agents there are in the United States, but one well-placed industry observer advised me there may be fewer than fifty officially in the business full time, and perhaps as many as three hundred if one includes those who do it part time. Each of those agents may represent from two to a dozen safari companies who in turn may each employ one or more professional hunters. Based on these figures, I'm sure there are hundreds of African hunts offered each year by agents, outfitters, and individual Professional Hunters (PHs). The number could be several thousand.

When planning my first safari in 1991, I wrote to the Professional Hunters Association of South Africa. I received a letter from them saying that they had over five hundred members. The association included my name in a periodical they publish, and some of their members contacted me.

By these various means I eventually developed a considerable amount of information that was at once both informative and overwhelming. I eventually made a big spreadsheet listing the most interesting companies and hunts offered, and the animals and fees they advertised. From that list I eventually selected one company. In appendix G, titled "Useful Contacts," I have included information on agents that can help the first-time safari hunter get started. All agents listed are highly reputable and have been in business for more than a decade.

The following are the basic issues one must confront when planning an African safari. These might be called the Big Five of safari planning.

1. Selecting a hunt location and game to be hunted
2. Selecting a safari company
3. Making travel arrangements, including health issues, passports, visas, and other documentation
4. Preparing gear and preparing oneself through physical conditioning
5. Making arrangements for any trophies taken, including shipment to your home country, and taxidermy

In the following chapters I will address these key issues in detail, but perhaps first getting some of the basic concepts and terminology straight will help the reader follow the discussion.

There are at least four clearly distinguishable levels of administration involved in arranging a typical safari: the client or hunter, the professional hunter, the safari company, and the booking agent. Below I give a brief description of the role of each one, except for that of the hunter since he or she is the subject of the rest of this book.

PROFESSIONAL HUNTERS

In the past, professional hunters, or PHs, as they are generally known today, were called white hunters, probably to distinguish them from the black hunters and trackers in their area of operation. Today, complicating the situation, I understand there are some black "white" hunters in southern Africa and even some female PHs. Whatever their racial or gender characteristics, all must pass a variety of practical and written tests to be licensed in a particular country, which qualifies them as professional hunters. Some are licensed in several countries. It is important that any outfit you book with provides professional hunters licensed in the country and for the game you plan to hunt.

J. A. Hunter, an experienced white hunter, characterized his role in his book *Hunter* as the person in charge of all the small "details which go toward making the client feel that he is getting his money's worth and having a good time." The details included providing adequate food and water for all hands, overseeing trophy selection and preparation, driving the safari vehicle, finding game, and "understanding something of photography, know[ing] half a dozen card games, and never, under any circumstances, [losing] his temper" (pages 117–119).

The PH is the hunter's guide, and a lot more. He is the person who directs hunting activities on the ground and may oversee camp services and activities, depending on how duties are distributed within a particular safari company. A good PH is an excellent field naturalist who can answer many of the client's questions about the local flora and fauna and the native people. He must have considerable patience and tact to deal with clients, and the best seem to have an exceptionally well-developed sense of humor. All of those whom I have met speak one or more of the local native languages.

Your PH will be responsible for selecting the animals you shoot and should be an excellent judge of trophy quality and know how to prepare them for shipment or mounting in the field, an activity usually called "field preparation" of trophies. He must know how to keep you out of unnecessarily dangerous situations, including how to help you avoid getting bitten by a snake, and knowing what to do about it if you do.

It will fall to him to troubleshoot any problems with vehicles or supplies in the field and to deal with any authorities you encounter on your travels. In a sense, the PH has almost as much to do with your safety and enjoyment as the pilot of the jet that brings you to Africa. Even if you don't hunt dangerous game, the PH still has to help you avoid being injured by these animals, and with luck, he will keep you from playing with the local cobras and mambas.

When you encounter dangerous game, in all likelihood your life will, quite literally, be in the hands of the PH and his staff. He will probably be the only one there who can stop a charge if you don't. Conversely, it sometimes happens that a client will shoot an animal to save the PH's hide after the PH has stepped in front of the charging buffalo to save the client's life. There is a degree of mutual dependence between the PH and client, particularly when hunting dangerous game.

In short, the selection of your PH is central to the enjoyment and success of your safari.

As in any profession, the skills, experience, and personal characteristics such as honesty and integrity will vary among individual PHs. It is important for the hunter to make some assessment of these characteristics prior to booking a hunt. That can be done by corresponding with the individual, talking to references, or even meeting the person at one of the annual conventions held for that purpose by organizations like the Safari Club International.

Some of us are easier to please than others. If you have particular requirements you'd like to have in a PH, ask those who know the PH and the PH himself if he can fulfill the requirements. In my experience, PHs are quite accommodating to clients' tastes and wishes. But it might be nice to know, before you commit to a particular hunt, whether you have a fundamental disagreement on some basic issue like smoking, use of alcohol, hunting methods, or firing finishing shots at your elephant (whether they appear to you to be needed or not).

Usually the PH has some important assistants who may prove to be crucial to the success of and satisfaction with your hunt. Such assistants include trackers, skinners, camp cooks, and various other specialists. Their job title pretty well describes what their role is. If you are fortunate, your PH may become a lifelong friend as a result of your experiences together on safari.

MIDDLEMEN: AGENTS AND SAFARI COMPANIES

Once they realize all the details that must be addressed in arranging a safari, many people will simply throw up their hands and place the whole matter in the care of an established safari booking agent. That is not a bad way to go. An experienced agent will know what questions need to be asked better than an inexperienced client. An agent will ask the client questions about what he wants to hunt, how much time and money he has to spend, what his physical condition is, and similar matters. Giving *honest* answers to those questions will go a long way toward arranging a truly satisfying hunt.

Agents work with clients as middlemen, booking hunts with PHs directly or with outfitters or safari companies who employ them. Outfitters, which may be called "safari companies" (I tend to use the terms interchangeably) may also book hunts directly with clients. Safari companies may employ several professional hunters and related staff, or they may be owned and run by one or more professional hunters.

These companies handle many of the administrative details involved in hunting in African countries.

Agents will book plane reservations, day rooms, and side trips if needed, while the safari company typically arranges for any necessary permits for firearms, and will act as a facilitator between the client and customs officials once they arrive at their Africa destination. Basically, the agent gets you to where you are to hunt and makes necessary arrangements with the safari company. Once the client arrives at the hunt location, his safari becomes the responsibility of the safari company.

Like any other travel agent, those that book safaris will have different personalities, skills, and experience. Some I have dealt with are personable and accommodating, others less so. I noted, for example, a distinct deterioration in the attitude of one agent I used when I told him I intended to book my own air travel. Another simply gave me the name of a travel agent he believed competent and invited me to have at it. Agents get a cut of some travel arrangements as well as the cost of the safari daily fees, and may not appreciate your denying them this piece of the action. On the other hand, I recently saw an offer by one agent to arrange air travel at what appeared to be a relatively low rate to anyone, regardless of whether someone booked a hunt with him.

Since I tend to be a do-it-yourself kind of guy, I wanted to provide enough information in this book so that people of similar bent could do much of the planning themselves. It's possible to do much of the research and planning for a hunt yourself while leaving some of the details, such as travel arrangements, to a qualified agent. Because circumstances within a particular country can change rapidly, it is a good idea to have at least a reliable contact in your destination country who is up-to-date on changes in firearms laws or procedures. Political unrest and similar factors can powerfully affect both the safety and satisfaction you get from your safari. If something goes awry on your trip, it's nice to have an agent to call to help sort things out.

Since this book is for the first-time African hunter, I believe it is safer for him to book a hunt through an experienced safari agent than to make all the arrangements on his own. On subsequent trips it might be appropriate to consider booking with a PH or safari company directly once you know the ropes of travel, preparation, and the various administrative details. I know people who have made a couple dozen safaris by booking everything themselves, never using an agent, and who have had completely satisfying trips.

With today's electronic media, including fax and the Internet, it is possible for a prospective hunter to contact companies or individual PHs directly, and with extraordinary speed by historical standards. In 1991, I exchanged letters with my African hunting contacts and found it typically took two weeks for a letter to make the trip each way. Now, some ten years later, I can contact many agents and PHs virtually instantaneously by using the World Wide Web. This should make it easier to book a hunt, and to get just what you want from the trip.

My own experience may not be typical, but the agents I worked with encouraged me to make direct contact by fax or letter with the PH they were booking me with. I sent both fax and letter. I believe this, along with speaking with references provided by the PH or his agent, helped me to make good decisions about where and with whom to hunt. The correspondence also gave the PH or safari company an opportunity to advise me what might be suitable as gifts for the staff at the end of the hunt, or to request that I bring some small items of equipment such as batteries or duct tape they couldn't obtain locally.

THE COST

The simple question, "How much does an African safari cost today?" is actually quite complex and impossible to answer by quoting a single number without considerably more information. The reasons for this will, I hope, become clear as the reader progresses through this book and are described more fully in the chapter devoted to that subject.

The short answer is, "It all depends." It depends on the country you hunt in, the game you hunt, how long your safari lasts, what amenities you are willing to pay for, and even the fame of the professional hunter you employ. All these factors are variables, not constants, and the way you fill in the blanks may make a substantial difference in the cost.

To provide some idea of what it might cost you to take an African safari, I am going to provide information later in this book on a hypothetical fourteen-day "standard" hunt for plains game in each country, using some typical charges. It will soon become clear why this can be no more than an estimate, but it will give the reader some idea of the costs involved, and help in planning his own safari.

Safari companies typically break down their fees into two general categories: "daily rates" and "trophy fees." Daily rates, sometimes called "safari fees" cover the basics of life on safari. Trophy fees are charged only if certain animals are killed, or wounded and lost. Safari operators, whether they are companies or individual PHs, should stipulate clearly what is covered by these fees so there won't be any unpleasant surprises or embarrassing moments at the end of a hunt when tallying up the bill.

Daily rates typically include the following: services of a licensed professional hunter, trackers, skinners, field preparation of trophies, sleeping, bathing and eating facilities, food, beverages, and laundry service. They may also include pickup and return to the airport or other place where the client enters the country, and transportation of trophies to a taxidermist or agency capable of shipping them to the client's home country. They may include alcoholic beverages.

They almost certainly will not include hotels before and after the hunt.

As in any contractual arrangement, the services and materials to be provided by the safari company should be specific and in writing. The company may even have some specific recommendations or expectations regarding the client's obligations, which you need to know before agreeing to a set program. The physical condition of the client may well be a consideration for a particular hunt.

Other details need to also be in writing, such as travel time. Does time spent traveling to and from the airport count as time to which the daily fee applies? Some companies start the clock running when they pick you up at the airport. But I recently saw an advertisement from a well-known Zimbabwe safari company stating that daily fees would begin on the day *after* you arrive in camp and end on the last day you actually hunted. Such an arrangement could save you several hundred dollars.

In appendix A of this book I have provided a table showing some daily rates charged for hunting various game animals. If, after perusing this table, the reader is *not* confused, you need to read it again! The way in which these rates are computed is complex, and the reasons for differences far from obvious. Essentially, these rates vary by country and by the game hunted, and even among safari companies in the same country hunting the same game. But the rates may also vary with the length of the hunt and living arrangements. In some countries safari outfits simply charge more than others for the services covered by this fee, for whatever reason. I believe this variation reflects supply-and-demand conditions both for the place itself and for the game available there, as well as the general cost of doing business in that area.

A common practice, which may provide an opportunity to save some money, is for hunters to share a PH. Most safari companies have reduced rates when two or more hunters share one PH. All the daily rates shown in this book, unless otherwise noted, refer to the daily cost for a hunter with his own PH. This is known as a 1 x 1 arrangement. If two hunters share a PH, it is known as a 2 x 1 hunt, and the daily rate is lower per hunter.

On a 2 x 1 hunt each hunter may be able to take the same game, but sometimes they must decide which one will take a particular animal if it is allocated on a *per safari* basis, rather than *per hunter*. For example, a safari with two hunters with a 2 x 1 arrangement may be allocated one lion and one leopard, total, for the two of them. They must decide who gets which animal. This arrangement seems made-to-order if the two hunters agree beforehand on which animal each wants to take. It also seems like a logical arrangement for a husband and wife, or a man and his son, if both intend to hunt. The savings provided by the 2 x 1 over the 1 x 1 arrangement may well be enough to make a noticeable dent in your airfare, allow you to take more animals for the same total cost, or even to extend the duration of your safari.

Another option offered by most safari companies is bringing along a nonhunting "observer" at a reduced rate. The charge for this observer is usually much less than for hunters and appears to run about $150 per day just about everywhere. Compare that to daily rates of $350 to $1,000 or more, and you can see it is an inexpensive way to bring along a nonhunting spouse, or perhaps someone to shoot videos of your trip.

As you sift through the various hunts offered today you may discover what I call the "luxury paradox." Historically, African safaris were so costly of both time and money that only royalty and the wealthy could take them. This class of people are used to having servants, gourmet meals, and their various personal needs catered to by their staffs. If they had an itch, they could afford to pay someone to scratch it. To meet those needs, safaris employed a large number of skilled black Africans as cooks, camp staff, waiters, and so on. Safaris typically were mixed-bag affairs and often moved camp several times to hunt all the animals sought by clients.

Today the situation is different. It is common to spend the entire safari in one location hunting from a single camp. These are often permanent or semipermanent affairs that often feature refrigeration, warm showers, flush toilets, and cold beer on demand. In many areas, these permanent camps are buildings of brick and mortar, and may even include the PH's house or that of a rancher where the client is hunting. In my experience, the food is adequate or better, if not five-star, the beer cold, and the wine often excellent. Fez-clad servants are scarce, though. If that sort of thing is important to you, you might slip the tracker or camp boy a few bucks and see if he'll wear one of those red-fez caps and some white gloves, like Juma did in the film *Out of Africa*. Otherwise, I wouldn't expect it.

I suspect you'll find that the food served on a typical safari today, particularly the relatively low-cost plains-game hunts most people select, is more like going to grandma's house or eating at a friend's than dining at the Four Seasons. Some of my meals on safari in South Africa were at the Afrikaner equivalent of Burger King as we were on a long road trip between hunting areas, which was fine with me. At other times they were home-cooked by my PH's mother or his wife, and the food was excellent. At one ranch where I hunted, the woman of the house was a professional cook and prepared everything on special ovens filled with glowing coals. We served ourselves and it was wonderful. Though it was not supposed to be included in the price, my PH in South Africa brought along a case of excellent wine that we enjoyed throughout the trip.

The older "tented" camp is still available, but typically at a higher price than hunts featuring permanent facilities. Peter Capstick observed that many ranchers in southern Africa regard it as bizarre that people would rather sleep, even eat, in a tent rather than in his comfortable ranch house, which he spent many years building. Some companies compromise by using tents, but at a permanent campsite. It is still possible to have an old-fashioned safari using tents and moving about to locate particular game. But it is here that one encounters the luxury paradox I referred to earlier: It frequently costs more to live in a tent on safari than in a nice house! Perhaps a parallel more familiar to U.S. residents would be going on a picnic versus eating take-out in front of the TV. Each has its charm. Today you can pay your money and take your choice, since both alternatives are available.

My safari camp in Zimbabwe was a permanent facility with piped-in water, flush toilets, hot showers, and permanent cooking and eating areas. The PHs and trackers slept in traditional green canvas tents, which I believe were removed after hunting season ended. By contrast, in South Africa, I stayed in several facilities, including a strange little converted motel, ranchers' houses, a bunkhouse-type facility, and commercial rondavels in Kruger National Park. While I think it would be great fun to have a traditional mobile, tented safari, I enjoyed getting to know the people and lifestyles of the residents I stayed with and would not have missed that for anything. The experiences are some of my favorite memories of those hunts.

In some countries with a relatively primitive road system or widely separated hunting areas, chartered planes are required to get the hunter from the airport where they arrive in the country to the hunting camp, or sometimes to move between camps. This is never cheap.

As another example of country-specific cost factors, I suspect that Tanzanian outfitters are able to charge a premium just for the privilege of hunting in that country, only one of two in East Africa today where one may hunt a variety of game in relative safety, including some animals available nowhere else. (The other is Ethiopia. I decided to include data from that country, as it is the only other country where certain East African species like lesser kudu and mountain nyala can be hunted today, even though hunting there is typically more expensive than in other African countries covered here.) Similarly, providing the same level of comfort in camp may be easier in South Africa than in Botswana or Mozambique because of the transportation infrastructure and overall level of development.

Another reason daily rates may vary, even with the same safari company, is that the game hunted often lives in different parts of the country, and on land under different ownership. An animal hunted on a "concession" (government-controlled hunting area) may have a higher trophy fee than the same animal hunted on a private ranch. The trophies that are scarce relative to demand for them will frequently require payment of higher daily fees, sometimes considerably higher, and will usually require longer hunts. Both factors increase the overall cost of the hunt without necessarily including any commensurate increase in, say, the quality of food and wine served or the coldness of the beer. It is just another way of rationing a relatively scarce resource.

One of the more confusing aspects of figuring the cost of a hunt is the way they are packaged today by the safari companies. I use the term "packaging" to mean the combination of animals hunted and the basis for the charges.

There are hunts available for a single species in many areas, usually for one of the Big Five. You will find exclusive hunts for elephant, lion, buffalo, and rhino, though less commonly for leopard alone. Some exclusive hunts are for rare and geographically restricted antelope species like bongo, sable, giant eland, sitatunga, the common nyala (in southern Africa) and the mountain nyala (available only in Ethiopia). The hunts usually offer an opportunity to take other plains-game species. The hunts are clearly designed for hunters with specific goals, perhaps attempting to complete a collection of a particular type of animal, in the same way North American hunters might try to bag a "grand slam" of sheep. Or perhaps they are trying to collect an animal that eluded them on an earlier hunt.

But the bread and butter of most safaris is the common plains and bush game. It is a frequent practice today for companies to package hunts for one of the Big Five together with plains game. I have also seen hunts for sable or sitatunga and plains game. This way of packaging hunts has become so popular that I suspect you could find, or negotiate, virtually any combination of animals you wanted.

Depending on the particular package, prices for these hunts vary extensively. I will refer to hunts combining one of the Big Five with plains game as "combos." Typically, the cost of the hunt is figured on the traditional basis of daily fees times the number of hunting days plus trophy fees for animals actually taken. Often these hunts have minimum lengths, say fourteen days if you want a sable, eighteen if you want both sable and leopard, or something along those lines.

Another kind of hunt increasing in popularity today is the "packaged" hunt. The entire hunt is sold as a package, including the daily and trophy fees, in a single price rather than separately, as has been the custom in the past. The duration of the hunt is also fixed, though sometimes it can be extended. Recently, I saw a package that even included the cost of shipping the trophies to the hunter's home country. Now that is a complete package!

For these packaged hunts, a group of animals is enumerated that may be taken for the fixed total hunt price. Sometimes substitutions are allowed, depending on the terms of the package. Typically, you don't get "credit" for any animals included in the hunt package that you don't shoot, since the price of the package is fixed. I have looked at many such offerings and have found that usually the total of daily and trophy fees amount to something less than you'd pay if they weren't bundled that way.

There has been some speculation about the motivation of the safari companies offering such complete packaged hunts to find high-quality trophies for the clients that book them. The concern is that the company will have little motivation to seek outstanding trophies since their fee for the hunt is fixed regardless of whether a particular animal is shot or whether those taken are above average. The comments I have seen from hunters who have booked such hunts indicate that outstanding trophies are frequently taken on them.

Perhaps the best approach for someone planning a safari is to decide which animals you feel you *must* hunt to make your safari worth the price; then try combining the various daily rates and trophy fees offered by several different companies to see which offers the most value for you. Don't forget to include the miscellaneous fees imposed by some countries like concession fees, firearms licenses, transfer fees, various permits, conservation fees, special fees for vehicles and staff to put out leopard and lion baits, and similar charges that may or may not be included in the daily rate as quoted. Like home-loan fees, hunt fees can add considerably to the cost and often are not included in the quoted daily rate. Be sure to obtain a *total-cost* figure before you book a hunt to avoid surprises when the time comes to pay the bill.

When you have decided what animals you want, what special services you want included, and so on, you can then shop the whole package among companies offering hunts where the animals you want are available. For example, if you just have to shoot a lion and a sable with everything else of secondary importance, refer to the tables provided to see where the two animals can be hunted on the same trip.

Suppose you go through this exercise, and it appears an animal you want is not available where you want to hunt because there is no trophy or daily fee for that animal in the tables I provide in the appendices of this book. A word of caution: Just because an animal doesn't appear to be available from the tables I have provided, it still is wise to ask an outfit you are comfortable with what they can do to accommodate you. Many companies have arrangements in several countries and can meet special requests if they know about your interest well in advance.

Using the daily-rate and trophy-fee tables, you should be able to come up with a ballpark figure of what the hunt you want should cost you on average. Of course, you'll need to add any airfares and hotels, meals, and other incidental expenses to get a final number. If money is a concern, you might find a travel agent who can save you enough on airfare so you can add that second buffalo or a leopard to your shopping list. Agents often have arrangements with airlines and hotel chains that result in considerably reduced fares and room charges for their clients.

The situation with trophy fees is not as complicated as with daily rates. Trophy fees are charged according to the game taken, as each has a price on its head, though the fee will differ between countries, between outfitters, and even in different areas hunted by the same outfitter. I suspect that the variation reflects the industry-wide supply and demand for the animals in question, as well as their relative scarcity in the particular area you hunt. Sometimes the fees are determined, at least in part, by the government, at other times by private owners of the property where the animals live.

Some countries adhere to an old East African tradition of charging *two* fees for each animal. In this system, the hunter is charged a license fee that entitles him to hunt for the animal and is typically nonrefundable if he doesn't shoot one. But an additional charge, a trophy fee, is paid only if the animal is actually bagged, or wounded and lost. Botswana and Zambia appear to use this method, as I saw some hunts indicating both would be charged. Other countries dispense with the separate license fee altogether and quote only a trophy fee payable when the animal is actually shot.

Either way, it should always be possible to get a breakdown of what these fees are for animals you want to take. A safari company should provide a list of the animals it offers and the trophy fee for each one. Sometimes the fee depends on the quality of the trophy taken, such as the weight of an elephant's tusks or the spread of a buffalo's horns. One company, for example, charges a trophy fee of $5,000 for an elephant with tusks weighing fifty pounds, but about $20,000 for tusks over seventy pounds.

Sometimes it is possible to take more than one animal of a species on a hunt. For example, it may be possible to negotiate with the safari company to forgo taking certain animals in order to take two of another. In the area of Zimbabwe where I hunted, there was an overabundance of impala, and I could take as many as I wanted for the nominal fee of $75. In other places the trophy fee for impala is three times as high, and only one is allowed per hunter.

Kudu, on the other hand, were generally limited to one per hunter per trip where I was. Governments sometimes impose quotas on the numbers of a given game animal that can be taken, and a private rancher will want to maximize his return on his game resources, so both may play a role in determining what animals you can take on a particular hunt. Supply and demand will probably dictate whether the hunter can take more than one animal of a species with a particular outfitter. If such an arrangement interests the hunter, he should inquire.

In addition to daily and trophy fees, often there are incidental expenses—sometimes well hidden and which may be considerable—associated with a particular hunt. Perhaps the most expensive would be chartered airplane flights to and from the hunting camp. Travel to camp or between hunting areas is typically referred to as a "transfer" by African safari companies. The hunter should know when the transfers are required, what they will cost, and less expensive alternatives, if any, that are available. Sometimes transfers by road are provided at no additional charge but take longer, while a charter flight might cost $1,500 or more but gets you to camp far quicker.

Some countries charge airport taxes to any foreigner entering or leaving the country. Others levy special taxes or fees on hunting safaris for gun permits and licenses in addition to the daily and trophy fees. All such charges should be made clear to the hunter before he signs up for a particular hunt. If they aren't shown in a company's literature or on your written agreement, you should ask about them.

PAYING FOR THE SAFARI

The method of payment for a hunt should be clear to all parties and should be in writing. Differences in terminology can lead to confusion. For example, does "bank check" and "certified funds" mean the same thing in Zambia as it does in Wyoming? Money orders, considered secure means of payment within the USA, may not be accepted by the outfitter in a foreign country. Charge cards, while readily accepted in many countries in urban areas, may not be acceptable to the outfitter in Botswana, or may involve an additional charge to compensate for the card company's profit. These are not the sorts of things one wants to discover at the end of his trip at a dirt airstrip in Maun or Mashonaland when attempting to settle up with the outfitter.

Another issue that should be clear is the policy on cancellation by either party. You will probably be expected to put up a substantial amount of cash, typically 50 percent of the daily rate for the entire hunt, when it is booked. If for some reason you can't make the trip, you should know what will happen to your deposit. Many companies offer to refund a portion of it if the hunt can be rebooked or if canceled, say, at least three months before the hunt. It may also be possible to purchase trip-cancellation insurance to cover your losses if you have to bail out before the hunt.

GUIDELINES ON TIPS

It is customary for a client to give gratuities, or tips, to the safari staff, including trackers, skinners, cooks, and other ancillary help. Unless a hunter has experience with this, he is likely to have little idea what is expected unless he asks his agent, the company, or PH about it, preferably before leaving home. I was so pleased with the performance of the trackers, cooks, and camp help during my safari in Zimbabwe that I was pleased to be able to present them with a special gift when my safari was over. My PH for that trip had suggested that a tip in the local currency would be appreciated, so I made sure I had some on hand when the safari ended. At that time the black camp staff lined up, in an enjoyable little ceremony orchestrated by the PH, to receive whatever I had to give them. I relied on my PH for advice on how much I should give to each person, depending on his job or my personal experience with him.

It is often appropriate, though not required, to give some gratuity to your PH at the end of a satisfactory hunt. I think it best to determine, if possible, what might be appropriate before leaving home so a suitable item can be procured. I suspect cash is always welcome, too. On only one occasion, and that recently, have I seen a safari company state in its advertisement a specific amount to be paid as a "gratuity" at the end of the safari. In that case it was not clear to me whether the amount stated was a requirement or a guideline. If required, I would consider it part of the fee and not a gratuity.

My PH in Zimbabwe fancied a gun case I had brought along to use while traveling in the safari car, and I was pleased to give it to him when my hunt ended. He gave me a gift, too: a pair of war-battered binoculars. My compact pair had failed the first day in camp, so he lent me and then let me keep one of his.

My South African PH, like most others I met, had a rather cheap scope on his rifle. I had brought along a spare Leupold in 3–9X, which was clearly not going to be needed at the end of my safari, so I gave it to him as a token of my appreciation for the fine experience he had provided.

It is not unusual for safari company personnel, including PHs, to travel to the USA to prospect for clients, enjoy a vacation, or hunt North American game. If you are in a position to do so, you might offer to assist them in such a trip, perhaps even welcome them to stay in your home while in the USA. I know this is done frequently and often leads to solid friendships.

HUNTING METHODS

There are basically four hunting methods in common use in southern Africa by safari companies. These may be called vehicle search, site hunting, tracking, and spot and stalk. I'll briefly describe each one.

The basic daily procedure on most safaris is for the PH, one or more hunters, trackers, and other staff to leave camp early in the morning in a four-wheel-drive vehicle. Sometimes the party simply drives around until some animal of interest is spotted. If further examination indicates the animal is a worthwhile trophy, the PH, hunter, and possibly a tracker will dismount from the vehicle and make a stalk to get into shooting position. At other times a specific animal is sought, so the party drives to an area where the animal may be found, and then either drives around that area trying to spot a trophy animal, or employs one of the other methods. (In his 1909 safari, President Theodore Roosevelt and his associates used horses instead of motor vehicles to reconnoiter for game each day, but the procedure was otherwise identical as far as I can tell.)

Photos I provide will in some cases show a seat in the bed of the safari vehicle. This resembles the arrangement used by some North American "road hunters." These guys put one or more shooters in this seat and drive around looking for something to shoot, and they plan to shoot from the vehicle. While illegal on public land everywhere I know of, it is still a popular method for meat hunters. In Africa the scat is reserved for the tracker or other game spotters and not the hunter. Once game is spotted, the hunter gets out of the vehicle to make a stalk in hopes of getting a shot.

By site hunting I mean waiting at a particular place in hopes the animal you're hunting will show up. I include in this method all forms of baiting and the common practice of watching a water or mineral source. Almost everywhere baiting is the method of choice to hunt lion and leopard. Site hunting is also a great way to get photos of game, particularly when a blind is used. In the USA this method is often called "trail watching," or baiting, and may employ tree stands or other blinds to conceal the hunters.

Tracking appears to be a common method for hunting elephant and buffalo as well as some plains game such as eland and bongo. Again, the hunters either drive or walk around until a promising track is located and a judgment made by the

PH whether it warrants going after the animal. Sometimes water holes are checked in the morning in hopes of finding a track worth following. This is probably the most physically demanding method of hunting used today and may require considerable effort on behalf of the hunter, as catching up with the animal may take hours, or even days, on its trail.

Finally, the spot-and-stalk method is similar to much North American hunting for sheep, deer, and pronghorn antelope. In this method, the hunter takes up a position where he can survey an expanse of country and expect to find the game he's after. Once a suitable animal is located, typically by the use of a binocular or spotting scope, a stalk is planned to get close enough for a shot. The stalk can be strenuous, depending on the terrain. In Africa the stalk is likely to be much less strenuous than approaching a Dall sheep and probably more like stalking a pronghorn since much of the hunting country is relatively flat.

Another method is simple "driving," which is well known to deer hunters in the east and south of the USA, and was commonly used in India, where it is called a "beat." Animals are simply driven toward a strategically located, waiting hunter by a group of "drivers" or "beaters," the latter in all likelihood deriving its name from the typical practice of beating drums or pots to frighten the animal. I have seen this hunting method used only once, in Natal, South Africa, on a hunt for the common nyala, but I wouldn't be surprised if the method occurs often since it can be highly effective.

Hunters often have strong preferences either for, or against, a particular method. Some, for example, would not like the idea of shooting all their game over the hood of a safari vehicle. I think this is one of those areas that would be good to discuss with the PH or outfitter before selecting a hunt.

There are, of course, specialized methods of hunting particular animals that don't fit the basic categories. A good example would be hunting sitatunga from a native dugout called a *mokoro*. These animals are also, it seems, hunted from large river craft that look like the pontoon boats used for family recreation on large U.S. lakes and rivers. But I believe most of the methods employed by safari hunters today can fit more or less comfortably into one or another of the main types.

RANCH VERSUS CONCESSION HUNTS

Hunting in Africa today takes place on two different classifications of property. One type is owned by the government and usually called a "concession." The government typically sets at least some of the fees for hunting on its land and decides which professionals are allowed to hunt there and on what terms. The government also receives some of the revenue.

The other type is privately owned land, which is typically a farm or ranch devoted to raising cattle or some other commercial product. Some of these ranches are devoted to raising game animals that are either offered to hunters or sold to other ranchers to stock their properties.

In my experience, hunts on government concessions tend to be more expensive than ranch hunts. It also seems to me that in many countries the largest game, specifically elephant, buffalo, and lion, are found primarily on government land.

Some hunters don't like the idea of hunting game that is "fenced in," and some game ranches do have high fences to prevent their stock from escaping. Others find the situation acceptable. Antihunting enthusiasts, and even some PHs, like to portray ranch hunts as canned, equivalent to shooting an animal in a cage. While such abuses of fair chase may take place, I don't believe that is an accurate portrayal of most of the ranch hunts I have experienced or heard about.

Virtually all hunts in Namibia are on private ranches. Many in South Africa and Zimbabwe are, too. Many of these ranches comprise tens of thousands of acres in size, and some apparently approach a quarter-million acres or more. Many have no high fences at all, so game is free to move between the ranches and adjacent private property or government concessions and parks. That's a pretty large and leaky cage in my opinion.

There are some important ethical issues involved in deciding whether a ranch or concession hunt is best for you, and I don't think this is the proper place to go into the matter in detail. Anyone who looks into the hunts offered in Africa today will soon realize that both kinds of hunts are available, and they will choose the kind they prefer.

Now that you have learned some terminology and, I hope, have an overview of the process of organizing and paying for an African safari, it's time now to focus on the questions of where to hunt, and what to hunt, which will be discussed in the next two chapters.

GAME:
WHAT'S AVAILABLE?

*The plains are alive with droves of strange and beautiful
animals whose like is not known elsewhere.*
— Theodore Roosevelt, *African Game Trails*

In spite of the continuous stream of alarming rhetoric
about the decline of Africa's wildlife, most of the animals that
could *ever* be hunted in Africa can still be hunted there today.

In *African Game Trails,* which describes his safari in 1909,
Roosevelt provided a list of seventy-four different game animals
taken on his trip, not counting monkeys and small predators.
Nearly all the animals on his list are still available today
somewhere in the area, with the exception of the black
rhinoceros, a species that has been declining for hundreds of
years. Actually, there are many more species of game available
than he collected because some occur farther south than he
hunted. The list includes all the Big Five and the most popular
of the antelope sought by hunters then and now. Today all the
Big Five can be hunted only in the Republic of South Africa.
There is reason to hope that this may be possible in other
countries in the region before too long, as there are efforts
being made to restore the rhino and elephant populations.

Looking back farther in history, F. C. Selous also provided a list
of the animals he had taken over the course of four years' hunting
(1877–1880) in *A Hunter's Wanderings in Africa.* With few exceptions,
including, again, the black rhinoceros, all the animals on his list are
still available as game throughout the region where he hunted.

Selous's list is similar to a game list from a country like Botswana or South Africa today. The animals on his list that are available today include kudu, eland, sable, impala, reedbuck, lechwe, warthog, hippo, elephant, lion, leopard, buffalo, and gemsbok, to name a few. There are also many lesser known, and often less coveted, such as oribi, steenbok, puku, klipspringer, and duiker.

These animals are still "on license," as the British used to say. That's because even though habitat has been reduced, good management has created a surplus of certain kinds of animals. Sport hunters are allowed to take some of this surplus without endangering a particular species in any way. It is not hunters who are responsible for the reduction in habitat; it is farmers and urban expansion.

The primary differences between 2000 and 1900 are the distribution of various species and the cost to hunt them. Many species occupy a smaller range today because of a decline in population or political factors limiting access. The latter can be a greater factor than animal population levels, and includes international preservationist activities, whether appropriate or not.

As this is written, it is likely that the number of game animals is actually *increasing* in southern African countries that welcome hunters. This is certainly true of both black and white rhinos where they are given adequate protection, and also of buffalo and many plains-game species. This is because over a significant part of this area ranches once cleared of game animals in order to raise cattle are now abandoning that enterprise and reintroducing native species to areas where they have been absent for decades. In many cases, fences that were erected to control the movements of cattle are being taken down, allowing the habitat for these game animals to return to a condition similar to its original pristine state.

As availability—a factor that depends on both abundance and accessibility—of any game animal is reduced, the cost of hunting it typically rises. This, of course, assumes a level of demand to hunt that animal as well as huntable population sizes. Both daily rates and trophy fees reflect this supply-and-demand situation.

An illustration of this is the availability of the rhino as a game animal. Today, virtually the only place they can be hunted is the Republic of South Africa. This is possible because that country has made a long-term effort to increase the number of white rhino and has succeeded in protecting them better than other countries have. Today, South Africa's effort makes it possible for a small number of mature males to be harvested each year.

But hunting rhino isn't cheap. Trophy fees are around $20,000, daily fees appear to average about $600, and minimum hunts range from eight to fourteen days. Therefore, if one just has to shoot a rhino today, for whatever reason, it could cost him $30,000 including travel, accommodations, and incidental fees. Again, this is because of the animal's limited availability, although they are readily accessible through the superior transportation infrastructure of the Republic of South Africa.

Another example is the bongo. This forest-dwelling, spiral-horned antelope has never been widespread and historically has been available only in Kenya and a few western and central African countries. Since Kenya has banned big-game hunting, this leaves the Central African Republic and Cameroon as perhaps the most common destinations for bongo hunters these days. Their fees are high even by African standards. Hunts may cost $1,300 per day, compared to perhaps $350 per day for hunting less glamorous critters in southern Africa. But if you want to bag a bongo, you go to those two countries or forget it. In this case, the high costs are a combination of very limited distribution, expensive access, and high demand by trophy hunters. Together they make bongo hunting an expensive proposition. To a lesser extent this might be said of hunting the sitatunga, a swamp-adapted animal that is available in very few locales.

A similar situation exists with the mountain nyala, which lives only in the rugged mountains of Ethiopia. Access is by pack stock and on foot, I understand, and hunting is said to be difficult. Again, the difficulties of getting into mountain nyala country—in this case seriously complicated by civil war and a primitive transportation system—and the very limited numbers and range of this animal, guarantee that a hunt for mountain nyala will be expensive, at least under the conditions existing today. (One of the few accounts I have read about hunting mountain nyala is in *A Treasury of African Hunting*, edited by Peter Barrett.)

The elephant, once widespread, has undergone a huge population decline in the last two hundred years. Even so, recently an authoritative source indicated that elephants exist today in approximately 75 percent of all African countries (see Paul Bosman, *Elephants of Africa*). Although hunters are blamed for the decline, the increase of indigenous populations and associated agriculture are the real culprits. Other villains, also gleefully referred to as "hunters" by the world press, are the gangs of poachers armed with military weapons who have decimated both elephant and rhino populations throughout Africa.

Elephants are destructive of their habitat, to the extent that they are able to convert one type of habitat into another, typically turning a forested area into grassland by their feeding habits. They destroy the trees and grass takes over. They especially like the easy pickings afforded by the natives' crops. These dietary habits do not coexist well with farming or even with living in a sanctuary of limited size.

Even in national parks and preserves set aside for the protection of elephants, their populations typically increase to the point where they destroy their own habitat and that of the other residents of the preserve. As a result, throughout the period of the animal's decline, elephant herds in Africa have been routinely reduced by government "hunters," a process often called "culling," to keep their populations at manageable levels.

As late as 1937, Mozambique considered elephants as nuisance in some areas, and in Zimbabwe and South Africa many thousands have been shot to protect their habitat. Some of the excess is made available to hunters in some areas, which is why the elephants may still be hunted in several countries today. The amount of foreign exchange these mostly poor countries can obtain from selective culling of elephant herds by sportsmen is substantial and is increasingly used to improve the lives of local native peoples so that they won't poach them or aid poachers in killing them. This is done by sharing the revenues generated by wildlife with local populations.

As a practical matter, these "glamour" species—namely the Big Five and the rarer antelope—are simply too expensive to hunt except for the wealthy. It's wonderful to report that this is not the case regarding many other game species. As I have no experience in hunting these glamour animals, I will have little to say about them, except to note where and at what cost they may be hunted. My own interest and the focus of this book is primarily the hunting of plains game.

Since this is a book about hunting rather than natural history, I won't give much information about the game animals in this region except for some general characteristics. I will touch on the habitat where they are typically found, where they may be hunted, and some representative daily and trophy fees currently charged to hunt them. This is not because I regard natural history as unimportant or uninteresting, but rather because I am not qualified to write about this subject in great detail in spite of being an amateur naturalist all my life.

I believe everyone going on an African safari, whether to hunt, photograph, or observe, will be well repaid for the time they invest in learning beforehand about the plants, birds, and animals they will see. To aid the reader in doing this, I have included in the bibliography several references I have found to be useful.

PLAINS AND BUSH GAME

The term "plains game" has become generic for animals other than the big cats and pachyderms, the latter two groups collectively being known as "the Big Five" or "big game." The Big Five has historically been the elephant, rhino, buffalo, lion, and leopard. All share the quality of being dangerous to hunt, at least under some conditions. Some would include hippo in this group, particularly if hunted on land.

The term "plains game" is misleading. That's because many of the species so grouped don't live on the plains at all, but in bush country. Once one has experienced the latter, he will never confuse bush country with plains. These are radically different habitats, though they frequently occur in the same general area, and this has a major influence on the choice of weapons and hunting methods, as well as the distribution of various animals. Still, since bush dwellers are commonly referred to by PHs and safari companies as "plains game," I will continue to use the term.

Because the plains or bush game are relatively abundant, and there is an adequate transportation infrastructure in areas they inhabit, these animals are certainly those most often hunted by both resident and foreign hunters. Safari companies typically charge less, often much less, to hunt most of these animals than they do to hunt the Big Five. The plains or bush game are also the group hunted most by Africa's four-legged predators such as lions and leopards, and hyenas and wild dogs. This is what comes of being at the bottom of the food chain.

Rather than attempt to present an exhaustive list of game animals that inhabit plains or bush habitats, I'll confine my discussion to those that are most often sought as trophies by paying clients.

There are numerous ways to categorize these animals, but one that makes most sense to me is size. I find it convenient to group the various nondangerous species into four categories: small, medium, large, and huge. I recognize that the dividing lines are arbitrary, but I hope they will be helpful to the reader. I also believe the classification I have used corresponds closely to common practice among experienced sport and professional hunters.

As a final note, by grouping these animals as I have done, I do not mean to imply that those in the same group necessarily have the same vitality or require similar calibers to hunt, although this is frequently done. While the correlation is far from perfect, there does seem to be a relationship between an animal's size and the difficulty of killing it with a rifle. Still, size is a convenient way of grouping the many animals of the area so the mind can grasp the variety of game available.

There are two broad categories of plains game typically hunted on an African safari today: pigs and antelope. (I have lumped the zebra in with the antelope because it is a variety of wild ass and it is also always associated geographically with antelope.) The antelope is much the larger class and constitutes the bulk of safari trophies. There are over seventy varieties of antelope in Africa, and only a total of eighty-four worldwide. The leading authority on antelope, Richard Estes, calls Africa "antelope heaven."

THE PIGS

There are two kinds of pigs hunted in southern Africa— warthogs and bushpigs; in central and East Africa, one can hunt warthogs, bushpigs, and the giant forest hog. Two reasons for their abundance may be that they are opportunistic feeders and that their litters are large, being four to a dozen.

Nearly everyone who watches TV has probably seen warthogs. This is because they are bizarre looking, widespread, and diurnal. The bushpig, however, inhabits densely vegetated areas, has a more limited range, and is nocturnal, which probably accounts for it being featured less frequently in TV nature shows. The giant forest hog is found in countries that attract few hunters and tourists. Countries in southern Africa—Tanzania, Zambia, Zimbabwe, Botswana, South Africa, Namibia, and Mozambique—which I refer to in this book as the Triangle, because of their collective shape, do not have the giant forest hog. Since the Triangle is the most popular area for safaris, and since the giant forest hog is not available there to hunt, I won't go into further detail about the animal.

Like all wild pigs, those in Africa have a reputation for being tough and dangerous if cornered. The tusks of all species can be fearsome and can inflict a severe wound. These animals also present some special problems in international transport. I only discovered this when my entire shipment of trophies from Zimbabwe was delayed because the crate, which contained my warthog cape, had not been properly documented for shipment. For a while I feared I'd never get the lot through customs. I describe this incident in more detail in the section on taxidermy in chapter 8. You'll want to ask your safari operator about shipment, though I have to assume it's not much of a problem since most hunters take one of these animals.

In weight, both warthogs and bushpigs fall into the medium-sized category as the largest males may weigh around two hundred fifty pounds. The giant forest hog is much larger and is believed to reach a weight of six hundred pounds or more. This swine is different not only in size but also in color since it tends to be black and is covered with long hair, whereas the bushpig and warthog are much less so.

Warthog

The warthog is more widely distributed than the bushpig and may be hunted in every country covered in this book, from Namibia to the subtropics of Mozambique, and from Ethiopia to South Africa. In size the warthog might be roughly compared to a small North American wild boar.

Warthogs are heavily preyed upon by lions, leopards, and other four-legged predators, as well as by people, who highly regard them as the main attraction at barbecues. The usual defense of warthogs is to go into an abandoned aardvark hole, which they typically back into so they can greet any pursuers with their sharp end. I understand that occasionally a PH is called upon to crawl into one of these holes after a wounded warthog, in which case I believe he can be said to have earned his pay.

Though often referred to as one of the continent's ugliest animals, I found warthogs very endearing and frequently comical. More than any other game animal, I observed, they added humor to my safari experience. The way they hold their tails vertically when running makes them look like they're all carrying CB radios, and that they frequently feed while on their knees was both a surprise and a delight. Their only serious competition as entertainment was from vervet monkeys and baboons, which are the wildlife equivalent of stand-up comedians. If none of these animals puts a smile on your face, perhaps you should see your doctor and have your sense of humor checked out!

Bushpig

The bushpig is more restricted in range than the warthog and is available in only about half the countries covered in this volume. Although the bushpig lives in the Caprivi Strip of Namibia and the far north of Botswana, it is not clear to me that it is classed as game in those areas. Apparently it is not well adapted to dry climates and lives mostly in the wetter areas.

Except for its remarkable mane and relatively long, streamlined snout, the bushpig looks more like a domestic pig than like the rather bizarre-looking warthog. Its tusks are much shorter than the warthog's but still capable of causing a serious wound. The animal also looks to me something like the small desert-dwelling American peccary or javelina but with a Hollywood hairdo. It appears the African animal can weigh considerably more than the average javelina, but those I saw were of roughly comparable size.

Bushpigs are omnivores, like bears and humans, able to eat all sorts of vegetables and fruits, and will eat meat when the opportunity presents itself. Because of their flexible diet, and skills as a rooter, they are considered a serious agricultural pest.

The animal is predominantly nocturnal, which poses some challenges if you want to bag one. I never saw one in daylight in either South Africa or Zimbabwe. The only live one I saw was while driving back to camp one night. I did have an opportunity to collect one while I was in Zimbabwe, but both my PH and I failed to take advantage of it. Another hunter in the same camp as I was primarily after leopard. I recall he and his PH commenting on the number of bushpigs that were eating on some of their leopard baits, but my PH and I could not take advantage of the situation before the chap got his cat. We just never thought to sit up near the leopard baits to bag a bushpig. I think that would have been my only chance to get one. Whether or not you hunt leopard, I believe this would be an effective approach to getting a bushpig.

SMALL ANTELOPE

The majority of animals sought on a typical safari are antelope of one sort or another. The size range of these animals is truly awesome, going from about ten pounds to around a ton. This large group can, as suggested above, be divided somewhat arbitrarily into four categories by size, specifically by weight.

In the "small" category I would include animals generally weighing under one hundred pounds. They actually range in size from around ten pounds up to the category limit or a little more. This would include, in no particular order, bushbuck, grysbok, klipspringer, dik-dik, duiker, oribi, vaal rhebok, mountain reedbuck, springbok, and steenbok. Some of these are so small they are referred to as "dwarf antelope." Several small cats, such as the civet, serval, caracal, and genet, would be in the same weight category.

There really are no game animals, deer or antelope, comparable to these miniature ungulates native to North America, at least I don't know of any, though the southwestern javelina probably falls in the same weight range. Some of them are not much bigger than a large jackrabbit. Even the Coues deer of the southwest would tower over a steenbok or duiker, both of which would probably come up only as high as that little deer's knees. The males of nearly all these tiny antelope have straight horns that stick more or less straight up from their skulls. Some have horns that are roughly parallel to the line of their faces, like the duikers'. Others have horns that project toward their faces at angles approaching 90 degrees. The differences can be useful field-identifying characteristics. The distribution of these little guys varies considerably with the species.

Duiker

There are at least sixteen species of duiker in Africa, the majority in central and western forests. In the southern Africa area there are three main species. They are the common duiker (also called the bush or gray duiker), the red duiker, and the blue duiker.

The common duiker appears to be the most widespread and occurs throughout the southern Africa region. It weighs about forty pounds and stands about twenty inches at the shoulder. It is hunted in all countries covered in this book. They are usually taken incidentally, since the sportsman is often hunting something else at the time.

The other two duikers in the region, the red and blue, are much less common. The blue variety is found in suitable habitat in central and western Africa, where it is widespread. The distribution of the blue duiker in southern Africa, however, is rather spotty and appears limited to parts of Zimbabwe, Zambia, Mozambique, and a thin coastal strip of South Africa. It is the smallest duiker, standing only about twelve inches at the shoulder and weighing in the neighborhood of nine pounds. It is considered a "rain forest" duiker because it is found in relatively wet and dense forest habitats.

There are at least two varieties of red duiker. One is restricted to parts of Tanzania, and the other appears to inhabit only a small area of South Africa in or near Kruger National Park and Natal Province and also in Mozambique. The red duiker falls between the blue and common at a shoulder height of seventeen inches and a weight of around thirty pounds.

Springbok

The springbok is the national animal of the Republic of South Africa. A beautiful little gazelle, the springbok is widespread and fairly numerous in Namibia, Botswana, and the Cape Province of South Africa. Although its horns are different and its size is larger, the animal resembles the Thomson gazelle of East Africa because of its distinct horizontal body stripe, and the two are in the same zoological tribe classification, the Antilopini. It is the only gazelle in southern Africa, though there are several species in East Africa and Ethiopia.

Unlike virtually all other small antelope discussed here, the springbok has attractive lyrate horns. This animal is at the upper-size limit of the small antelope group, being around thirty inches at the shoulder and weighing about ninety pounds. One of its characteristic behavioral displays is "pronking" or "stotting," which is a stiff-legged bouncing gait engaged in when alarmed, or at times apparently just for the fun of it.

Klipspringer

The curious little klipspringer, which in Afrikaans means "rock jumper," is unique because it prefers a habitat more suitable for a mountain goat or marmot than an antelope. It typically inhabits the rocky hills widely scattered over southern Africa known as *kopjes* (pronounced "copies") and sometimes steep cliffs.

Weighing about twenty pounds and standing around twenty inches at the shoulder, it is one of the smallest antelopes. Its distribution is surprisingly broad because it lives wherever it can find food. Because kopjes occur somewhat sporadically, so does this antelope. It apparently also inhabits some cliffs along the Zambezi River in Zimbabwe, which is a somewhat unusual adaptation for it. There are also small populations in East Africa, Zambia, Zimbabwe, Namibia and the Central African Republic.

Dik-Dik

The dik-dik, one of the smallest of the dwarf antelopes, is available as a game animal in only three countries I'm concerned with in this book: Ethiopia and the southern African countries of Tanzania and Namibia. The dik-dik in these countries are of different species and are not equally abundant. They are about the same shoulder height as a red duiker, about sixteen inches, but weigh around ten pounds. There are several other species of dik-dik found mostly in East Africa. According to Estes, all species of dik-dik originated in the area now called Ethiopia.

Bushbuck

The bushbuck is one of the prettiest and most intriguing of the small antelope. Zoologically, it is classified with the nine spiral-horned antelope in the Tragelaphini Tribe, which includes sitatunga, mountain nyala (available in Ethiopia only), common nyala, and the greater kudu and lesser kudu. The bushbuck has an unusual coat with white spots and vertical stripes, like a bongo or kudu, that blend in well with the thick, typically riverine, habitat it prefers.

Smaller than a springbok, it stands around twenty-four inches at the shoulder and typically weighs about one hundred pounds. It is, I believe, the smallest of the spiral-horned antelope. To me it looks almost like a miniature sitatunga, but without the shaggy coat. Since the bushbuck is more abundant and widespread than the sitatunga, perhaps it would be more appropriate to say the latter looks like a large, shaggy bushbuck.

The bushbuck's habitat preferences limit its range to the wetter parts of the region. Their habitat stretches as far west as the Caprivi Strip of Namibia, as far northeast as Ethiopia, and southeast in Zambia, Zimbabwe, Mozambique, Tanzania, and South Africa. There are many varieties of bushbuck, and a person could make a hunting career of collecting them all. Some of these get considerably larger than the upper limit of one hundred pounds for this group, but they fit better here than in the next weight category.

Mountain Reedbuck and Vaal Rhebok

The mountain reedbuck and the gray or vaal rhebok share the distinction of living primarily in a small part of South Africa. They are grouped with the common reedbuck, kob, bohor reedbuck, puku, lechwe, and waterbuck. I have lumped the mountain reedbuck and vaal rhebok together because they inhabit the same general area and are about the same height at thirty inches, though at sixty pounds the mountain reedbuck weighs about twice as much as the vaal.

While the vaal rhebok has the straight horns typical of the group of small antelope, the horns of the mountain reedbuck resembles those of its lowland relative, the common reedbuck, and are heavily ridged like those of the impala, though the shape is quite different.

Grysbok

The grysbok appears to have limited range, the Sharpe variety being more widespread than the common grysbok. The latter occurs only in a small coastal strip near Cape Town, South Africa, and the Sharpe appears to range throughout Mozambique, much of Zimbabwe, and parts of Zambia. This animal stands only about eighteen inches at the shoulder and weighs around sixteen pounds.

Oribi

The oribi is fairly widespread but spotty in its distribution. It stands about twenty-four inches at the shoulder and weighs about thirty pounds. It occurs primarily in the wetter parts of the region where it inhabits open grassland. It occurs as far north as Ethiopia and as far south as South Africa. There is a small population in the Caprivi Strip and northern Botswana as well as in Zimbabwe and Mozambique.

Steenbok

The steenbok is about as widespread in its distribution as the common duiker. It is present in all the southern countries, from the edge of the Namib Desert to the coast of Mozambique, and from the Zambezi River to the southern coast of South Africa. The steenbok ranks in the middle of this group both in height—about twenty inches—and in weight—about twenty pounds.

Its straight horns are set on its head more perpendicular to its skull than a duiker's, which should help distinguish it in the field. It also appears to be better balanced since its forequarters and hindquarters are more alike in size than a duiker's, which show a characteristic overdevelopment and elevation of the rear end.

SMALL CATS

In this general size class there are several small cats available to hunters. I saw most of them but had no interest in hunting them. I know little about them except that most are nocturnal and some are not technically felines—like the genet and civet—even though they look, more or less, like cats. Two of the ranchers I visited in South Africa had genets for pets and they appear to be easily domesticated if caught young.

MEDIUM-SIZED ANTELOPE

The medium-sized group includes a large number of animals that range in weight from one hundred pounds (comparable to the North American black-tailed deer) to four hundred pounds (comparable to the caribou). This group includes some of the most common and some of the rarest of African antelope, such as the impala, reedbuck, sassaby, black wildebeest, hartebeest, common and mountain nyala, bontebok, blesbok, and sitatunga.

Impala

Undoubtedly one of the most widespread of the group is the impala, which is available nearly everywhere in the region, though it is most common in the eastern part. They are a strikingly beautiful animal in both their appearance and their remarkable springing gait, which I found a joy to watch. They are probably most recognizable when leaping high into the air while running, though the reasons for this behavior are unknown. The impala is one-of-a-kind and has no close living relatives.

An impala's coat is sleek and shiny, with mixed shades of brown and dark accents on its rump. Its horns are striking in appearance, and its movements range from graceful to acrobatic. They are at the small end of this category, weighing up to one hundred sixty pounds and standing three feet at the shoulder. It has been said that if this animal were not so common, it would be among the most prized of African antelope trophies, and I agree. Even a moderately good specimen makes a beautiful trophy. The East African variety, found in Tanzania, carry much larger horns than those in the southern countries.

Reedbuck

Another common antelope about the same size as the impala, the reedbuck favors wet areas such as flood plains that include tall grass and, surprise, reed beds. In appearance it closely resembles the smaller mountain reedbuck, and they are close relatives, being in the same genus. The mountain reedbuck, however, is only about half the size of the common variety. In spite of their similarities, the two animals have different habitat preferences, as their names suggest, but their ranges do appear to overlap in parts of South Africa.

To me the common reedbuck is a rather plain-looking animal with unimpressive horns, but is generally a well-balanced antelope. I doubt they are high on anyone's list of priority trophies, but I think they make an attractive addition to one's trophy room, particularly if rendered in a shoulder mount where their delicate and pretty facial features can be seen.

Blesbok and Bontebok

I have grouped these two together because they are similar in most every way except their color. They are subspecies of the same genus. Both stand about three feet at the shoulder and weigh about one hundred fifty pounds.

The chief difference in appearance is that the hide of the bontebok is much darker in color, which contrasts sharply with its white belly fur. It is a strikingly beautiful animal, except for its face, which I think is homely. The body of the blesbok is more uniformly tan, and the contrast with its white belly is, therefore, not so striking; its face is just as homely as the bontebok's. Both have a broad white patch that runs the length of their faces (horses with this feature are said to have a "blaze"), which may have been the basis for their name.

Though the blesbok is more widely distributed than the bontebok, both occur primarily in South Africa. Both were nearly hunted to extinction but, because of the efforts of a few South

African farmers, the bontebok has now recovered to the point where a few can be made available to sportsmen. The blesbok has recovered strongly and has even been introduced in places where it never existed before, including Namibia and Zimbabwe.

Black Wildebeest

The black wildebeest, or white-tailed gnu, looks very different from the blue variety, though both are members of the same genus. Except for its bushy tail, the black would probably not be recognized as being related to the blue. The horns of the black sweep forward and upward, rather than sideways like the blue, and the black sports a bizarre brushlike clump of stiff, black hair on its nose. This is about as attractive as a pretty girl with a big black mustache—not that any sort of wildebeest is pretty! They are quite ugly to my eye, but they are also an important and highly visible member of the African antelopes. The black variety are exotic looking and restricted in distribution, making them an unusual trophy.

At an average weight of nearly four hundred pounds and a shoulder height of four feet, the black wildebeest's size puts it at the top of the medium-sized antelope class, but it is smaller than its cousin, the blue wildebeest. The black's range is also smaller than the blue's, being restricted to South Africa and Namibia. The habitat preferences of the black make it a true plains-game species.

Red Hartebeest and Sassaby

These two animals look similar to me, but are not as closely related as they appear to be. They are members of the widely distributed group of antelope that look generally like hartebeests. The group includes the Lichtenstein hartebeest of Tanzania and Zambia, and the East African topi, wildebeest, and even the blesbok. They all share the hartebeest's peculiar structural features of having their back legs appear to be shorter than their front legs, giving them a decidedly rearward slope. All, I believe, have a pronounced hump at the withers. To my eye, they are also remarkably ugly, but that is clearly a personal matter. They are said to be among the fastest of African antelope and are widely sought as trophies by hunters. These are among the true plains antelope and prefer open woodlands and savanna.

The red hartebeest is a large animal, weighing about four hundred pounds and standing four feet at the shoulder. This animal appears to be largely restricted to the general area of the Kalahari Desert region and similar habitat in Namibia and South Africa. There are other hartebeest species in practically all the countries in the southern region.

The sassaby looks like a hartebeest, but to me has the least interesting horns of all the medium-to-large antelope. Its distribution is spotty, but it appears to be most common in northern Botswana, central Zimbabwe, and Zambia. It is about the same height as the red hartebeest, but generally weighs around three hundred pounds.

Hartebeests have a reputation of being fast runners and fairly tough. In areas of tall grass, they have been known to climb up on anthills to get a better view of their surroundings.

Sitatunga

This antelope probably has the most restricted distribution of any in the medium-sized antelope group, at least among those classified as game animals. Although it does have a fairly wide distribution in central and western Africa, its occurrence is spotty due to its preferred habitat. In the southern and eastern countries, which are the focus of this book, it occurs only in a small part of northern Botswana, in parts of Zambia, and Tanzania.

The sitatunga looks like a cross between a bushbuck and a waterbuck, with spiral horns and a shaggy coat. The horns of a sitatunga are larger than a bushbuck's and similar in size and shape to those of the common nyala.

This animal stands about three feet tall at the shoulder and weighs around two hundred fifty pounds. A member of the prized spiral-horned group of antelope, it is adapted to wet terrain and is said to be "semiaquatic" for this reason. The area of Botswana it inhabits, the Okavango Delta, is like a marsh dotted with islands. They have greatly elongated hooves that appear to be an adaptation to this environment and apparently are excellent swimmers. They are said to be able to submerge themselves completely except for their nostrils when wounded and trying to escape, and they rest on floating mats of reeds.*

Hunting sitatunga sometimes requires the use of a native boat made from a hollowed log called a *mokoro,* or some other watercraft. The video *Botswana Safari* by Sportsmen on Film, featuring Peter Capstick, is the best I have seen illustrating this method of hunting. Other methods include hunting from elevated blinds or driving.

Common Nyala

I believe the common nyala would be better known if it occurred more widely, but it is confined to a few spots in

---

*See Smithers, *Land Mammals of Southern Africa,* p. 193.

southern Zimbabwe, Mozambique, and South Africa. When a person first sees this animal, he knows he is looking at something unique among African antelope. It is so exotic it could be from the moon.

They share several features with others of the spiral-horned group, but none of the others have all the characteristics of the common nyala in one package. The shape of the horn is like that of the sitatunga and bushbuck, typically a single twist of horn with ivory-colored tips in a mature specimen. They also have a shaggy coat similar to the sitatunga but considerably darker, which appears black under some field conditions. They have the vertical stripes of the bongo and kudu, and spots like a bushbuck, which their facial markings also resemble. Their generally dark coat of long hair contrasts sharply with their very trim, almost dainty, legs, which are smooth and a contrasting brown. They are able to erect their dorsal hair when displaying to others of their species. The females look nothing like the males, and one could hardly imagine they belonged together when seen apart. She looks more like a female bushbuck or a bongo than the male common nyala.

South Africa, specifically Zululand in Natal Province, is the primary location for hunting this animal today. It may be that Mozambique has a bigger population, but it's hard to know what remains after years of civil war.

LARGE ANTELOPE

Among the large antelope I include the greater kudu, gemsbok, roan, blue wildebeest, waterbuck, sable, and zebra (because of its size and because it lives on antelope ranges.) All these animals are roughly elk-sized, and some have a reputation for being extremely tough. They range in weight from four hundred to six hundred fifty pounds. You do not want to make a bad first shot on any of these; trust me on this one!

One of the features that stands out about this group of animals is that they are not only large, but also striking! Every one of them is a head turner in my book. All are stately, elegant, majestic, and beautiful. This group contains some of the premier trophies available in Africa.

Greater Kudu

This big, beautiful antelope is regarded by many as the finest trophy in Africa. It is a matter of considerable good fortune that it is also one of the most widespread and plentiful. The greater kudu occurs in all the countries under discussion, from Ethiopia to South Africa, from Namibia to Mozambique. Several varieties are recognized but all appear to be similar. And he is one grand animal in every way wherever he is found.

Absolutely nothing looks like a greater kudu even though the animal shares features of several other spiral-horned antelope. It is a large animal, about as tall as the roan, but lighter in weight. It has spiral horns similar to the sitatunga and common nyala, but instead of stopping after a single turn, the kudu's just keep going, and going, and going, forming an incomparable corkscrew shape. A fine common nyala might have thirty-inch horns, but a large kudu's horns will approach sixty inches or more measured around the curves. They are simply spectacular.

The greater kudu is a tall animal, standing nearly five feet at the shoulder, with large bulls weighing up to seven hundred pounds. This makes him about the same height but considerably lighter in weight than the largest North American bull elk, which average well over six hundred pounds and can weigh a thousand pounds.

Both sexes have a prominent hump at the withers. Males have a striking, multicolored mane or beard that hangs below the neck at the midline, and a narrow white chevron crosses the nose below the eye. The mane is beautiful and more attractive than the similar feature on a bull elk, which is typically shaggy and brown. Kudu cows have the same ungainly look to me as cow elk, but considering their numbers, they must look just fine to kudu bulls.

Kudu have a wonderful, springy, fluid gait that is as pretty to watch as that of any antelope I have seen. Based on what I have observed, they are also good jumpers. Their body color varies somewhat but is typically grayish or brownish. Their ears look like something drawn onto them by a cartoonist, as oversized looking as a donkey's or a bat-eared fox's. They are said to have excellent hearing, and I am inclined to believe it. When danger is near, they are the very picture of alertness.

Kudu are plentiful enough that they are relatively inexpensive to hunt, and they are wonderful on the table. I would not consider making a safari where they were available without at least attempting to take a kudu. I have known men who have made over twenty African safaris who hunted nothing but kudu most of the time.

Sable

Another contender for Africa's finest trophy is the handsome sable antelope. A strikingly beautiful animal, bulls are virtually black with white accents, and have majestic, backward-sweeping horns sometimes reaching forty inches or more in length. Their facial markings are unusual and, like some others in this group, look painted on. Both sexes have horns, but the males' are larger.

Sable belong to the group of "horse antelope," which also includes the roan and oryx. They may be so classified because of their horselike build and speed, and their long, horselike tails, similar to that of a wildebeest.

Unlike the kudu, unfortunately, the sable has a rather restricted range. Although its range is not as limited as the sitatunga or common nyala's, the sable is apparently not abundant anywhere; hence, it tends to be expensive to hunt. Safari companies often package sable and the Big Five with animals requiring hunts of greater length. For example, sable are packaged like lion and elephant into hunts for "sable and plains game." Hunts are typically fourteen days or more and carry fairly high daily rates. In most places today a trophy fee on one sable is equal to that of two or three kudu. There are many hunts available on which you can take a kudu in as little as five to seven days, but if you want a sable, you're probably looking at fourteen days minimum.

The main destinations today for sable are Botswana, Zambia, and Zimbabwe. There is a race with larger horns in Angola, but hunting has not been permitted there for many years because of continuing civil war.

Gemsbok

This is another strikingly beautiful "horse" antelope, and it's one of my favorites. It has the look of power and speed I associate with the American quarter horse. Gemsbok are stocky and powerful, with massive front shoulders, and look like they are born to run, which no doubt they are. They have a reputation for being dangerous to hunters or their dogs, or anything that tries to make a meal of one of them. My experience suggests that it is a bad idea to make a poor shot on one of these guys.

The animal is also known as the giant oryx, since it is the largest of the several oryx types. It is similar in appearance to other varieties of oryx occurring in Tanzania, Kenya, and Ethiopia, as well as in the northern African deserts and in parts of Asia. The most striking characteristic of this oryx group is their long, rapierlike horns that are among the most spectacular of all antelope. Only sable and kudu have horns as grand as the gemsbok. Both sexes look alike and both have horns, the female's often being longer than the male's, though less massive. The gemsbok is one of the heaviest in this group at around five hundred pounds, and on average stands around four feet at the shoulder.

Like the sable and roan, this antelope has striking contrasts between lighter and darker skin and vivid black-and-white facial markings sometimes referred to as "clown paint" because it seems so artificial and garish. They are well adapted to desert environments and are numerous in Namibia and the Kalahari as well as the northwestern Cape Province of South Africa.

Roan

The roan is one of the largest antelope in Africa, exceeded in weight only by the eland. It weighs around six hundred pounds and may stand five feet at the shoulder, which places it at the high end of this grouping, though far below the eland in size. Its horns are similar in shape to those of sable, though they never approach the latter in length or massiveness. Like several others in this group, the roan has white facial markings, present at birth, which resemble those of the gemsbok and sable. Overall coloration is tan without the striping and contrasts seen in some others in this size class.

The roan has a rather wide distribution but generally in central and western Africa, including Cameroon and the Central African Republic. It occurs in the Caprivi Strip of Namibia, in northern Botswana, along the Zambezi River valley in northern Zimbabwe and southern Zambia, and along the border of Mozambique with Zimbabwe and South Africa. There are some in Kruger National Park on the border between South Africa and Mozambique. The habitat they prefer is similar to that of eland, but not far from water in open grass and woodlands. It appears to be sensitive to habitat changes, which may account for its relative rarity today.

Waterbuck

Although the waterbuck lacks some of the colorful features of the other glamour animals in this group, it has always been one of my favorites among African antelope. There are several varieties of this animal in western and central Africa, but the most widely hunted in the southern African countries is probably the common waterbuck.

A large animal, the waterbuck may weigh close to six hundred pounds and stand over four feet at the shoulder. It prefers to live near open water and is seldom found more than a mile or so from it. Like the reedbuck, it is an animal of wet areas such as grassy floodplains and river valleys, which probably accounts for its name. Like the common nyala and sitatunga, it has a long, coarse coat, even on its face. One of its most curious and distinctive features is a light-colored circle on its rump, seen on both sexes, with its tail roughly at the center, which is unmistakable as a field-identifying feature. I think of them as "bull's-eye" butts. Other varieties of waterbuck have a solid white patch on their rump instead of a circle.

The common waterbuck is widely distributed but spottily because it needs to live in a wet region. It appears to be common throughout Mozambique, the Zambezi River Valley in Zimbabwe and Zambia, northern Botswana, and in the northern Transvaal of South Africa along the Limpopo River and the border with Mozambique.

One curious feature of the waterbuck is that, perhaps unique among African antelope, it is not good to eat. It has an oily coat with a distinctive smell, which its meat is said to share. I have read that if the animal is carefully skinned so that the hide does not touch the meat, it is perfectly edible. I think the jury is still out on this one.

Blue Wildebeest

The blue wildebeest, or gnu, as it is also known, is one of the most familiar of all African antelope. It occurs in several variations and may be the only animal in Africa that still makes an annual migration in such huge numbers as to be a spectacle much sought after by tourists and photographers. The best known migration occurs on the Serengeti plains of Tanzania and the Masai Mara, the adjoining part of Kenya.

The horns of this species are reminiscent of Cape buffalo but much less massive. They sweep out of the animal's head at right angles to its line of travel, dropping down near the head and rising to a pointed tip. Both species of wildebeest have long, horselike tails, and both sexes have horns described by one source as "cowlike."

A large antelope, the blue wildebeest stands around five feet at the shoulder, and a large male will weigh between five hundred and six hundred pounds. They have a reputation of being one of the toughest of the African antelope, and are undoubtedly one of the ugliest. Blue wildebeests seem to enjoy romping and bucking when not immediately concerned with feeding or escaping predators, and many people find them comical for this reason.

ZEBRA

The zebra is one of the most unique-looking large ungulates on earth. Most school children around the world could probably recognize and name one immediately. Zebras have always been a favorite of sport hunters, probably because of their distinctive hide, and lions love to eat them, particularly the little ones.

Essentially a wild horse or ass, the zebra has the reputation of being tough and a hard animal to kill, particularly if your first shot is not properly placed. The most common variety is among the largest animals in this group and may weigh seven hundred pounds or more and stand over four feet at the shoulder. All have remarkable "potbellies" that give them a bloated appearance.

There are at least three varieties of zebra in southern Africa, including two species of mountain zebra, and the most widespread of the three, the Burchell's. Other varieties occur in countries farther north, like Kenya.

HUGE ANTELOPE: THE ELAND

The eland has this class all to itself. Both the common eland and its relative, the giant or Lord Derby eland, may be over three times as heavy as the largest animals discussed so far among the plains game. It is the largest antelope in the world; a large bull can weigh over two thousand pounds and may approach six feet at the withers. Even cows may weigh half a ton—as heavy as a big bull elk. In spite of its name, the giant eland is no larger than the common eland but does have larger horns.

The eland is the largest of the spiral-horned antelope, the bushbuck being the smallest. It is the only one of the group that is truly gregarious and at times forms into herds numbering in the hundreds. All other spiral-horned antelope are more solitary or form only small groups.

I found it one of the most difficult antelope to hunt. When I asked the agent for my safari in Zimbabwe what my chances were of bagging all the plains game species I wanted, which included most of the animals found in Zimbabwe except sable and some of the rarer small antelope, the only one about which he expressed any doubt was the eland.

The size of a domestic bull but much taller, the eland bears a greater resemblance to a Jersey bull or domestic ox than any other antelope. I believe eland are the only large antelope that have been domesticated, both for its meat and milk.

Eland are notoriously shy and alert and augment their own senses by associating with other animals that help sound the alarm if approached. They also can travel long distances and are inclined to do just that when spooked. Eland are widely believed to be capable of jumping over an eight- to ten-foot-high game fence from a flat-footed start.

I found that you can spend considerable time and energy trying to catch up with a spooked herd of eland to try for a shot, and there is no guarantee you'll be successful. The walk of the animal is at least as fast as an average man can jog. When trying to keep up with an eland herd in thornbrush country in temperatures often over 80 degrees, the hunter can quickly become exhausted.

Although local residents hunt eland with whatever they use for the larger antelope, when it comes to safari clients, you'll find many PHs recommending the .375 H&H for these animals. Some PHs even recommend solids, assuming any shot is likely to be at a departing animal.* Eland do not have the reputation for toughness that, say, zebra do, but it should be remembered that they may be three times the size of a kudu bull or bull elk and more than twice the weight of a zebra. I know many are shot with garden-variety .30-06s and even smaller calibers by residents, but the traveling sportsman would be wise to use a larger caliber. Eland also lack the reputation for ferocity that the gemsbok and even the little bushbuck have, and are often described as gentle by residents of African countries where they occur.

One thing about which there is no disagreement is their ability, and inclination, to cover ground when alarmed. Our native white-tailed deer has what is known as a short escape or flight distance. When alarmed and caused to flee, unless pursued, the deer soon slows to a walk and either beds down or continues doing what it was doing before being alarmed.

*See Peter Barrett, *Treasury of African Hunting,* p. 220

Elk have a longer flight distance, and I have seen them run clear out of a mountain basin in which they have been shot at and cross the ridge into the next one, a distance that can be a mile or more.

I don't really know how far an alarmed eland will travel because I never could catch up with the herd on the one occasion when I attempted it. It was far enough that they got away from me, and I believe it was a mile or more over level ground. Estes says their flight distance is about five hundred yards, but I suspect this is subject to renewal at the will of the herd leader. The point is, they will go a long way and are not easy to catch.

BIRDS

Not everyone is aware of the excellent bird shooting available in Africa, so it is probably worth a brief mention here. During my winter safari in Zimbabwe I saw an abundance of game birds that I could have hunted. These included guinea fowl, doves, pigeons, grouselike francolin, and some waterfowl. Because of limited time, further restricted by having to retrieve my lost baggage, I shot just one bird on that trip, a guinea fowl, with a shotgun borrowed from my PH.

As the word has got out about the fantastic bird shooting available, some outfitters have begun offering bird-only safaris. Those I have seen offered cost about as much as a plains game hunt, and frequently require groups of four or more hunters. But I don't believe it's necessary to book one of these hunts to sample the bird hunting available.

If you are a bird shooter, I would suggest you mention that fact to your agent or outfitter and ask if some bird shooting could be arranged during your hunt for plains game. Some ads for African hunts have started to include birds in their literature, but prices vary greatly. I have seen offers for some bird shooting at no extra charge, and some for $450 per day. Sometimes there are even trophy fees for birds. It appears that if bird shooting is done within the time frame of your hunt, the cost may be included in your daily rate. If the safari is extended to hunt birds, it may be at the same or a different rate. I certainly would explore this possibility if you are a bird hunter.

Most safari operators have shotguns available for use by clients if the operators are advised of the need before the hunt. My PH let me use his Brno double to shoot my guinea fowl. Since most hunters are restricted by law or practicality to two long guns on a hunt, one of these could very well be a shotgun if you take your bird hunting seriously. By all accounts, though, it is better to buy your shells in Africa than to bring them with you because of the weight involved. I understand that 12-gauge is the only size commonly available, but your outfitter should know if ammunition for smaller gauges can be purchased where you'll be hunting in case you'd like to bring something else.

WHERE TO HUNT

The hunter who wanders through these lands sees sights which ever afterward remain fixed in his mind.
—Theodore Roosevelt, *African Game Trails*

There are at least two commonly used ways to plan an African safari. One way is to first decide which *animals* you want to collect and make the necessary arrangements to hunt where these animals are available as game. The second way is to select a *place* to hunt, such as a particular country (e.g., Zimbabwe) or region (e.g., the Kalahari Desert), and then select from among the animals available in that location. Perhaps you particularly like desert habitats, or have relatives or friends somewhere in Africa who might influence your choice.

Either way may be described as a "general bag" hunt strategy since a variety of game is typically available in every country covered in this book, although not all animals can be hunted everywhere. In some places one can hunt practically all the main species of plains or bush game, for example. In fewer places such a general bag hunt can be combined with hunts for one or more of the Big Five as well as plains or bush game.

Both ways are valid approaches. In practice, the first, I'll call it "animal priority," is likely to be more expensive and restricted as to species than the second approach, especially if there is a particular, presumably somewhat rare, animal that is the first priority for the hunter. Often this implies a special habitat where there are fewer game species than in other places.

Hunting the forest-dwelling bongo or mountain nyala come to mind as examples.

The animal-priority approach has been used for years by wealthy sportsmen engaged in competition with their peers for the largest or most unusual trophies. For these people, money and time are typically not a problem, as they have plenty of both. Spending in the five-figure range to bag a rare sheep or a forest dwelling antelope is not a serious obstacle to them. These individuals, however, are unlikely to be reading this book. (For an excellent account of how wealthy hunters approach African hunting, see Barrett, *Treasury of African Hunting*.)

But the approach isn't necessarily appropriate for only the wealthy seeking rare trophies. Recently, I noted that comments on a World Wide Web message board devoted to African hunting included one fellow who wanted *only* a zebra, and another wanted primarily a large kudu. To these guys everything else seemed either off-the-menu or of little importance. A fellow in my safari camp in Zimbabwe came from Italy, and taking a leopard was clearly his highest priority; he hunted little else until he got what he came for. I don't really understand such a narrow focus, particularly in African hunting, but there are safaris out there for people of that mind-set.

The second approach, which I'll call "place priority," is generally more appropriate for the rest of us. An example of this approach would be to decide that a hunt in Zimbabwe would be just your cup of tea, and then to look for hunts there offering the game you are interested in. A final decision could be made on the basis of cost, rapport with the safari company, accommodations, or whatever is most important to you.

My experience suggests it is possible to combine elements of both methods. I wanted both gemsbok and kudu, but this combination on a single hunt is not available in the eastern or northern part of the Triangle because of the gemsbok's limited range. But areas of Namibia, Botswana, and South Africa have both, as well as many other plains-game species. A general bag can, therefore, be had in these countries even with certain animals designated as priorities.

The best place to hunt in Africa, in my view, is the Triangle—southern Africa. I believe the countries of the Triangle—Zambia, Zimbabwe, South Africa, Botswana, Mozambique, and Namibia—host the majority of safari clients today, at least from the United States. (I have included Mozambique, even though hunting there has been difficult and dangerous for many years because of political turmoil, including civil war and the associated risks. Presently, a number of hunts are again being offered in that country.) Countries outside the Triangle that are worth hunting in are Tanzania and Ethiopia; only in these countries can one hunt certain East African species, such as the lesser kudu, and the fringe-eared and beisa oryx.

I also decided to provide some information on Cameroon and Central African Republic, for they offer the most accessible areas for the fabulous giant eland and the elusive bongo. Both countries may be too risky today for a family safari, based on information provided by the U.S. State Department, but may be more appropriate for a second or third hunt for the adventurous.

Altogether these countries represent a vast cornucopia of African game and nongame birds and animals. Except as I have noted, all the countries provide numerous professional hunters and related staff, grand wildlife parks and preserves, good transportation infrastructures, relative safety, and abundant natural beauty. Because of these factors, and competition, the cost of hunting in most of these countries is within reach of many working-class people in the USA, though not all realize it. As will become clear, however, the cost associated with hunting in different countries for the same animals varies considerably.

In the Triangle, one may hunt all the common species noted in chapter 2, and some not mentioned, as well as view and hunt a variety of birds, and enjoy numerous fishing and photographic opportunities.

Some animals considered rare in the traditional safari countries of East Africa—Kenya, Tanzania, and Uganda—are abundant in this southern Africa region. The greater kudu, for example, regarded by many as the finest of African trophies, may be hunted in all the countries in this region except Cameroon. It's a situation too wonderful to believe! In the case of kudu, at least, it is true. Fortunately, this wonderful antelope is plentiful and frequently of trophy class all over southern Africa, and cheaper to hunt there to boot, than in East African countries.

Other animals available in several of these countries, though not necessarily of equal quality or at the same price everywhere, include elephant, Cape buffalo, lion, leopard, hippo, crocodile, impala, hartebeest, warthog, zebra, bushbuck, eland, wildebeest, bushpig, klipspringer, duiker, baboon, jackal, hyena, and various lesser cats. Since there are usually varieties of particular animals in different countries, the waterbuck hunted in South Africa won't be the exact type of waterbuck hunted in Ethiopia.

There are several animals in the Triangle found virtually nowhere else, including the fabulous gemsbok, giant oryx, three species of lechwe, and the common nyala. Even the sitatunga—the swamp-adapted, spiral-horned antelope—is available in some parts of the Triangle. Also, there are various exotic or rare species available, mostly on game farms, such as fallow deer, black wildebeest, and bontebok.

Since this book is being written for the average person making his first or second safari, rather than for the wealthy, I won't spend too much time on the most expensive of African game—the Big Five, bongo, mountain nyala, and giant eland.

Of the Big Five, the Cape buffalo is one of the most widely available and cheapest to hunt of the dangerous-game animals. Leopard are also widely distributed over the region and relatively cheap to hunt. Elephant and lion are available in several of the countries mentioned, though often on a limited basis, and they aren't cheap to hunt anywhere. Hippo and crocodile are available in a few places. Elephant are generally the most expensive, but all the others are available at "reasonable" prices and in some quantity. Rhino are, as far as I know, available only in South Africa, thanks to that country's efforts at conservation and dissemination of this animal. If current efforts to enhance protection of these animals are successful, these animals could be reintroduced to their original range and become available for viewing and hunting in other countries.

What game a person decides to hunt and where to hunt it is a highly individual matter. Some would never feel satisfied with a safari that did not include one, or perhaps all, of the Big Five. A safari for all of them is almost certain to involve hunting in at least two countries, but it can be done if you have the time and considerable cash. Others feel cheated if they don't bag one or more animals that "make the book," that is, are sufficiently grand to warrant inclusion in one of the registries of African trophies, such as Roland Ward or Safari Club International. Inclusion into the registries isn't too difficult if you put your mind to it, and many animals are placed in the record books each year by clients on ordinary plains-game safaris.

I confess that this getting-into-the-record-book mentality preoccupied me during my two African safaris. My original goal was to simply have an enjoyable hunt and bag solid "representative" examples of plains game. But I soon found myself believing that I had to have at least a fifty-incher! Knowing the animals I wanted were plentiful caused me to raise my standards. That attitude was agreeable to the safari operators since their reputations depend to some extent on the quality of the animals their clients shoot.

In the same way that individual U.S. hunters prefer to hunt elk or whitetails, some will be drawn to certain African species. I have known men who specialized in kudu and returned to Africa many times and hunted virtually nothing else. Others were especially excited about lion, leopard, or buffalo.

During my own safaris my preferences evolved considerably. Some that became my favorites were animals unfamiliar to me before seeing them listed on safari operators' trophy lists. The bushbuck comes to mind as an example. I knew little about this beautiful and interesting animal before planning my hunt in Zimbabwe. Another is the common nyala, which I consider one of the most exotic and beautiful trophies in the world. Both these animals are found in brushy country similar to where I hunted black-tailed deer in California as a kid, which may account for my attraction to them. My own experience suggests that a general bag hunt is a good idea for a first safari, since it's always possible to specialize later—if you are fortunate enough to go on more than one African hunt—in those animals that especially strike your fancy. Hunting and taking a variety of game can also make your safari a richer experience.

If you prefer a particular trophy, before booking your safari, ask potential outfitters how available that animal is in their hunting area, and the quality of that species taken by their clients. You may find there are large differences in the trophy fees charged by outfitters for a particular animal, depending in part on how plentiful it is in the hunt area, supply-and-demand considerations such as quotas, and the costs of doing business in a specific area. A high trophy fee may indicate that exceptional trophies are available, or that the animal is scarce in a certain location. It's probably a good idea to inquire about the success rate for hunting that species as well.

Namibia, for example, appears to have abundant gemsbok, most of which are hunted on large ranches. Trophy fees as well as daily rates there are relatively low compared to, say, Botswana, which also has gemsbok. Similarly, kudu are plentiful in Zimbabwe and costs are low, so trophy fees are low compared to some other countries.

The reasons for these differences in fees are not always clear, but the fact that they exist makes it worthwhile to look at the entire package price for a hunt. The cost of taking the same mix of animals of similar quality might be hundreds or even thousands of dollars different, depending on what country you hunt and what outfitter you choose.

Let me share a few thoughts about deciding which outfitter to book a hunt with. Many hunters simply pick an agent based on the advice of a friend, in much the same way one might pick a dentist or auto repair shop in an unfamiliar area. The agent will recommend a hunt from among those outfitters and PHs he represents that seem to suit the client's needs. This clearly works well for many, but is not necessarily the best approach.

Agents are compensated based on the cost, primarily the daily rates, of the hunts they book for clients. Agents typically represent a few outfitters or PHs with whom they are familiar and with whom they have negotiated satisfactory payment arrangements. Naturally, they will want to sell their more expensive hunts, other things being equal, since they make more money this way. Some would deny this, but that is the way the incentives are stacked.

To the extent that the quality of a hunt is related to its cost, this may not be a problem. You pay more, you get more, sometimes. There are several U.S. agents who have been booking hunts for many years and have hundreds of satisfied clients. Some of these are shown in the appendix on useful contacts. Often the agents themselves have hunted with the outfits they book hunts for, or have at least visited their facilities to make an evaluation. A hunter is, I believe, probably pretty safe booking with one of these agents, though it is hard to know just how good a job they actually do.

You should always ask a potential booking agent or safari company for references, and you should contact several. You can be sure that the names you get will be of people who have had a satisfactory experience with that agent or safari company. The difficulty is that if some client had a bad experience, it will be difficult to learn about it from the agent or outfitter since they will in all likelihood not provide that name as a reference. One way to circumvent this is to ask an agent or outfitter for the names of *all* their clients for the last two to five years, though I'm not sure many would comply with such a request. Then the prospect could contact them on whatever basis he chooses. In the case of the largest agencies, this might be a hundred or more names per year. This is, clearly, the most objective way to assess an outfitter's ability to please their clients, but I know few will be that thorough.

Another excellent approach is to contact nonprofit groups that can provide information on hunts their members or subscribers have taken. There are organizations listed in appendix G, "Useful Contacts," that function as independent third-party sources of information, in much the same way as consumer advocate associations do for purchasing run-of-the-mill goods and services. I think it's an excellent idea for those planning a safari to check with these sources, before committing themselves to a specific hunt to find out what other hunters' experiences have been with a particular outfitter, agent, or professional hunter. As time goes by, I expect the various hunter-oriented chat groups and message boards on the Internet will also increasingly serve this function.

Some agents may book hunts for only one safari company and others with several. Often they will offer a range of hunts, depending on the animals to be hunted and the amenities provided. Many offer both high-end (i.e., higher cost) and low-end "budget" (i.e., lower cost) safaris. The cost may be based on amenities provided, quality of animals available, the fame of the PH involved, and the country or the particular game hunted.

Elsewhere in this book I provide tables showing where some of the most commonly sought African game may be hunted today and the associated costs. But it's important to point out that such a static description, while of some use in planning a safari, cannot be considered comprehensive or even accurate much beyond the date it was prepared. This is true for several reasons.

One reason is related to the availability of game. Depending on population levels, political conditions, and other unpredictable factors such as weather, game that is available today in a particular country may not be available there a year from now, or even a few days from now. A period of severe drought may substantially reduce the numbers of a particular animal you want to hunt. For that matter, whole countries may be off-limits in the future for one reason or another. In Africa, civil war, or more generally politics, is probably the most common event taking a whole country entirely out of the hunting business.

Another reason, on a more positive note, is a trend throughout the southern African region to convert cattle ranches to game ranches. Some of the latter allow hunting, and most provide animals for stock to establish breeding herds on other ranches. Animals that were not available in a specific area at one time may be reintroduced for the purpose of breeding or hunting and could be huntable in the future where they aren't today.

Yet another factor limiting the accuracy of this information is the method I used to screen the entries, and the particular hunts I used as a basis for the tables. Sometimes it was not possible using the data I had to list the trophy and daily fees for one reason or another. This might result in a blank cell in, say, the trophy-fee table, suggesting the animal was not available at all in the country indicated. Also, the database I used to develop the tables represents a convenient nonrandom sample of hunts that I found by writing to several prominent booking agencies, searching the Internet, and using other sources that were easy to access. This method could only produce a true picture of the industry by accident since the fees I show in the tables are indicative of only the hunts available through these sources. Nevertheless, I believe they make an excellent basis for planning a first safari.

The basic costs of an African hunt have remained pretty stable over the last decade, according to the information I have gathered. Daily rates I found in 1999 were similar to those prevailing in 1991, at least for plains game. Trophy fees seem to have increased a bit, but not dramatically in most cases.

The general rule in using the information I have provided is that a blank in a table doesn't necessarily mean the animal isn't available in that country. It may mean only that I did not find one being offered there that I could break down into daily and trophy fees. If in doubt, ask your agent or outfitter.

In the daily- and trophy-fee tables my intention was to list only animals native to the area shown, as opposed to having been introduced in modern times to places where they never existed naturally. For example, one can find lechwe and fallow deer in South Africa, but I do not believe original wild stocks ever existed there. Some hunters want to restrict their hunting to animals native to the region they hunt, others do not or don't care. I believe some of the organizations that keep records of trophies won't allow animals to be entered if they have been taken in an area where they were not originally found. Safari Club International has special rules for entering such animals in its record book.

COUNTRY PROFILES

In the following pages I will give a sketch of each of the countries discussed in this book. The information has come primarily from two sources. First, the U.S. State Department provides information both in print and on the Internet on many countries, and I have drawn heavily from that source. Second, several of these countries have World Wide Web sites that have been useful. Information about hunting per se has come from advertisements, hunting literature, and my own experience. (The Web sites and agents I have used are listed in appendix G, "Useful Contacts.")

The primary reason I wanted to provide this information is to allow a person to plan a hunt in the kind of place he really wants to go and is likely to enjoy the most. The country in which you hunt is likely to materially affect your experience, for better or worse, depending on your preferences and goals.

For starters, there is a huge difference in the overall level of development, education, income per capita, and other socio-economic factors between these countries. They also have different colonial histories, so there may be language problems in one that don't exist in another. Infrastructures, like social institutions, roads, and airports differ considerably, too. The countries also differ in their level of safety.

For example, in Cameroon and Central African Republic, which were once French colonies, French is the most common European language. Compare this to a country such as Botswana, Zimbabwe, or South Africa, which were British colonies, and where English is widely spoken. Unless you speak French, it's probably easier to travel in a former British colony than a former French colony. The language of a country can have a significant effect on one's hunting experience.

Another factor to consider is the state of development in the country where you want to hunt. If, for instance, you want to experience Africa like it was in the early days—as characterized in films and adventure stories—you may be disappointed by a hunt in South Africa or Namibia. South Africa is highly developed and has the highest standard of living in Africa. Most hunting there takes place on private ranches or "farms," as they are usually called there. Other countries in the region may have a more primitive, authentic "feel" that some people are looking for. If you plan to take your wife and young children on safari with you, the relative safety and comfort provided by ranch hunts in South Africa and Namibia may be just right.

One way to evaluate the economies of each country and their level of development is by comparing their total government expenditures. As a standard to evaluate these numbers, keep in mind that in fiscal year 1996–97, the smallest and least populated states in America—including the Dakotas, Wyoming, and Vermont—had total government expenditures of $1 billion to $2 billion. (The data is from the U.S. Census Bureau.) Economic structure, literacy rates, and life expectancy can all give some indications about a country's development.

Figures on population density help measure the "wildness" of a country as a whole, but would not reflect accurately an area like a hunting reserve, which may have no permanent residents. Still, comparing the population density (the number of persons per square kilometer) of states in America with African countries may be helpful when deciding in which countries to hunt. In 1800, the population density of the United States was about 2.4 persons per square kilometer of land area. By 1900, it had increased to nearly 10. By 1990, U.S. population density was about 28 person per square kilometer. By comparison, the population density of Alaska in 1990 was only 4.7 and South Dakota was about 219.

The brief summaries that follow are meant to give you some general guidance in planning a trip to Africa, and may give ideas about what questions to ask of your agent or outfitter.

Botswana

This southern African country, once known as Bechuanaland and whose official name is the Republic of Botswana, is located north of South Africa and west of Zimbabwe. Its western border is with Namibia. The country gained its independence from Britain in 1966.

Botswana is one of several states in the region that are landlocked by having no seaport. In size, the country is slightly smaller than Texas, or, to give a relative size in Europe, about the size of France and Beligum. Its capital city, Gaborone, is near the southern border of South Africa. The Limpopo River forms a long common border between the two countries farther to the northeast. Most of the population of 1.5 million, about the same as Nevada or Vienna, the capital of Austria, is concentrated along its border with Zimbabwe and South Africa. The country's population density of only 2.4 person per square kilometer makes it one of the most sparsely populated in the region.

Economically, Botswana has only 1 percent arable land and is about equally divided between permanent pasture and forests and woodlands. Most of the population work as subsistence farmers, including cattle raising. Mining produced 35 percent of the gross domestic product in 1997, with agriculture contributing 4 percent and services 51 percent. Seventy-one percent of its export value is from diamonds. Government expenditures in fiscal year 1996–97 were about $1.8 billion (all dollar amounts are U.S. dollars,) about like that of Wyoming.

The population is composed almost entirely of native groups, with whites constituting only 1 percent of the population. Half are Christian while half profess "indigenous beliefs". Even with this population mix, the official language is English along with Setswana. The literacy rate is nearly 70 percent, among the highest in southern Africa. Life expectancy is about forty years.

Its terrain is predominantly flat. The northern part is better endowed with water and contains the Okavango Delta, a good deal of which is swampland. This region appears to have most of the elephants and is home to the unusual sitatunga, a swamp-dwelling antelope. The southern part includes the Kalahari Desert, which is said to have no permanent surface water. The south also has the true plains species, including giant oryx or gemsbok, red hartebeest, and springbok. Climate over most of the country is considered semi-arid.

Botswana is considered one of the finest safari destinations. Although historically rather expensive for hunters, I found some plains-game hunts that make a safari there competitive in today's market. A special appeal of this country for hunters is that bushmen trackers are sometimes employed, thus providing an opportunity to watch these legendary hunters in action.

Cameroon

The Republic of Cameroon is a central African country about the size of California or Spain. In colonial times France and Britain claimed parts of the territory. Cameroon is located on the west coast of Africa, with a small section of its southwest border on the Atlantic Ocean. Besides the ocean, Nigeria is its western border, and most of its eastern border is with Central African Republic and Chad. Its capital city is Yaoundé, which is located in the southwestern part of the country. French Cameroon became independent from France in 1957.

The population of Cameroon was estimated to be just over fifteen million in 1998, about the same as the state of Florida or Spain, with a population density of about 32 persons per square kilometer. Less than 1 percent of the population are non-African, the remainder being a mixture of native groups. About half the population professes indigenous beliefs, 33 percent are Christian, and 16 percent Muslim. The literacy rate is about 63 percent and life expectancy is approximately fifty-one years. Coastal climate is considered tropical but the north is semi-arid. Much of the country, nearly 80 percent, consists of dense forest and savanna.

Its oil reserves and seaport strengthen Cameroon's economy, but nearly a third of the economy is in the agricultural sector. Most of its exports are minerals or crops, but also include oil and petroleum products, lumber, cocoa, aluminum, and coffee. Government expenditures in fiscal 1996–97 were about $2.2 billion, about the same as New Hampshire.

Like the Central African Republic, travel within Cameroon is said to be hazardous by the U.S. State Department due to "armed banditry" on the highways, in tourist areas, and in major cities. Persons are said to be "at extreme risk from armed banditry" when traveling outside major towns. Even so, both hunting and game-viewing safaris are routinely booked in Cameroon. Pygmies and lowland gorillas are two of the attractions for visitors.

Cameroon has huntable populations of both giant eland and bongo. It also has northwest and dwarf buffalo, forest elephant, sitatunga, several species of duiker, western roan, and western kob. Some of these animals are generally not available elsewhere except, in some cases, in neighboring Central African Republic.

Central African Republic (CAR)

This central African country is not one of the historically familiar safari destinations like Kenya or Tanzania, at least for U.S. residents. Under French rule it was part of French Equatorial Africa. The country is landlocked and about the size of Texas or Spain and Portugal combined, and in 1998 it had an estimated population of 3.4 million. Population density is low at 5.4 persons per square kilometer. It was proclaimed an independent republic in 1958, and it declared independence from France in 1960. The capital is Bangui, in the southwest part of the country.

Ethnically, less than 1 percent (about 6,500 persons) of the population is European. The balance is made up of various native groups, the largest being the Baya, which, along with the Banda, make up over 60 percent of the population. In this former French colony, French is the official language but Sangho is the lingua franca and national language. The country has one of the lowest life expectancies in the region at less than forty-seven years by the most recent estimate. The literacy rate is 60 percent.

Economically, CAR's population is largely dependent on subsistence agriculture and forestry with over 70 percent living in rural areas. The agricultural sector produces about half the GDP with timber producing about 16 percent of the export value. Over half the value of exports is from the mining industry, especially diamonds. Government expenditures in 1994 were about $2 billion, close to that of North Dakota.

Conditions in the country have been somewhat chaotic for the last several years. There have been mutinies by members of the armed forces over pay, and armed robbery is apparently common even in the capital city. Travel outside major cities is considered dangerous for tourists. The U.S. State Department has recently advised its citizens to "defer travel" to the country because of "highway banditry." The government of CAR recently restricted tourist travel because it was unable to guarantee their safety.

In spite of the apparent dangers of travel today in the CAR, it does offer hunting of African species not available farther south, including the giant eland, bongo, forest and dwarf buffalo, giant forest hog, kob, and western roan.

Ethiopia

Ethiopia achieved its independence at least two thousand years ago, making it one of the oldest countries in the world, and the oldest independent country in Africa. The most recent political arrangement came about as the result of civil war and produced a new constitution in 1994, followed by national elections in 1995. The capital is Addis Ababa, located about center of the country. Its official name is the Federal Democratic Republic of Ethiopia.

Ethiopia is located west of Somalia and, like Botswana and CAR, is landlocked. It has shared borders with Kenya, Somalia, Eritrea, and the Sudan. It is nearly twice the size of Texas, or approximately the size of France, Germany, and Romania combined. Its population today of approximately 58 million is almost twice that of California, since 1990 the most populous U.S. state. Ethiopia's population density is nearly 52 persons per square kilometer, the highest of any country in northeast Africa.

The population is a mixture of several native groups, half being Muslim and 35 to 40 percent being Ethiopian Orthodox. Non-Africans make up less than 1 percent of the population. The official language is Amharic, but several others are spoken, including Arabic, Somali, and English. The literacy rate is about 36 percent, one of the lowest in that region of Africa. The climate is quite variable, described as tropical in some areas, but conditions are strongly influenced by terrain. Life expectancy is a bit less than forty-one years.

Economically, the country is one of the poorest and least developed in the world. Its economy is primarily agricultural, which accounts for over half the GDP, 80 percent of employment, and over 90 percent of exports. The government runs over 90 percent of large industry but only 10 percent of the agricultural sector. Its chief exports are coffee, leather, and gold. The total expenditure budget was $1.5 billion in fiscal year 1996–97, close to that of Vermont.

Today Ethiopia does not attract nearly as many hunters as states farther south. The State Department advises against U.S. citizens traveling to the country because of a decades-long conflict along its border with Eritrea.

The chief attractions for hunters appear to be the mountain nyala and certain East African species not readily available elsewhere, except in Tanzania. It does not appear that there ever were many safari outfitters serving Ethiopia, and the situation is the same today. As a result, hunts offered are limited in number and tend to be quite expensive.

Mozambique

Known as Portuguese East Africa in colonial days, the Republic of Mozambique borders a country regarded as part of eastern Africa (Tanzania), one considered part of central Africa (Zambia), and three considered part of southern Africa (South Africa, Zimbabwe, and Swaziland). Its eastern border is the Indian Ocean, its seacoast being about fifteen hundred miles.

Mozambique is one of the few countries considered in this book to have a tropical to subtropical climate, most others being largely semidesert. But even in this coastal country severe drought is a problem in some areas. The mouths of both the Limpopo and Zambezi Rivers are on the coast of Mozambique.

The country gained its independence from Portugal in 1975. Its capital city is Maputo, which is located in the extreme south of the country near Swaziland. Its population was estimated to be 18.6 million in 1998, roughly that of the state of New York. In total area it is about twice the size of California, or nearly the size of France and Italy combined. Population density is about 23 persons per square kilometer.

Ethnically, the population is virtually all from various native groups. Less than 1 percent of the population is European, and Portuguese is the official language. The population is 30 percent Christian, 20 percent Muslim, and 50 percent have indigenous beliefs. The literacy rate is 40 percent, one of the lowest in the region, and life expectancy is forty-five years.

Mozambique's terrain is predominantly coastal lowlands, with uplands in the center of the country, and mountains in the west and northwest. Fifty-six percent of the country is in "pasture," which may mean marshes or natural grass plains, and 18 percent is classified as woodlands.

Economically, Mozambique was one of the poorest on the globe prior to the end of a civil war in 1992, but conditions are said to have improved since then. Both its infrastructure and economy have been devastated by many years of civil war. Government expenditures in fiscal year 1996–97 were only $600 million, about half that of South Dakota in the same year. Thirty-five percent of the economy is devoted to agriculture which provides the country's principal exports, including shrimp and other crops. Over 50 percent of the GDP is produced by the service sector.

After years of civil war, Mozambique is reawakening as a hunting destination. The country has many of the most desirable game species, including four of the Big Five, nyala, kudu, and sable. At present there appear to be relatively few safari operators in the country, though I hope this will change if the country remains peaceful.

Namibia

The Republic of Namibia, formerly known as South-West Africa, gained independence from the Republic of South Africa in 1990. Its western border is along the South Atlantic Ocean and is 1,572 kilometers long. Paradoxically, the land adjacent to the ocean is very dry; virtually all of it consists of the Namib Desert. The central part of the country is highlands, and the Kalahari Desert forms part of its eastern boundary with Botswana. The capital is Windhoek, located in about the center of the country.

Namibia is about half the size of Alaska, slightly larger than Spain and Italy combined. Its climate is largely desert, with "sparse and erratic rainfall." Even so, 46 percent of the country is pasture and 22 percent woodland. A small part of the country known as the Caprivi Strip projects eastward like a narrow finger along the border with Botswana. This area is different in character from the rest of the country, being much wetter largely because of the Cubango River flowing out of Angola, which forms the Okavango Delta in Botswana.

Namibia's population of 1.6 million is comparable to the state of Nebraska. With a population density of about 2 persons per square kilometer, it's one of the most sparsely populated countries in Africa.

Much of the country was settled by people of German descent, and it has a relatively high proportion of Caucasians at about 7 percent. About half the population belongs to the Ovambo tribe, with much smaller percentages divided among several other native groups. Three percent are classified as Bushmen, which many regard as the original people of the area. Christians, mostly Lutheran, make up 80 to 90 percent of the population. The official language is English, spoken primarily by the white residents. Afrikaans, the common language of South Africa, is spoken by most of the population. German is spoken by about 32 percent. Literacy is estimated at 38 percent and life expectancy is forty-two years.

The economy is highly dependent on extraction of minerals, which account for about 20 percent of the GDP. The country is the fifth largest producer of uranium, is a primary source of diamonds, and produces a variety of other minerals for export. Still, about half the population depends on subsistence agriculture for its livelihood. Total government expenditures were estimated to be $1.2 billion in fiscal year 1996–97, less than that of North Dakota.

Namibia's huntable game is largely on private property, and all hunts I have seen advertised in Namibia are ranch hunts except in Caprivi. It has a somewhat limited range of game available because of its very dry climate, except in the Caprivi Strip, as noted. Accommodations are frequently in cattle ranchers' homes or in rondavels (thatched huts) constructed specifically for hunters and other tourists. According to all accounts I have seen, accommodations are always adequate and the hospitality of the ranchers outstanding. In the section on Africa in *The Best of Jack O'Connor,* O'Connor gives the best description I've read of hunting in Namibia, and it is as relevant today as it was when written over twenty years ago.

The accommodations and relative safety of Namibia make it a good choice for a family safari or a place to take your wife, whether or not she hunts.

Because of its climate, the country hosts mostly animals adapted to arid conditions. It has cheetah, eland, gemsbok, kudu, springbok, hartebeest, wildebeest, zebra, and other game. In the past, elephant have been available to sport hunters in the Caprivi Strip and today are offered on a limited basis. It's one of only two countries, I believe, where it's possible to hunt cheetah.

I have heard that the Bushmen are often used as trackers there, as they are in Botswana, which for many will be a special attraction.

South Africa

South Africa is probably the best known country in the region because of the press coverage of its recent transition from white to black rule. It is by far the most highly developed country in southern Africa. The country, as the Union of South Africa, declared independence from Britain in 1910.

Historically, it was settled by a succession of European colonial powers, including the British, Germans, and Dutch. As a result, a visitor will find South Africans with surnames associated with each of those countries, plus France, whose families have lived in the country for generations and who consider Afrikaans their mother tongue. In 1910 the various independent provinces were united to form the Union of South Africa. Officially, the country is known today as the Republic of South Africa.

This country forms the southern tip of the African continent, and stretches from sea to sea, from the Indian Ocean on the east to the South Atlantic on the west. It has nearly 3,000 kilometers of coastline. Its residents often refer to it as a "world in one country," and its climate varies from semiarid to subtropical. The country is nearly twice the size of Texas, or slightly larger than Sweden, Norway, and Finland combined. Its capital city is Pretoria, which is in the far north, but its legislature is in Cape Town, located on the Cape of Good Hope at the extreme southern tip of the African continent.

The country's ethnicity is diverse, with blacks constituting 75 percent of the population. Whites make up nearly 14 percent, which is much higher than any other African country and about twice that of its closest competitor, Namibia. About two-thirds of the population is Christian, nearly 30 percent traditional native religions, and small percentages are Muslim and Hindu. The population in 1998 was estimated to be nearly 43 million, larger than that of Spain, resulting in a population density of 35 persons per square kilometer.

South Africa's economy is largely dependent on mineral extraction. It's the world leader in the production of gold, platinum, and chromium and has substantial industrial assets. Minerals constitute nearly half the value of its exports. It has more arable land than all other countries in southern Africa. Its stock exchange ranks among the top ten in the world. Its expenditure budget in fiscal year 1994–95 was $38 billion, slightly more than the states of Florida or Texas for the same period. This is well over twenty times that of most countries in the region.

Politically, the country is still somewhat unstable, something its officials would no doubt deny. Its first elections including blacks were held in 1994, and the associated constitution was installed as recently as 1997. As an indication both of its history and continuing ethnic and racial turmoil, the country has eleven *official* languages, including Afrikaans and English, and nine native languages.

I was in South Africa before the 1994 elections, when there may have been more political violence and tension there than there is now. I was never aware of being in any danger, nor did I observe any kind of overt hostility, although signs of tension were clearly evident. The relatively peaceful transition to black majority rule is considered miraculous by many, and resulted in at least three Nobel Peace Prizes being awarded to political and spiritual leaders in South Africa.

Because of the many hunters who travel from the USA to South Africa, and the large number of professional hunters and safari companies operating there, it's probably easier to arrange a hunt there than in any other country in the region. Only Zimbabwe and Namibia appear to compete with South Africa in this respect. The quality of accommodations, availability of services, recognition of English as one of the national languages, and other factors all make South Africa one of the best places for a safari for a couple or family.

It's possible to fly nonstop, from the USA to South Africa, avoiding the increasingly tedious problems associated with taking flights through Europe. Johannesburg and Cape Town are the primary destinations in southern Africa for flights originating in Europe and the USA. People planning to hunt in Namibia, Botswana, and Mozambique often link through Johannesburg International Airport (formerly Jan Smuts Airport). Because of its extraordinary infrastructure it's much easier, and probably safer, to get from one hunting venue to another in South Africa than in any other country discussed here, with the possible exception of Namibia.

South Africa has the distinction of being the home of many animals that are not available anywhere else. All the Big Five, including the rhino, may be hunted there, the only country to my knowledge where this is possible. The blesbok and bontebok, which looks like a color phase of the blesbok, and black wildebeest are available nowhere else to my knowledge, except possibly neighboring Namibia. It has the most accessible population of common nyala. Some small antelope such as the vaal rhebok are not available anywhere else that I am aware of. The mountain reedbuck is available in a few locations farther north, but most are probably taken in South Africa. The country has most of the desirable plains and bush species that form the backbone of most safaris.

Tanzania

The United Republic of Tanzania is one of only two East African countries included in this survey. It is one of the most significant hunting destinations in Africa and has been since foreigners began coming to that continent to hunt or to observe and photograph wildlife over a hundred years ago. It is home to the famous Serengeti Plains and Mt. Kilimanjaro, the highest point on the African continent.

Formerly known as Tanganyika, the United Republic of Tanzania is bordered on the north by Kenya and Uganda, on the east by the Indian Ocean, on the west by Rwanda, and on the south by Zambia, Mozambique, and Malawi. Because of the maritime influence, Tanzania, like Mozambique, has a tropical climate along the coast with more temperate highlands in the interior. The capital is Dar es Salaam, which is on the Indian Ocean. The country is more than twice the size of California, or the combined size of France, Germany, and Belgium. It gained independence from Britain in 1961. The present structure of the country resulted from union with Zanzibar in 1964.

Tanzania does not appear to have as serious a problem with recurring drought as many countries in the region, and, as noted earlier, its climate varies from tropical along the coast to temperate inland. But it is still plagued by the scourge of early European settlers, the tsetse fly.

With a population estimated at 30.6 million in 1998, about the size of California's, it has a population density of 32 persons per square kilometer.

Economically, Tanzania is one of the poorest countries in the world. It is heavily dependent on its agricultural sector, which accounts for over half of its gross domestic product and 85 percent of its exports, and which employs 90 percent of the population. Its expenditure budget in fiscal year 1996–97 was just over $1 billion, roughly half that of New Hampshire during that period. Life expectancy is less than forty-seven, and the literacy rate is less than 68 percent.

Tanzania's ethnicity is almost 99 percent black Africans, 95 percent of whom represent various Bantu tribes.

Europeans, Asians, and Arabs together make up only 1 percent of the population. Swahili, the lingua franca of eastern and central Africa, is, along with English, an official language in Tanzania. If you hear an African language spoken in a film, it will undoubtedly be Swahili, or Zulu if set in South Africa.

The landscape of Tanzania, of all the countries discussed here, probably most epitomizes the African safari as most people think of it. It seems likely more people associate the open plains and savannas of the Serengeti with safari hunting than with any other kind of terrain.

Regarding hunting in Tanzania, there is both good news and bad news. Part of the good news is that the country is home to all the Big Five and other animals associated with safaris. The only thing missing today for hunters is the black rhino, which has been driven to the edge of extinction by machine-gun-toting poachers, and those animals that are, and always have been, are found farther south. It is likely that, with these exceptions, some variety of the animals typically sought on safari can be hunted in Tanzania. There are both greater and lesser kudu, sable, fringe-eared oryx, bushbuck, zebra, wildebeest, and many other species available.

One factor that made Tanzania and the former French colonies, Cameroon and Central African Republic, different from other countries is the way hunts are priced. Outfitters in these three countries seem to charge the same daily rate to hunt all game, including any of the Big Five, rather than different rates for elephant, buffalo, lion, plains game only, and so on. In all three countries, trophy fees tend to be a little lower, daily rates higher, and minimum hunts longer than in countries farther south. High daily rates plus long minimum hunts make expensive total safari costs.

Part of the bad news is that this is one of the most expensive places to hunt, ranking third in my survey behind the two former French colonies mentioned above. In this book I use a "standard" hunt (see next chapter) as the basis for comparing the costs of a hunt in different countries. Using my standard hunt as the criterion, I found that a hunt in Tanzania can cost twice what it would in some other countries of the region. If money is no object, or the appeal of this great, traditional hunting country is irresistible, I have no doubt you can have a fine and memorable hunt there. But you will pay a premium for it.

Zambia

Formerly Northern Rhodesia, the Republic of Zambia is a south-central African country about the size of Texas, or the combined size of Sweden and Finland. It gained its independence from Britain in 1964, nearly twenty years before the southern half of Rhodesia, now known as Zimbabwe, achieved its independence from Britain.

Zambia is another landlocked country, without a seacoast. Its rather unusual shape and size results in its having many bordering countries. To the north are the Congo and Tanzania. To the west it has a long border with Angola, and to the east it borders Malawi. Mozambique and Zimbabwe form its southern border. Its capital is Lusaka, located in the southern part of the country near the border with Zimbabwe.

Like most of the countries in the region it has little arable land, only 7 percent, and is 40 percent "permanent pastures," which often means native grasslands, and about the same percentage is forests and woodlands. Its population of over 9 million, comparable to that of Michigan, is spread rather thinly, resulting in a population density of about 13 persons per square kilometer. Life expectancy is slightly over thirty-seven years, and the literacy rate is nearly 80 percent. The population is 50 to 75 percent Christian, the rest mostly Muslim and Hindu.

Economically, Zambia earns 80 percent of its foreign currency from the export of copper. Agriculture accounts for about one-fourth of the GDP, and industry contributes nearly 40 percent of the total. Other exports include various minerals and tobacco. Government expenditures in 1995 were only $835 million, about one-half that of South Dakota.

Drought seems not to be as big a problem in Zambia as in most countries of the region. This is due to the country's seven-month-long rainy season, caused by the country's elevated terrain. The climate in most of the country is tropical, and tropical storms are the main natural hazard.

Like most of the countries in the region, Zambia is 99 percent black with the rest being of European descent. The official language is English, with over seventy-seven indigenous languages spoken throughout the country. The literacy rate is said to be about 80 percent, the second highest in the region, but life expectancy is low at slightly more than thirty-seven years.

As a hunting destination, Zambia has much to offer. There appear to be a number of experienced safari companies operating there, which should mean more hunts and more choices, which in turn should lower prices. Still, Zambia is one of the most expensive countries in the region to hunt.

The country is home to the Big Five but neither elephant nor rhino can be hunted there at this time. Lion, leopard, and buffalo are available. At least three varieties of lechwe—Kafue, black, and red—occur in Zambia, and the black and red are available nowhere else I know of. It is one of only two countries where puku are available, as that animal only shows up on trophy-fee lists for Zambia and Tanzania. Zambia has some of the most desirable plains species such as sable and greater kudu, and is one of the few places in the region where you can take roan antelope.

Zimbabwe

Formerly Southern Rhodesia, Zimbabwe is yet another landlocked southern African country somewhat larger than the state of Montana or Germany and Belgium combined. Like its northern neighbor, Zambia, the country has a colorful colonial past. As Southern Rhodesia, the country declared its independence from Britain in 1964, but a civil war raged for sixteen years between native factions and the white Rhodesian government. The country came under black rule on 18 April 1980, which is considered the country's Independence Day. During the long civil war, international sanctions were imposed that seem to have fostered a strong ethic for independence among the population of Zimbabwe.

The country borders several of the other significant hunting countries in the area, including Zambia, Mozambique, South Africa, and Botswana. Zimbabwe has a population of 11 million, about the same as that of Illinois or Ohio. Population density is 28 persons per square kilometer. Its capital city is Harare, which is in the northeastern part of the country.

Ethnically, the population is virtually 98 percent native African, with only 1 percent white. The largest native group is the Shona tribe (71 percent), with the Ndebele tribe considerably smaller (16 percent). Literacy is the highest in the region at 85 percent, and life expectancy is about thirty-nine years. The official "commercial" language is English, but both Shona and Sindebele are also officially recognized.

Zimbabwe's exports include minerals at 20 percent but this sector constitutes only about 5 percent of the GDP and employment. Just over a quarter of the population is employed in agriculture, which provides nearly 40 percent of its exports, and manufactured goods contribute another third. Until recently the government has had a decidedly Marxist bent, but like many other African countries it is trying to develop a market-driven economy. Government expenditures in fiscal year 1996–97 were less than $3 billion, which is lower than that of Rhode Island for that period.

Zimbabwe is one of the most popular safari destinations. I suspect this is true because the country has a variety of game, and it is relatively inexpensive to hunt there. The cost of hunting in Zimbabwe appears comparable to Namibia and South Africa, measured by the sample standard hunt discussed later in this book.

All the Big Five live there, but rhino cannot be hunted now. Several ranchers in the southern part of the country are making considerable efforts to convert their properties from cattle to game production, and it appears their effort is paying off in larger populations of game animals, including endangered ones like rhino. Because of this effort, it's possible that rhino might again be available at some time in the future.

WHAT DOES A SAFARI COST?

By now, you probably realize that the question asked in the title of this chapter cannot be answered quickly. Some of the issues have already been addressed in chapter 1; in this chapter I will go into more detail, but keep in mind that the cost of the safari you plan may be quite different because of a variety of factors.

CLOTHING AND EQUIPMENT

I'll start with special equipment and apparel that you'll need for hunting in Africa. The good news is, there isn't any. I will ignore the issue of guns and ammunition, which is covered in chapter 7. Aside from guns and ammo, though, many people can outfit themselves with what they have on hand by simply taking a few articles of clothing from their closets, grabbing their binoculars, sunscreen, and insect repellent, and getting on the plane for Johannesburg. Overall the process is far simpler and cheaper than outfitting for a hunt in Wyoming in November for elk. As the chapter on rifles and ammo indicates, there is an excellent chance you already have what you need in that department, too.

Chapter 6 includes some clothing recommendations, and appendix E provides a safari checklist. In brief, a couple pairs of shorts and long pants, a quilted jacket, a baseball cap, a T-shirt or two, and some well-broken-in running shoes make a fine basis for a safari in most areas. Cost? Let's be generous and say $200 if you have to buy it all from scratch. I paid about that much just for the waterproof leather boots I use for elk hunting! Never mind what I've spent on horses, tents, and foul-weather gear. In spite of what you may have heard elsewhere, a monocle and bush coat with cartridge loops are *not* necessary!

If you want to go whole hog and buy new clothing for your African hunt, you might look at the line of safari wear sold by Cabela's. They have clothing for men and women in appropriate colors at very reasonable prices. A complete outfit from hat to boots would cost you less than $300 per person. I have used this clothing on safari and found it completely satisfactory.

Some items you *will* need are a passport and perhaps a visa. Add a few bucks for vaccinations and malaria pills, and whatever medication you'd need if you never left the house. Cost? At most a few bucks for postage and the cost of the medications, which is pretty nominal.

One item of equipment you will surely need is a sturdy gun case to take on the plane. In my view, the flimsy plastic cases available at discount stores are risky. My recommendation is to purchase a heavy-duty case made of aluminum, to minimize weight, that is lockable. Whatever you decide, be sure it meets the requirements of the airline on which you will be traveling. A good case of this type starts at around $200, and Cabela's carries those as well as other fine outdoor gear. You will also need an outdoor kit, the contents of which I list in appendix E.

AIR TRAVEL

One big-ticket item you must have is a round-trip plane ticket. All fares mentioned here are "economy class."

One factor influencing travel expenses will be any layovers, dayrooms, or other special features you want to incorporate into your itinerary. I have omitted flights from your initial African destination to the actual site of your hunt. To keep it simple, I have used New York as the departure point for flights that go through Europe, and Miami for direct flights. In all cases the African destination is Johannesburg, South Africa.

For residents of the USA, the recent addition of direct flights to Africa may be the most significant development in travel options. This is an important development because flying direct avoids the hassles associated with linking flights through Europe, particularly Great Britain, which one correspondent referred to as a nightmare. Direct flights also completely avoid the considerable chance of lost or delayed baggage. If the baggage gets on the plane with you, you'll see it at your African destination. I regard this as a huge benefit and would not even consider the alternative when traveling to Africa.

If you plan a stopover in Europe, the situation is quite different. In that case you'll need to deal with the problems associated with that kind of flight. I would only advise you to minimize the opportunity for serious problems. This is where an experienced travel agent can really be helpful, whether it's the same person who books your safari or someone else.

Today, I have seen round-trip, direct flights from Miami to Johannesburg quoted as low as $800, though the average seems closer to $1,300. In 1991 my round-trip airfare on Lufthansa from Los Angeles, via New York and Frankfurt, to Johannesburg was just over $2,500. In Frankfurt I had a layover of several hours, and continued on a different Lufthansa flight to Johannesburg.

My 1991 flight was before the first all-race elections were held in South Africa, and many airlines and other companies refused to do business with the country. Now the situation is different. I recently checked a Web site that claims to provide economy fares to Africa, and the site showed no less than eleven airlines flying from New York to Johannesburg. Fares for one adult ranged from about $1,000 on Ethiopian Airlines to $1,600 on Delta, round-trip. Lufthansa was in the middle of the pack at about $1,400.

In addition to the cost of traveling from your home to the departure city for your flight to Africa, some hunts may *require* that you charter an aircraft for travel to your hunting area once you arrive in Africa. Some safari camps even have their own airstrips. These flights can be very costly. One outfit charges $6,000 just for flying into and out of its camp, for one person. Observers are extra. This is very nearly enough for a complete plains game safari in some other countries, including international airfare!

Air charters are usually *optional* and save time compared to travel by road. Sometimes ground transfers to and from the hunting camp are included in the daily rate, whereas air charters always appear to cost extra. If minimizing travel time is important enough, perhaps these charters are worth the cost.

Sometimes it's necessary to travel from one safari camp to another to obtain all the animals a hunter wants. Frequently, one is given the option of doing this by road or locally chartered aircraft. You may have to decide at the time the hunt is booked which you prefer.

THE HUNT

So you have all your items together. Your unloaded rifles are sighted in and locked in a heavy-duty case. You've had any required shots, started your course of malaria medication, and assembled all medications you need for the entire trip and have prescriptions for each one. You have your visa (if required) and passport, and customs documentation of the guns, cameras, and similar equipment you will be taking so that you can bring them home without difficulty (which I detail in chapter 5). So what about the safari?

The first thing you should realize is that you will be asked, in all probability, to deposit 50 percent or more of the total daily fees at the time you book your hunt. Depending on how lavish an affair you are planning, this is likely to be several thousand dollars. This money will probably not be refundable unless you cancel within a specified time frame, and only then, perhaps, if the safari company can rebook the hunt.

The balance, which includes trophy fees, will generally be paid at the end of the hunt. (The cost of preparing and shipping trophies is discussed in chapter 8.) But I have seen some hunts offered that require full payment some time before the safari begins. Unless you do pay for everything in advance, the method of paying the balance after your safari ends should be clearly spelled out, in writing, before you leave home. Specifically, you need to know what method of payment will be accepted. Some safari companies probably accept Visa or MasterCard today, but I'd guess most don't. They are likely to want cash, traveler's checks (they may even specify the brand or issuer), or some equally secure form of payment. Don't plan to write them a personal check on your bank at home unless they have agreed to that beforehand, in writing.

Often, safari companies in the former French colonies of Cameroon and CAR require payment in French francs, which just serves to illustrate that one needs to know precisely what form of payment is acceptable to your safari outfit. These outfits, and their agents, sometimes quote their fees in French francs as well. There are Web sites that will convert these fees from francs (abbreviated "ff") to U.S. dollars, and the value will fluctuate with the prevailing rate of exchange. Major newspapers will often list current exchange rates, too.

COST OF A STANDARD HUNT

Since there is a nearly endless variety of combination hunts for the Big Five and plains game, and many types of plains-game hunts, it would be impossible to determine "the" price of a hunt without a clear definition of what I'm talking about. One way to illustrate the differences in cost between countries is to price the same hunt in each of them. My approach has been to price a hypothetical plains-game-only hunt for specific animals and of fixed duration. I call this the "standard" hunt.

This general bag of plains game will be quite similar anywhere in the region, though in a few cases I substituted a comparable animal when it wasn't available in a particular country. In some cases I couldn't decide on a comparable animal to substitute, so I used the average trophy fee for the missing animal. If you want to include one of the Big Five or glamour plains game, the charts on daily fees (appendix A) and trophy fees (appendix B) should give you an idea of what such a hunt would cost.

In the daily rate table in appendix A, I refer to the hunts combining *one* of the Big Five with plains game as "combo" hunts, but there are many other combinations offered or which may be negotiated. An example might be buffalo plus leopard and plains game. Since such combinations are practically endless, I have not tried to establish a standard hunt of this type.

My standard hunt is for fourteen days, and includes all basic services customarily included in the daily rates (see chapter 1) plus special fees, and trophy fees for the standard bag. When they were stated in ads for a particular hunt, I have included things like license fees and conservation or concession fees—everything not associated with a particular animal—in the total figure as part of the daily fee.

I want to emphasize that a hunt at the daily rate in the table and for the length of time indicated *might not actually be available.* The daily rates and trophy fees shown in the tables are *averages,* and may not represent any actual daily or trophy fee charged in the area. For example, in the same country there may be only bargain hunts priced relatively low and others priced much higher, so the average of the two might represent an intermediate daily rate that no existing company actually charges. Also, minimum hunt lengths may be longer in a particular country than the *shortest* one I found, which is what I listed in the daily rate table. Another factor is that some animals in addition to my standard bag, like sable or sitatunga for example, may not be available on a fourteen-day hunt, though most plains game and frequently one of the Big Five, can be taken on hunts of that length.

Another requirement to standardize the hypothetical hunt was to include the same group of animals in each one. This was not too difficult since *some variety* of each animal I've included was nearly always available in each country. When there were animals on the menu in a particular country that were not available in most countries, I listed them separately and called them "special animals." I believe in nearly all cases these could be taken on a fourteen-day hunt, too. The total cost of a hunt that included one or more of these special animals can be estimated by adding the trophy fees for them to the total standard-hunt cost. For instance, if you wanted to take a klipspringer in addition to the standard bag, you would just add the trophy fee for one of these little antelope to the price of the standard hunt where you are going.

As with daily rates, the trophy fees used to calculate the standard-hunt cost were averages for the country where the hunt takes place. For example, to calculate the total cost of a standard hunt in Namibia, I used average daily rates and trophy fees for that country.

As a review of the information provided indicates, a hunt of the same length for the same animals can vary considerably from country to country. The cost of this standard plains-game hunt ranges from a low of about $10,000 in Namibia to a high of about $31,000 in CAR. This does *not* include airfare, transfers, and expenses before or after the hunt. It may not include the cost of *field preparation* of trophies either if this was not included in daily rates. Charges for that service vary considerably and today are not always included in the daily rate. If the outfitter does not state the charges for field preparation up front, the hunter should ask about them. Similarly, the cost of preparing trophies for international shipment can differ greatly, and I suggest a hunter get this information before a hunt is booked.

It is a fact that if you want certain animals, your choice of hunts may be very limited. If you have your heart set on bagging a grand slam of lechwe, you are going to have to hunt in Zambia, period. Similarly, if you want a black wildebeest or a springbok, you will of necessity limit yourself to the general area of the Kalahari Desert in Botswana and South Africa or Namibia. If you want a lesser kudu, you will probably have to hunt in Tanzania or Ethiopia, and so on.

Some safari companies have affiliates in more than one country, so it may be possible to travel between countries to obtain a specific animal. This is likely to increase the cost considerably, so I believe most people will be better off choosing a country where most of the game they want is available. You can save the animals you don't get on your first hunt for your next safari. But if you would like to take an animal that does not appear to be available where you plan to hunt, it doesn't hurt to ask the outfitter or agent about the chances of including one somehow.

Cost, of course, is always an important consideration. Below are 2000 costs for a standard hunt in the African countires discussed in this book. The duration for each hunt is 14 days, and the animals included in each hunt are the following: bushbuck, duiker, hartebeest, greater kudu, warthog, waterbuck, wildebeest, and zebra.

Botswana

A standard hunt in Botswana costs $12,900. The special animals that can be hunted there are sitatunga, gemsbok, red lechwe, and springbok.

Cameroon

A standard hunt in Cameroon costs $25,550. The special animals there are bongo, giant eland, northwestern buffalo, dwarf buffalo, duiker, forest elephant, kob, roan, sitatunga, and giant forest hog.

Central African Republic

A standard hunt in Central African Republic costs $30,930. The special animals in CAR are bongo, giant eland, sitatunga, northwestern buffalo, dwarf buffalo, forest duiker, roan, kob, and giant forest hog.

Ethiopia

A standard hunt in Ethiopia costs $17, 860. The special animals that can be hunted there are lesser kudu, mountain nyala, besia oryx, and dik-dik.

Mozambique

A standard hunt in Mozambique costs $17,860. The special animal that can be hunted there is common nyala.

Namibia

A standard hunt in Namibia is $10,310. The special animals there are mountain zebra, roan, springbok, gemsbok, black wildebeest, blesbok, cheetah, and did-dik.

South Africa

A standard hunt in South Africa costs $11,620. The special animals there are common nyala, black wildebeest, blesbok, bontebok, mountain reedbuck, vaal rhebok, springbok, gemsbok, and mountain zebra.

Tanzania

A standard hunt in Tanzania costs $21,340. The special animals available there are did-dik, fringe-eared oryx, lesser kudu, East African impala, and sitatunga.

Zambia

A standard hunt in Zambia costs $19,480. The special animals that can be hunted there are red lechwe, black lechwe, kafue lechwe, roan, sassaby, and sitatunga.

Zimbabwe

A standard hunt in Zimbabwe costs $10,760. The special animals there are common nyala, sassaby, Sharpe grysbok, and cheetah.

* * * * * * *

I thought it would be interesting to compare the costs of a safari today to a similar hunt in the past. Elmer Keith's book *Safari,* published in 1968, provided information that makes it possible to make some comparisons. Unfortunately, there was not enough data provided to price a "standard" hunt, including trophy fees, as I have done for current conditions. But there was enough information to compare daily rates in several of the countries shown above for 1968 and 2000.

Here is how daily rates in 1968 compare to the average daily rates shown in the table in an appendix of this book. The figures from 1968 are based on only one or two safari companies, while those in the table are often based on four or five companies. Since all the fees shown in Keith's book permitted hunting some, if not all, of the Big Five as well as all plains game, I have used daily rates (see appendix A) from the "combo" hunt for buffalo. Recall that this would entitle the hunter to take a buffalo and an assortment of plains game. Daily fees in 1968 ranged from a low of $112 in South Africa to a high of $227 in Zambia, with the CAR a close runner-up at $225, but the average was $168 for the eight southern African countries for which I had data.

Historical Perspective: Comparing 1968 Safari Prices with 2000 Prices

Year	1968	2000
Botswana	$167	$1,100
CAR	$225	$1,680
Ethiopia	$180	$1,500
Mozambique	$190	$ 760
Namibia	$116	$ 860
RSA	$112	$ 600
Tanzania	$130	$1,020
Zambia	$227	$ 940
Average	$168	$1,058

The average daily rate from 1968 to 2000 has increased 530 percent.

It is also interesting to compare trophy fees from 1968 to those charged today for the same animals. Data for this comparison comes from Keith's book but was only available for two countries, Tanzania and Mozambique. It is somewhat difficult to compare these fees of yesteryear with Mozambique's today since in 1968 several plains-game species were included in the basic license without any additional trophy fees. Apparently Tanzania charged trophy fees for all animals taken.

Comparison of Trophy Fees
Mozambique

Year	1968	2000
Elephant [1*]	$123	$NA
Lion	$ 53	$3,750
Kudu	$ 42	$ 650
Leopard	$ 53	$3,250
Eland	$ 42	$1,500
Common nyala	$ 71	$1,130
Sable	$ 42	$2,820
Average	$ 61	$2,183

Tanzania

	1968	2000
Elephant [2*]	$210	$4,780
Lion	$143	$2,230
Leopard	$129	$2,200
Eland	$ 29	$1,030
Buffalo	$ 14	$ 780
Average	$105	$2,204

[1*] It appears this was a flat rate and not dependent on ivory weight.
[2*] Trophy fee based on weight of ivory. A seventy-five-pound tusk would cost, for example, about $1,300.

Lion can be hunted in all the countries featured in this book. Many consider it the most dangerous of the Big Five.

Like the hartebeest, the sassaby (left) has a hump at the withers and a sloping back

Steenbok, available in all the countries featured except Ethiopia, Cameroon, and CAR, are an example of the small antelope.

Acute hearing and camouflage are two of the kudu's primary defenses against predators.

Keeping the safari vehicle running became a family affair when we stopped at a PH's house located on the ranch where I hunted.

Travel on roads in Zimbabwe was often nerve-racking because of the large number of people walking along them, day and night.

The Land Rover's tire is covered with thorns collected while driving through the bush. This resulted in flats almost every day.

A reminder of the recently ended civil war. Wire mesh covers the windows of this Zimbabwe ranch building.

The bungalo is for clients at a Zimbabwe safari camp. With its thatched roof and brick construction, it is built in the style of local structures.

The brick bathhouse, complete with shower and flush toilet, helped make us comfortable at Turgwe Camp.

This young kudu bull on the left is much less impressive than the trophy-class bull on the right.

Turgwe Camp was clean and accommodating.

The local Zambezi beer was cold and of high quality, a welcome treat after a hot day afield.

The curious "Blue Motel" in Zululand. Note the high electric fence.

My PH and his father at their game ranch in South Africa. They are watching a herd of kudu bulls grazing outside the ranch's front gate.

Today, some African game species are actually increasing, resulting in cattle ranches being converted into game ranches.

Four-wheel-drive vehicles made remote areas accessible to sportsmen, and today are a central feature of most safaris.

This comfortable bar is one of the amenities of permanent safari camps.

Concrete patio with firepit overlooks the Turgwe River at a Zimbabwe safari camp.

Common waterbuck, available in all the countries featured, displaying the characteristic bull's-eye rear end. Waterbuck prefer habitat that has a lot of water.

Impala are numerous, and even a slightly above-average specimen makes a fine trophy. This is a young impala that, if taken, would probably not be for trophy but for bait or for its beautiful hide.

In some African countries, elephant have been protected so successfully that thousands have been culled to keep the population from destroying habitat.

Here, elephant have pushed over a tree to get at its fruit and leaves.

Blue wildebeest are a familiar African antelope, living in large numbers in some areas of southern Africa.

Most safaris today are conducted from permanent facilities like this one rather than from mobile tents, as they were in the early days of the safari industry.

The mesh enclosure is the skinning and caping area at Turgwe Camp, complete with cement floor, drain, and running water.

Greater kudu are considered the finest trophy among the common antelope.

Common reedbuck favors relatively wet areas, so its distribution is spotty in the dry habitat in southern Africa.

The ground hornbill is one of many nongame bird species encountered on safari.

Trixie, the Lion Dog.

The warthog is common to all the countries featured.

Ranch hunts typically offer amenities not available in mobile tented safaris, such as this cement game-cleaning area.

After a gut shot, this kudu bull was brought to bag only because of skillful tracking

Handling trophies is considerably easier on ranch hunts than in field camps. Here my PH's father and a farm hand skin my waterbuck.

Zulus were recruited to pack out my nyala from the canyon.

Common duiker, representative of the small antelopes, are the most widely distributed of the duikers, living in huntable numbers throughout southern Africa.

On my bargain-priced hunt in South Africa, the PH performed the caping and skinning of trophies.

Zebra is one of the heaviest of plains game. Five people are needed to load this one into the safari vehicle.

Two men from a rancher-supported antipoaching team with a rhino skull.

Thorns like these make taking a rest on the local vegetation a tad difficult.

Below is a list of the African countries covered in this book, ranked by their hunting fees from most expensive to least expensive:

1. Central African Republic (CAR)
2. Cameroon
3. Tanzania
4. Zambia
5. Ethiopia
6. Mozambique
7. Botswana
8. South Africa
9. Zimbabwe
10. Namibia

Note that the ranking reflects the total cost and that, in many cases, the difference in the price of a standard hunt between any two adjacent countries in the rank order was only about $1,000.

There were several surprises in this ranking for me. Botswana, which I have always considered an expensive place to hunt, ranks seventh on the list. This was because I found some plains-game-only hunts offered at much lower daily rates than is typical for combo hunts in that country. I was also surprised to see that South Africa ranked so low. Keep in mind that these rankings would very likely change, possibly dramatically, if a different combination of animals was included. At best, this kind of analysis can only give a rough idea of the relative cost to hunt these "basic" plains game animals in these countries.

It is interesting that daily rates rather than trophy fees account for most of the higher cost to hunt these countries. This is evident even when using my hypothetical fourteen-day hunt and ignoring situations where minimum hunts were actually longer. There was far more variation in the set of total daily rates than total trophy fees.

Trophy fees for the standard fourteen-day hunt ranged from $4,120 in Tanzania to $7,410 in the CAR, a range of about $3,000. At the same time, daily rates went from a low of $5,180 in Zimbabwe to $23,520 in CAR, a difference of more than $18,000! However, these rates are not entirely comparable because of differences in the way daily fees for various animals are set in the different countries. In CAR, for instance, daily rates for buffalo or lion are often the same as what you'd pay to hunt only plains game. A similar situation prevails in Cameroon and Tanzania.

As a closing thought on the subject, it would, I believe, be a mistake for most people to base their choice of a hunt on cost alone. Most of us will make only one safari in our lifetime, I suspect, and there are several factors that should be considered in making this decision besides the expense. Note also that the costs are very similar in several cases, often differing by only a few hundred dollars, and should probably be considered equivalent because of the many ways total costs can vary based on your particular choices. Still, I trust this analysis will be of some value to the hunter committed to making an African hunt in deciding where to go and what to hunt when you get there.

TRAVEL AND HEALTH

In the early twentieth century, the only way to get to Africa from America was by boat. Now, at the beginning of the twenty-first century, I doubt seriously if anyone would consider any other mode of travel than jumbo jet.

At present there are at least eleven airlines offering flights from the USA to southern Africa. The traditional route is through Europe, mostly through London or Frankfurt, thence to points south. Which route is preferable for a particular hunter will depend on several factors. Clearly, if you want to combine a stopover in Europe with your safari, linking through an international airport there is the way to go. If you are not planning a stopover on the Continent, however, you should consider one of the direct flights offered by South African Airways.

A transatlantic flight from New York to Frankfurt takes approximately seven hours, and from Frankfurt to Johannesburg about ten hours. Since there is often only one flight per day to South Africa by each airline, there may be a substantial layover in Frankfurt. South African Airlines has a direct flight to South Africa from Miami that goes initially to Cape Town and then to Johannesburg. Based on their published flight schedules, the direct route is approximately six hours shorter than going via Frankfurt, but it still takes around seventeen hours, including a layover in Cape Town. That's a long time to be on a plane.

Anyone who has traveled internationally by air realizes that there are certain hardships involved in doing so that need to be addressed. Perhaps the most important of these, on a personal level, is sleep. I found it virtually impossible to sleep on the plane going to or from Africa, and others I've talked with admit to the same problem. I also had to fly across the USA since I lived on the West Coast. Actually, I lived in Alaska at the time, so just getting to the Lower Forty-eight was a matter of a few hours by air. There weren't any suitable direct flights to New York available.

I stayed up late getting gear ready, and my flight left Juneau early in the morning. I also had to make two plane changes within the USA en route to Frankfurt. As a result, when I arrived at that German airport, I had not slept for nearly twenty-four hours and was exhausted. Like many other weary international travelers, I simply curled up on one of the benches along the corridor of the terminal and slept for a while. I can't say I'd recommend these particular accommodations though.

The flight to Johannesburg was similarly exhausting, and by the time I arrived in South Africa, I was a zombie from lack of sleep and the stress of the trip. That none of my baggage, including my rifles, made it to Johannesburg International Airport when I did, didn't help my mood or stress level. Desperately needing some rest by then, I rented a dayroom in a hotel at the airport, where I took a shower and slept for a few hours before my flight to Harare, Zimbabwe, where my safari was to begin. This experience made me a believer in the idea of booking a room in advance to get caught up on sleep after long legs of a flight.

Since many people find a long trip by plane stressful and travelers are often deprived of sleep, travel agents often suggest reserving a dayroom and scheduling extra time to recuperate after each extended leg of the trip. I decided not to avail myself of this luxury because of the cost and extra time involved. But after my first experience of traveling to Africa, I highly recommend that you pamper yourself and include at least a brief respite in a dayroom, and a layover of several hours or even overnight stay if possible. I believe doing so will help in overcoming the physiological effects caused by jet lag in traveling to the Southern Hemisphere. Having adequate rest will also enhance your hunting enjoyment, not to mention your shooting ability. Remember, this trip requires a nearly complete reversal of your normal waking-sleeping cycle because of the time changes involved (Johannesburg is about nine hours ahead of West Coast time.) Some adjust to this change easily, others do not. If you already know how your body responds to time changes, you can plan accordingly. If not, I suggest you plan a rest stop if you go through Europe.

Perhaps the only thorny issue facing hunters traveling to Africa today is the transportation of their firearms. There is some uniformity among the airlines flying to Africa in the way they handle firearms, but from what I understand their attitudes toward *people* flying with firearms may differ considerably and may change over time. Therefore, it is imperative that you inquire, close to the time of departure, just what is required by the airline you'll be flying. Get their guidelines in writing if possible.

I have a vivid memory of an experience at Anchorage International Airport in September 1965 involving air travel with guns. I was waiting to board my flight to Seattle when I observed a young man in his twenties, his wife, and small child walking up the ramp into their waiting jet. Over his shoulder the young man carried a Winchester Model 71 in .348 caliber. No case, no panic, no problem. I'm guessing he just held the gun between his knees during the flight. Well, pilgrim, we live in a different world today.

An experience I had while doing research for this book will illustrate how confusing the situation can get, and why it is imperative that you use a travel agent, or consult with someone if you book your own flight, who is up to snuff on your airline's policies about traveling with guns.

When I was planning my first safari in early 1991, I learned that British Airways had for years been considered by hunters and travel agents I spoke with a "firearm friendly" airline. They have a long history of transporting hunters to Africa, and I'd always heard they were accommodating regarding the shipment of sporting weapons as checked baggage.

But when I was doing the research for this book in 1999, I was told by a British Airways ticket agent that the airline currently has a "total embargo" on firearms of any type, including sporting rifles. This meant, he advised, that no firearms could be taken on any British Airways flight, period. For verification I was referred to the cargo division.

When I inquired about this policy of the local British Airways cargo office, the gentleman I spoke with confirmed it and read a bulletin to me issued by the British Airways home office in London. It clearly stated that no weapons of any sort would be accepted by that airline. I was told by the agent that this total ban on firearms was the result of the Dunblane massacre, in which a deranged man killed several children in Scotland.

After several phone calls and international exchanges of E-mail, I determined I had been misinformed by the ticket agent I had initially contacted. Later I confirmed to my satisfaction that British Airways will accept firearms as checked baggage, though, as with other airlines, there are very specific requirements on how the guns should be packed and handled. If I had actually booked travel on British Airways for a safari, the misinformation I received initially would have been disturbing, to say the least.

The British government today is very hostile to the private ownership and use of firearms as are many of the former colonies of Britain, like Canada and Australia, which find new ways to express their hostility on a regular basis. As a result, if you intend to route through Britain, you must be very sure you comply with the rules and regulations in force at the time. This is advisable when traveling with any airline but seems especially true in the case of British Airways, or any airline that goes through Britain en route to Africa.

After considerable air travel within and outside of the USA, I have concluded that the chances of delayed or misrouted baggage increase with the number of times it must be handled by the airline, as it must be if you change planes. I suspect baggage problems also increase when airline companies are changed from one leg of a trip to another.

I was required to change planes and airlines several times on my trip to South Africa and had serious problems in getting my baggage on time, both going and coming. The difficulty en route to Frankfurt appeared to be that my baggage was not available for me to identify prior to boarding my flight to Johannesburg. I later learned it was regarded as "unclaimed," and the airline refused to put it on a different plane than the one I was boarding, out of fear of terrorist bombs. My baggage apparently arrived after my flight had left. Everyone who travels by air knows that baggage frequently arrives late when one has reached the destination. In my situation it was a disaster.

On my way home to Alaska, after a layover of a week in Los Angeles, the airlines sent me home but sent my rifles to Mexico! I consider myself lucky my guns weren't lost or stolen in the process. If it's at all possible, I would suggest you take a direct flight from the USA rather than going through Europe.

One requirement common to all international airlines, I believe, is that ammunition and firearms be transported in separate containers. It would seem obvious that all firearms be *unloaded* prior to shipment, but some idiots still show up at airports with cartridges in the magazine and even in the chamber. If you do this today, the consequences may be severe, and might include confiscation of the weapon and a trip to jail for the offender. In any case, the situation is likely to be unpleasant. I took the bolts completely out of my rifles, stored them in the case, and still rechecked them repeatedly to be sure they were unloaded before I headed for the airport.

It appears that all international airlines also limit the amount of ammunition you can take as checked baggage to eleven pounds (five kilos). This is not much of a problem, as it amounts to several boxes of ammunition. It would be a problem if you wanted to take your own shotgun ammunition. It's probably better to buy that in Africa.

Gun containers should be of sturdy construction and locked. I think it's best to have all your guns in a single case, separate from the ammunition and other gear. Guns may be subject to special security measures not accorded a suitcase. If two people are traveling together and both intend to hunt, I think two separate cases would be better, as a hedge against one being lost in transit.

I've seen rifles arrive in remote airports in Alaska in cheap gun cases made of thin plastic that were secured with duct tape. These are fine for transporting rifles between your home and the rifle range, but you're simply asking for trouble trying to get by on the cheap in international travel. I spent nearly $300 for a very heavy-duty, riveted aluminum case that looked like it could survive a drop from several thousand feet or trampling by a herd of elephants without damaging the contents. Whether it could, I can't say, but when the case finally caught up with me in Zimbabwe it had been handled roughly enough that several of the rivets holding the hinges in place had been jarred loose so that they rattled. Aside from the airline's requirements, if you want to get your guns to Africa and back again in good shape, get a good case.

My ammunition and clothing were carried in a soft duffel bag. Although the duffel bag was not designed to be locked, I found a way to do it. It would take only a few seconds for an unscrupulous baggage handler or customs official to reach into an unlocked bag and pilfer your binoculars or other valuables. Money, passports, medications, visas, and other important papers should, I am convinced, be carried *on your person* if at all possible. I used a sort of travel wallet that hung around my neck inside my clothing. If you can't carry everything, put it in your carry-on, not checked, baggage.

You should give some thought to what you put in your carry-on. I took a compact binocular, main camera, film, shaving kit, toothbrush, and change of underwear. I had enough gear and clothing that I was able to hunt and take pictures for several days before my checked baggage arrived. You never know when you might be forced to lay over a day or more for some reason and need a few personal items. A book, preferably a long and engrossing one, would be a good item to put in your carry-on, as would a small tape recorder and a writing pad and pen.

DOCUMENTS, INSURANCE, AND HEALTH CARE

There are three important kinds of documents you may need for your African trip: a passport, a visa, and certificates of vaccination. To travel internationally you *must* have a passport. Don't leave home without it! I believe it's a good idea to carry a copy of it with you as well, separate from the original, in case the original is lost or damaged and you need to replace it. It often takes weeks to obtain or renew a passport, so this is not a task to be left until the last minute. Be sure to allow several weeks to get a new passport or have one renewed if necessary.

Countries appear to require visas of visitors they want to keep track of. In practice, this means people from countries they consider in some degree hostile to their own. Getting one may be relatively simple, like picking it up at the airport on arrival, or it may require correspondence with the country's embassy in the USA. Either way, be sure to know whether you need one, and allow sufficient time to get one if you do. It's also possible to obtain multicountry visas if you plan to visit more than one country on the same trip to Africa.

All countries in southern Africa recommend that you take medication to prevent malaria, especially if you plan to travel throughout the region. This medication may need to be started weeks prior to your trip and continued after your trip to be effective. Some countries require vaccinations for yellow fever under certain circumstances, usually if you are arriving from an area where the disease is endemic. Since this does not include the USA or Western Europe, you probably will not need to be vaccinated against yellow fever unless you stop for some time in an endemic area, which is mostly South America and parts of Africa. Exceptions are Cameroon and CAR, both of which currently *require* yellow fever vaccination for everyone over one year old who enters the country.

The Centers for Disease Control and Prevention (CDCP) provides up-to-date information on this and other health matters, and you or your doctor should obtain the latest information from one of these centers before your departure. Ways to contact CDCP are listed in appendix G.

Don't assume that your health insurance coverage in the USA will cover you in Africa. Inquire, and if necessary, purchase additional insurance. It's also possible to buy "trip cancellation" insurance that covers some circumstances. Doing so may save you a bundle if something goes haywire and the hunt is scratched, which happens. You should also insure your firearms against all-cause losses. This kind of insurance is good worldwide and includes loss or damage in transit.

If you have chronic health problems that could require care while in Africa, you should inquire about available medical facilities. In many cases, the nearest trained medical personnel may be a long way off, and the facilities that do exist may be poor. Read what the U.S. State Department has to say about medical facilities in Cameroon and CAR and you'll see what I mean.

Just how important medical care can be is illustrated by the experience of an acquaintance of mine. This fellow and his son went on a dream safari to Tanzania. Considering that they were after lion and, I believe, leopard and buffalo, the cost of the trip must have been impressive. Both got sick with some unknown disease after a week, and it was determined they could not receive adequate medical care anywhere in Tanzania.

By then they had taken a few animals but not nearly what they'd hoped for. They were flown to Amsterdam, where they spent several days in a hospital recovering and were not able to continue their safari. I assume the guy had paid at least 50 percent of the daily fees in advance, nonrefundable, which likely amounted to $10,000 or more. After recovering back home, he tried to work out a deal with the safari company he'd booked with originally, to get credit for the amount he'd already paid up front, but was not successful. I believe he eventually took another African safari with another company.

I don't know if he had insurance to cover the expenses involved in this fiasco, but this guy had pretty deep pockets anyway and didn't let on if it had caused him any financial hardship. If the average guy had to pay his bill, however, it could have been ruinous.

I have listed below some things you need to do before your trip that concern travel and health.

THINGS TO DO

1. Be certain your travel agent is familiar with the needs of hunters and the requirements of your airline for transporting firearms. Most agents that book safaris are knowledgeable, but don't assume all travel agents know these things.

2. If you can, arrange to fly direct to Africa, without any changes of plane or airline. If this is not possible, keep flight changes to a minimum.

3. Pay close attention to what you put in your carry-on bag. In it (or on your person) you should have your money or traveler's checks, medications, passport, visa, custom's firearms form, a toothbrush and shaving gear, and a change or two of underwear. It's a good idea to wear comfortable shoes you could use in the field. Your carry-on bag and the clothes you have on may be all you have when you get to Africa.

4. Book a room for at least a few hours at the end of each long leg of your trip and at your point of arrival in Africa so you can rest before your hunt.

5. Purchase insurance for your guns, trip cancellation, and health care, and be certain all apply where you are going. Be sure you know the coverage you have and how to make a claim or receive services during your trip.

6. Start your malaria medication before you leave on your trip and obtain any required vaccinations and documentation that you've had them.

7. Start your passport and visa applications months before your trip.

8. Make arrangements to visit at least one of the wildlife parks before or after your safari.

RECOMMENDED GEAR AND CLOTHING

There is considerable information available about what gear and clothing to take on safari. I have read dozens of lists provided by safari companies of what items they recommend to take along, and I have found the lists to be very similar. Once you have booked your hunt, your agent, safari outfitter, or PH will undoubtedly provide you with such a list.

As in other matters relating to African hunting, there is some variation as to what is recommended. For what it may be worth to the first-time African hunter, I decided to include my own experience, which may differ slightly from recommendations found elsewhere.

Whatever you ultimately decide to take along, you should consider yourself lucky that you don't have to contend with what poor Gordon Cumming had to when outfitting for his multiyear safari in South Africa in 1843. He traveled by horse and oxcart and wanted to be completely self-sufficient in all his food and equipment. His kit included "2 large casks of tar to be mixed with hard fat for greasing the [wagon] wheels when required, 6 dozen pocket knives, 24 boxes of snuff, 300 pounds of [colored] beads . . . a vice . . . 10,000 prepared leaden balls, [400 pounds] of gunpowder, 50,000 percussion caps,

2,000 gun flints . . . [and] several large jars of pickles" (Gordon Cumming, *A Hunter's Life in South Africa*, pp. 16–17).

GUN CASES

Elsewhere I have recommended that you purchase a lockable, heavy-duty, aluminum gun case to transport your firearms by airplane. I also brought along a couple of soft cases to carry the rifles in while traveling in the safari vehicle. Much of the area is dusty, and a soft case will help keep your guns clean and functional. Of course, scope caps are a necessity. The cases I used were padded and covered with a medium-weight canvas. They worked fine but were unnecessarily bulky. I believe something lighter, just a sleeve to protect my guns from dust, would have been adequate. Since the tracker usually held onto any rifle I wasn't holding, protection from impact wasn't a concern.

CAMERAS

A camera should be part of your safari kit. Today many will take a video camera, or camcorder, which I considered but decided against because of its bulk and weight. If a hunter is traveling alone, a video camera would be a considerable burden. But if two or more persons are hunting together, it would probably be a good idea to bring one along. You should give some thought to who will do the photography, but don't rely on your PH or tracker to do it. On a 2 x 1 safari, where only one hunter at a time is the shooter, the other can operate the camera. So could a nonhunting wife or companion.

For most people a still camera is the equipment of choice. I took three and would not have left one behind without a fight.

For those times when I wanted the best possible pictures to illustrate articles or dazzle my friends I brought a Pentax single-lens reflex with a normal and a zoom telephoto lens, the latter with a range of 70–210mm. Of course, I also had extra batteries for the camera, along with lens-cleaning materials. This camera fulfilled its role perfectly.

Since I didn't know what the skill level of those who would be taking my picture with my trophies, I wanted a camera as foolproof as possible. For this role I purchased an Olympus weather-resistant, point-and-shoot 35mm camera with built-in flash. My thinking was that anyone who could look through the viewfinder and press a button could take an adequate photo with that camera. This camera perfectly fulfilled its role, too. As it turned out, all the safari staff I hunted with, including the trackers, were familiar with 35mm cameras and could have used my Pentax, though there would have still been the problems of focusing and using the manual through-the-lens light meter.

The third camera I took was the simplest and cheapest Polaroid I've ever seen. It had autofocus capability but no flash or other gewgaws. In some ways it was the star of the show. I soon learned that the native staff loved having their picture taken with the animals I killed or holding one of my rifles. The staff was often photographed by clients who from their home country eventually sent prints to each staff member. But it was a clear hit to be able to hand them a photo of themselves in a few seconds, and it gave me great pleasure as well. Another benefit of having this Polaroid along was that I could have my own picture taken in flattering poses. Being a cautious sort, I figured that if the processor lost my 35mm film, or if it was fried by an airport security scanner, I would still have some pictures of my safari. I brought enough film for forty Polaroid prints, and I could easily have used twice that much.

For 35mm film, I was advised that color prints could be readily processed, at least in the cities of South Africa, whereas slide film could not. Having film processed locally meant I would not only see the pictures sooner, but also not have to worry about those airport scanners damaging my undeveloped film. I was expecting to need slides of the trip, and so I took mostly that kind of film instead.

Since I planned a trip to a game park and anticipated using my telephoto for most of my "shooting" there, I took twenty rolls of 400 ASA Fujichrome slide film. I shot ten rolls before I ever got to Kruger Park, on two separate safaris, but the ten remaining proved adequate for the three days I spent there. I carried my film in a lead-lined bag, hoping to avoid damage from airport security scanners, but I'm not sure this was necessary.

A JOURNAL

People who wouldn't think of going on safari without writing material don't have to be reminded of this, but for the rest I suggest taking something compact, preferably self-contained, to write in. I took a waterproofed write-in-the-rain notebook, which filled the bill for me. I'm relying on my journal for much of the information used to write this book, many details of which I'd never have remembered without my notes.

In addition to this notebook, I took along a small microcassette recorder and extra tapes. This whole outfit, including a dozen tiny tapes, takes up no more space than many compact cameras, and hardly more than a pack of cigarettes. I was often able to record impressions and experiences faster than would have been possible writing longhand. You can talk into one of these recorders while traveling in a vehicle, or even in the dark, when handwriting would be nearly impossible.

CLOTHING

I present a detailed list of clothes to take on safari in appendix E. In this section I want to pass along a few general observations.

Many hunters will have a vision of an African hunter dressed in a tan bush coat complete with waist belt and shell loops holding cartridges the size of hot dogs, and wearing shorts and a wide-brimmed felt hat decorated by a strip of leopard hide. Although such attire may be functional, it isn't necessary. And I would have some problem with the hat.

When you choose clothing for your safari, consider the weather and temperatures you are likely to encounter in southern Africa during the winter hunting season, as well as the requirements of the hunting itself. Also relevant are the services likely to be provided by your safari outfitter.

Years ago a gent, frequently a wealthy businessman or royalty, gearing up for a safari would simply go to the Ambercrombie and Fitch store on Madison Avenue in New York City. There a bwana and his memsahib could find everything they needed for their trip to the Dark Continent. On one floor, there was all the khaki a heart could desire, along with those hats with the leopard-skin band, or a pith helmet if that struck the hunter's fancy. Elsewhere there was luggage of fine leather suitable for travel by oxcart, and footwear of the finest sort made by English boot makers. Up a floor or two was the world-famous Griffin and Howe gun shop where, with enough cash in his jeans, the hunter could purchase anything from a Purdy 12-bore to a .416 Rigby, or, if there was time enough, have the rifle or shotgun built to order especially for the safari.

Having been to that wonderful store on many occasions before its sad demise and subsequent reincarnation, I can imagine how pampered and courted the privileged and wealthy would have felt during this process. Those who can afford this kind of luxury can probably find a similar store even today. Fortunately, for people of ordinary means, there are cheaper alternatives, which will give complete satisfaction.

It's common for laundry to be done daily even in a primitive safari camp, which makes it unnecessary to bring many changes. Your outfitter or agent can detail your needs in this regard, but typically two or three changes of clothes to wear while hunting is sufficient. Women, almost certainly, will require more.

Much of the hunting in the brush and thorn country in this region makes a wide-brimmed hat something of a liability. I believe you will find that the ordinary baseball cap will meet your basic needs for a hat, and you'll probably find that your PH and the locals wear them, too. I noticed that several of the Zulu and Shona trackers and bearers I worked with did, at least when they weren't wearing something warmer like a knitted watch cap.

Not much has been written about footwear for use on safari. The animals you hunt and the methods used will influence your choices. If you plan to do a lot of walking in pursuit of buffalo, elephant, or eland your footwear should be as light and comfortable as possible and provide adequate support in the dry and soft soils of the region. Hip boots would not be a good choice here! Eight-inch-high boots commonly worn in North America for big game and bird shooting would be awfully hot and are seldom seen among clients or professionals in Africa. Whatever you wear, it must be well broken in before the trip, preferably during the many miles you walk getting in condition for your safari.

I looked at some expensive, handmade boots such as the PH model by Russell, which are beautiful and undoubtedly will meet most requirements. I ended up with an inexpensive pair of lightweight hiking boots made by Coleman. These had a light-duty lug sole and were lined and padded. I had been convinced that it was desirable not to wear socks while hunting to avoid getting sharp-pointed seeds of the local grasses stuck in them, which could cause a painful scratch. As it turned out, these seeds were rarely a problem, and I wore medium-weight, cotton athletic socks on numerous occasions without difficulty. My shoes did have a soft, suedelike lining that made them comfortable without socks, and I found the shoes worked well that way, too.

In South Africa, my PH wore *veldschoenen*, Afrikaans for "field shoes." These boots were similar to a chukka and appeared to be unlined and had a crepe sole. My PH in Zimbabwe wore a similar shoe, and both types reminded me of the Clark's "desert boot," which was popular when I was a kid. I gather that many clients coming to Africa wear running shoes, which I've noted are recommended by many safari outfitters, and seem to work fine.

The nights are cold in southern Africa during the primary hunting season, which is winter there. I never saw a thermometer, but I believe temperatures often went down to the forties at night. But once the sun comes up, temperatures can quickly rise into the seventies or higher—sometimes much higher. Coping with this temperature range on a daily basis is not difficult but does require some planning. The bottom line is that you need to prepare for a rather extreme temperature range during the course of the day which, I believe, translates into dressing in layers.

Though it may seem paradoxical, wearing shorts and a down jacket in the morning while traveling in the safari vehicle to the hunting site often makes a lot of sense. My legs don't seem to mind the cold as much as my upper body does, so wearing shorts usually caused no discomfort even in cool-morning temperatures. At times I wore long pants over my shorts and a bush jacket over a T-shirt, stripping off the outer layers as the day warmed. The new pants that allow removing the lower trouser leg by means of a zipper, leaving you with a pair of shorts, make a lot of sense in this application, though I haven't actually tried them.

If you sweat a lot during exertion as I do, I recommend you bring along a bandanna to use as a sweatband to keep the salt from dripping into your eyes when you are trying to catch up with that herd of eland or buffalo. Of course, the bandanna needs to be tan or green and not a farmer-style red one.

I found that a pair of tight-fitting leather gloves made of elk hide were useful for taking a rest on the extremely thorny trees and brush of the area. I rarely wore a glove on my right hand unless I was cold because that's my trigger hand, and I can't feel the trigger as well as I like with a glove on.

GRATUITIES FOR YOUR PH

It is customary, though not mandatory, I believe, for the client to give a gift or gratuity—i.e., a tip—of some sort to his PH after the safari. Clearly this will vary according to the client's means and the PH's needs and preferences. I think it is best to inquire of the PH himself or someone who knows him as to what might be appropriate. I was surprised to learn what my own PHs wanted.

My PH in Zimbabwe took a fancy to a soft rifle case I had brought along for travel afield in the safari vehicle. The case had cost me little, but would have cost considerably more in that country. Besides, he had two small children and a wife to provide for, and I suspect he had more important things to do with his money. I was happy to give him the case when I left, and I am sure it was appreciated. Since guns traveled to and from Africa in a rugged, locked, aluminum case, once the safari was over I had no further use for the soft case.

I noticed that nearly all the PHs I met had rather cheap scopes on their rifles. By U.S. standards they were far below the quality a serious hunter who could afford a guided hunt for anything would use. I made one PH the proposition that, in lieu of $200 paid as a tip at the end of my safari, I would instead purchase a Leupold scope and send it to him after I got home. I later found out that this would have made him liable for paying a substantial duty on the item, or anything else I sent him, so the deal never got done. Since I was planning another hunt before leaving Africa, I didn't want to part with the scopes on my rifles or the spare I'd brought along. Perhaps the lesson should be that gratuities are both highly individual and negotiable.

My PH in South Africa also had a rather cheap scope on his primary weapon. Since I was heading home after this safari, I gave him a Leupold 3–9X in excellent condition, with which he was clearly delighted. Had I realized the situation beforehand, I would surely have brought a nice scope for each of my PHs.

GRATUITIES FOR THE NATIVE STAFF

My South African PH suggested I bring some good sporting knives for the trackers and skinners, so I purchased several excellent Buck folding hunters with superb hollow-ground blades. Two of them went to the senior Zulu trackers who located my beautiful nyala and arranged to have it packed out of the deep canyon where I shot it. Others went to trackers who helped locate a wounded gemsbok. My PH liked them so much that he kept one for himself and used it as a caping knife.

I had no clue what to bring for the native staff in Zimbabwe on my first safari. On the advice of my PH, I changed some of my U.S. dollars into Zimbabwe dollars and distributed varying amounts to the staff at the end of my safari. They had done such a great job for me that I was only sorry I didn't have more to give them.

A pair of binoculars might be a useful gift for a head tracker or game spotter. Most of the glasses I saw in use in Africa were not of the highest quality. Virtually all were compact and rubber armored. Your PH might be able to use a pair, too.

RIFLES AND AMMUNITION

The choice of a rifle is almost as much a matter of
idiosyncrasy as the choice of a friend.
　　　　　　　—Theodore Roosevelt, *African Game Trails*

GENERAL OBSERVATIONS

Choosing one's guns and ammunition for a safari is one
of the more controversial subjects in the hunting field, and for
me among the most interesting and enjoyable. In addition to
being challenging and entertaining, the choice of guns and
ammunition can play a significant role in the success or failure
of a hunt. The choice of a safari rifle can, and I believe should,
also be a very personal matter that will vary depending, among
other things, on the tastes and desires of the hunter.

It has been said that a man's choice of weapons is a portal
into his thoughts, his values, his character, and his experiences.
Whether it's true, I can't say, but it is part of hunting lore that
these choices, particularly of big-game rifles, identify him as a
person of taste and judgment or a boorish oaf, a sensible
conservative or a dangerous radical, a tough hombre or a wimp.

Whatever truth there may be to these presumptions, I think
it's wise to employ considerable objectivity when selecting a rifle
for what will probably be a once-in-a-lifetime safari. One should
not be seduced by the idea that your manhood (or womanhood)
demands the use of a larger caliber than you can shoot effectively.
Equally flawed is the idea that it's necessary to use exotic calibers
and rifles by foreign makers to hunt African game.

In his history-making book about hunting in Africa, President Theodore Roosevelt observed that hunters of great experience— such as F. C. Selous, Samuel Baker, and other professional hunters— disagreed radically on which of the Big Five they thought was the most dangerous.* Roosevelt wrote: "The experts of greatest experience thus absolutely disagree among themselves; and there is the same wide divergence of good hunters and trained observers whose opportunities have been less (*African Game Trails*, p. 79).

As far as I know, Roosevelt did not ask this group which rifles they thought were the best for various kinds of African game, but it would not surprise me to learn that there was considerable disagreement on that matter as well. He clearly appreciated a man who could be objective in his observations, as his remarks in this book repeatedly demonstrate. He had some clear preferences of his own, but recognized these for what they were and usually labeled them as such. Not all experienced hunters are that objective.

In spite of over one hundred years of data on the subject, the selection of rifles and ammunition for African game still gives rise to a seemingly endless dialog—sometimes amiable, sometimes downright hostile, and often confusing to those new to the debate. The debate centers around the following question: What calibers are suitable for which animals under what conditions?

Historically, the questions relating to calibers have centered around bore size, bullet weight, velocity, energy, stopping power, knockdown effect, and similar issues. All of these issues are related to the "adequacy" of a particular caliber for a particular purpose.

---

*J. A. Hunter, in his book *Hunter*, provides an interesting discussion on this subject, based on his having taken hundreds of the Big Five and on his guiding clients to many more.

Some additional questions I believe are important for the hunter to ask are *not* typically raised in this context, but I think they should be. These include:

1. Which calibers are available as factory loads with premium bullets?
2. How heavy a caliber can the hunter consistently shoot well?
3. How available are parts for his rifle if something breaks during his safari?
4. How available is ammo for his rifle where he plans to hunt if his is lost or damaged?
5. What does the hunter now own and how well does he shoot what he has?
6. Where should he place his bullet?
7. What bullet should he use? The answers to these questions tend to point to certain choices for the safari-bound hunter.

A BRIEF HISTORY

Hunting in Africa for sport began in the mid-nineteenth century, when sporting firearms were fearsome cannons. All were muzzleloaders and fired round balls, often from smoothbore guns. Some were even designed to use exploding bullets! To be effective on the large game of Africa, these projectiles were made larger in diameter and heavier than had been required for hunting elsewhere. A similar development took place in North America as trappers and settlers moved west and encountered larger game like elk, moose, buffalo, and grizzly bear.

The term "bore" is often encountered in the literature on African hunting. This term, which I believe was invented by the British, does not refer to bullet diameter, as the terms .35 caliber or 8mm do today. Instead, like the method we still use to designate shotgun gauges, the bore designation refers to the number of balls you can make of a given diameter from a pound of lead. Bore size, then, is the number of round balls of a given diameter it takes to make a pound. The weight of a 12-bore round ball could be figured as follows: 16 ounces divided by 12 = 1.3 ounces; or one could figure the weight this way: 7,000 grains (16 ounces) divided by 12 = 583 grains. A 4-bore, therefore, fired a round ball weighing 4 ounces, or 1,750 grains. By way of comparison, the modern "elephant gun" typically uses a bullet weighing from 400 to 500 grains, or a quarter as much, and a .450 caliber would be a 75-bore.

There are reports that rifles designated 4-bore were used by some early European hunters in Africa. Using today's methods of naming cartridges, a 4-bore would be a .93 or .94 caliber, and bullets would be around an inch in diameter. By comparison, a 10-gauge shotgun, or ten-bore, has a bore diameter of .77 inches, and a 12-gauge has a bore diameter of .729 inches. In the second half of the nineteenth century, 8- and 10-bores were frequently recommended for hunting Indian and African game.

W. W. Greener, in *The Gun and Its Development,* described one of these brutes:

> The double 4-bore with barrels 20 inches long will weigh from 14 to 18 lbs., and fire a charge of 12 to 14 drams [of black powder] and a spherical bullet of 1,510 grains. The recoil is undoubtedly heavy, but an Indian hunter of great experience in their use states that it is not noticeable when firing at game, and that on one occasion a rifle with 12 drams and a four-ounce bullet went off both barrels together, but he did not notice the recoil. The great weight of the rifle, as much as its recoil, is against its general use.

Excuse me, but I believe I would have noticed!

The great hunter-naturalist F. C. Selous had a somewhat different reaction. In his book *A Hunter's Wanderings in Africa*, Selous wrote that the 4-bore "kicked most frightfully, and in my case the punishment received from these guns has affected my nerves to such an extent as to have materially influenced my shooting ever since, and I am heartily sorry that I ever had anything to do with them."

Greener thought the 8-bore was a better game rifle than the 4-bore, and the particular one he recommended, which used a brass case, was capable of shooting a round ball weighing 2 ounces, and a conical bullet of 3 ounces, or 1,313 grains! These rifles had to weigh around 15 pounds for the recoil to be tolerable, he said.

During the last half of the nineteenth century there were two significant developments in firearms technology that profoundly changed the nature of sporting weapons. These were the development of breechloading and smokeless powder.

Breechloading made it possible to load, or more important, reload, one's weapon quickly after firing it, and also permitted the use of bullets that were a tighter fit in the rifling and that could be made of harder materials. Loading from the muzzle required a soft projectile of a size less than the "groove" diameter of a rifled bore so that the projectile could be seated with relative ease on the powder. This undersize feature was particularly important when the bore was fouled from previous shots, and undoubtedly resulted in poor accuracy. The chief contribution of smokeless powder seems to have been that it permitted higher velocities than was possible with black powder.

Breechloading also made it possible to use self-contained ammunition, or cartridges. By that time projectile shapes had been redesigned even for muzzleloaders to a more aerodynamic form than the round ball. These bullets were elongated rather than spherical, and are often referred to as "conical," or shaped like a cone. The minié ball, developed, I think, about the time of the American Civil War, is an example of a projectile of this type.

An early development using the technology of fixed-cartridge ammunition and breachloading was the repeating "magazine" rifles such as the familiar lever-action Winchester, and the bolt-action rifles used by the military of many countries. The latter included various Mausers, Mannlichers, and Enfields. These soon largely replaced the single-shot and double-barrel rifles used by early sport hunters, as well as the lever actions.

Most of these repeaters were chambered for calibers much smaller in bullet diameter than those used in the muzzleloading era. Because of advances in firearms technology, the projectile diameter of European military rifles developed during the nineteenth century declined from around .750 or 11-bore in 1850 to less than .32 caliber, or 150-bore, by 1889.

At the dawn of the twentieth century, in place of the .94 caliber, 4-bore muzzleloader, hunters began to use breechloaders with bullet diameters in the range of .303 to .600 inch. The smaller of these were military calibers such as the 6.5x54mm Mannlicher, 7x57mm Mauser, .303 British, .30-40 Krag, and .30-06 Springfield, all adapted to bolt-action "magazine" rifles, all introduced in the 1890s to early 1900s.

Near the turn of the century, a class of cartridges developed specifically for hunting the dangerous game of India and Africa was developed in the United Kingdom and in Europe. These were often referred to as "express" or "nitro express" calibers to indicate that the cartridges were loaded with smokeless powder (nitro) and attained higher than usual velocities (express), frequently with lighter than normal bullets.

It was at that point that the great bore-diameter, bullet-weight controversy in its modern incarnation probably began.

BIG, MEDIUM, AND SMALL BORES

The more conservative hunters of the day insisted that a large bore rifle shooting relatively heavy bullets—the old muzzleloading formula for power—was the only reliable weapon for use on dangerous game. The more progressive argued that, at least in the hands of a good shot, the much smaller "long-range express" calibers gave satisfactory results. Some of these progressive thinkers were elephant hunters and used the 6.5mm, 7mm, and .303 military cartridges with great effect to prove their point. The exploits of "Karamojo" Bell comes to mind in this regard. It appears that many hunters adopted these military small bores when they became available.

Hunters came to think of rifles as small, medium, and big bores; these categories, however, were highly fluid over the last century or so. It's probably fair to say that in recent times big bores have typically been thought of as .45 caliber or larger; medium bores, from .33 to .44 caliber; and small bores, .32 caliber or 8mm and under. During the transition from muzzleloaders, a .45 caliber was considered a small bore, which it was, compared to its predecessors.

The controversy as to which of these classes of cartridges is most effective still goes on with some vigor today. Enough evidence has been acquired by hunters collectively over the last one hundred-plus years, though, that some conclusions can be drawn on the subject.

The "heavy" or big-bore express rifle did not continue to just get larger in caliber and push bullets of ever-increasing weights to higher and higher velocities without limit. The power levels that were reached required rifles approaching a weight that was too heavy to carry and a recoil that was intolerable; eventually, power levels hit a ceiling. Recoil and weight were the reasons monster muzzleloaders were abandoned in the first place. One rarely hears of calibers above .475 being used today even by professional hunters, though some apparently still cling to their .577s and .600s for backup. Most use about .45 caliber for the heaviest game. In general, development of cartridges for dangerous game has largely stopped at calibers half the size of the monster 4-bore, firing projectiles at one-quarter the weight, though at higher velocities.

The largest calibers have usually been preferred only for the largest game, namely elephant, under the "worst conditions," generally meaning a charge at close quarters. Under these circumstances, the sheer impact of the big bore is said to be capable of turning a charge, giving the hunter time to shoot additional shots, or perhaps climb a convenient tree. In open country at least, the military small bores seemed very satisfactory to many experienced African hunters, even those who specialized in elephant teeth.

Early in the twentieth century, medium-bore, bolt-action, express rifles began to displace big-bore doubles, even in their traditional role. Calibers such as the .318 Westley Richards, .333 Jeffery, .375 H&H, .416 Rigby, and many others could be made lighter in weight and still have tolerable recoil. These were all introduced about 1910.

In the hands of professional hunters, African residents and clients alike, the medium-bore, nitro-express calibers, from about .350 to .411 or so in bore diameter, proved satisfactory on all game under any but the most desperate of conditions. And the small-bore military calibers proved very satisfactory for game other than the heavyweights. To this day many professional hunters will recommend these medium bores for their clients, but a few still prefer big bores for their own use when backing up clients against dangerous game. Clearly, these men think that doing so gives them an edge.

BULLET WEIGHT AND DESIGN

In spite of all the concern expressed over the last 150 years or so about bore size and bullet weight and how these relate to effectiveness on game, much of this discussion may have been misdirected. I believe there is some evidence to suggest that at least some of the calibers that gave the most satisfactory results owed their success to the *construction of the bullets* they were supplied with by the factories, and not to these other factors. The performance of the calibers was mistakenly attributed to their bore diameter or bullet weight when the significant factor was the structure of the bullet itself. It turns out that the way a bullet is constructed can often outweigh other factors such as weight and diameter when it comes to determining the bullet's performance on game. John Taylor's comments, in *African Rifles and Cartridges,* on the bullets that Rigby supplied for its proprietary calibers is one example.

Put another way, it's possible to achieve greater penetration by using today's best game bullets of lighter weight at higher velocity than by using a heavier bullet of the same caliber but of conventional construction at lower velocity. This is the opposite of what one expects based on older formulas. This has been found true of the Barnes X, Winchester Fail Safe, and the H-Mantle, but more on that later.

When a cylindrical ball, which was used in muzzleloaders, is made of homogeneous material like lead, its weight increases in proportion to its diameter. In other words, to allow for more weight, bore diameter must increase. The weight of a round ball that a given rifle can use is fixed.

When bullets began to take on conical forms, this was no longer true. Within a given caliber, one could choose among bullets of different weight. This was a revolutionary development. It was no longer necessary to use a larger caliber to gain bullet weight. With the diameter constant, longer bullets were generally heavier and by definition had greater sectional densities. These longer, heavier bullets were found to give deeper penetration, other things like construction being equal, than lighter bullets.

The famous British firm of Westley Richards clearly understood the requirements for a sporting softpoint bullet by 1912. In a catalog celebrating its one hundredth year, the company had this to say: "The two essentials of a sporting bullet [are] high penetration and instantaneous expansion." They clearly believed that their version, a capped hollow point, met these requirements at that time. Though the requirements of such bullets have remained essentially unchanged, it has taken the better part of a century to perfect softpoint and solid game bullets.

As velocities increased in the early years of smokeless powder, even hardened lead proved unsatisfactory at higher velocities. "Jackets" of harder material were developed, therefore, to allow the use of softer alloys for the cores, among other things. These jackets were an advantage because lead and its alloys tended to foul bores and left much to be desired in their terminal performance. The old bullets also "striped" in the rifling, or failed to be adequately gripped and rotated by the lands and grooves of rifled barrels. The new bullets used a cover of metal, a jacket, over the lead core to improve performance, particularly to prevent leading or striping the barrel and to provide greater penetration.

Development of the jacket was new technology, and there was considerable experimentation with bullet design in Britain and Europe, which continues today. Various point designs were tried to ensure expansion of softpoints. Perhaps the most common was the hollowpoint, with or without a covering over the cavity, and various sizes and shapes of the cavity itself. The other was the amount of lead exposed at the tip and not covered by the jacket. These are still two of the most common ways bullet makers solve the same problems today.

By leaving more or less of the soft lead core exposed at the bullet's tip, the rate of expansion, and hence the amount of penetration, could be controlled somewhat. More expansion meant less penetration, and vice versa. Bullets with less lead exposed at the tip, other things being equal, started to expand later and expanded less and thus penetrated more than bullets with more lead exposed. Such bullets were often referred to as having "controlled" expansion but I believe could more accurately be called "delayed" or "reduced" expansion.

The Winchester Silvertip is an example of a delayed-expansion softpoint with the exposed lead coated with a tougher material to retard expansion. The Remington bronzepoint and the Nosler ballistic tip use an insert into a hollow cavity in the bullet's nose, made of "bronze" or plastic respectively, to accelerate expansion. The Winchester Fail Safe and Barnes X-Bullets have hollowpoints. Similar methods were used nearly a hundred years ago by casting various materials into lead bullets.

Various jacket and point-covering material were tried, including paper, brass, nickel, iron, and copper, and alloys of these and other materials. The silver color of older softpoints reflects the use of nickel as the jacket material. Eventually an alloy of various proportions of copper, nickel, and zinc—sometimes called cupronickel or guilding metal—proved best, and a similar alloy is still the most common material in use today for jacketed bullets. It appears that copper may have been the first material used as a jacket, and is still the most important material used in bullet jackets. Some of the best bullets made today are made entirely of pure copper or have pure-copper jackets.

But serious bullet failures still occurred on a regular basis with the early jacketed softpoints and solids. Bullets just misbehaved, and the faster they were going, the more often this occurred. The technology for making bullets go faster had gotten ahead of the technology for making them behave.

Softpoints designed to expand either didn't or expanded too much and disintegrated, sometimes causing a superficial wound. Solids, developed for use on the pachyderms, sometimes were bent and deflected or shattered without penetrating as deeply as required. There were several high-profile cases where sportsmen were killed using small bores, and the blame was often placed on high velocity per se, or a lack of bullet weight. It may be the fault was really with the construction of the bullets they used.

One early success in jacketed bullet design was the H-Mantle, a German partition bullet designed to expand readily, but which had a rear portion that did not and would continue to penetrate. These bullets are still in use today and may have been the first successful solution to the twin problems of expansion and penetration, and they were available in factory ammunition as well. In one recent penetration test conducted by a much respected gun scribe, the H-Mantle proved it is capable of giving much greater penetration than smaller or larger calibers firing the best premium bullets of greater weight and sectional density. In terms of penetration, it outperformed most of the premium bullets we have today except, possibly, Winchester's Fail Safe.

There is little disagreement today about "terminal" bullet performance—that is, what happens when the bullet hits the target. The clear consensus is that a bullet must perform like it is supposed to, and do it consistently. Softpoints must expand and penetrate deep enough to reach vital areas. This requires that the bullets don't blow up, which in turn means the jacket and core must not separate from each other. Keeping the two parts together allows them to retain a large percentage of their initial weight. And they must expand against light resistance, as when fragile animals are shot, or at long range where velocity is reduced. Solids must give great penetration and not be diverted from their intended course because of being deformed by hitting extreme resistance or other factors.

A softpoint that disintegrates before it reaches a vital area or doesn't expand at all, or a solid that doesn't travel in a straight line, not only is unacceptable, but also the cause of considerable grief and, not infrequently, the demise or injury of the hunter who experienced either. Although bullets are available today that virtually eliminate these problems, there are still pitfalls for the unwary.

Another controversy that has gone on for at least one hundred years is whether it's more desirable for a bullet to exit or remain in the animal. An exit will presumably provide a better blood trail to follow if the animal runs off. Others argue that it's better for a bullet to expend all its energy inside the animal rather than "wasting" some of it on the landscape after it exits. There's something to be said on both sides of this issue. Which side you come down on may depend on how certain you are that the animal will drop soon after being hit and not run off and possibly be lost.

Which performance you want will dictate to a considerable extent which bullet you'll select. Today you can choose bullets that excel in penetration and frequently exit, or bullets that expand to greater diameter, limiting penetration, making them more likely to stay in the animal.

Even the grand old master and champion of the big bore and heavy bullets, Elmer Keith, experienced near catastrophic failure of the carefully selected softpoints that he chose for his first African safari in the 1950s. He was using 300-grain, .333-caliber bullets from a famous maker (Kynoch) with sectional densities well over .300 at modest velocities. I'm confident he expected these to penetrate like crazy. Instead, his bullets simply broke up against minimal resistance and gave insufficient penetration. He finally resorted to solids even on plains game to achieve adequate penetration.

Keith had far more experience as both a hunter and guide than virtually any American who has written extensively about his experiences before or since, and was in close touch for many years with African professionals with regard to calibers and bullets for African game. He knew enough to choose the very best available, at least according to a consensus of the experts he relied on. If he could make such a mistake, rest assured that a novice is at much greater risk of doing so. His experience should give pause to the man who thinks he's an expert on such matters. Fortunately, developments in bullet technology have largely eliminated this kind of risk *if the hunter will take advantage of what we have learned.*

In the United States, I believe the first successful softpoint game bullet that solved the twin problems of failing to expand or disintegrating without adequate penetration was the Nosler Partition. The Nosler Bullet Company was founded in 1948 by John Nosler to market a bullet that he designed to perform better than the conventional softpoints of that era. More than fifty years later it is still one of the finest available.

Before the H-Mantle and Nosler Partition, the primary ways used to improve softpoint bullet performance were to use jackets of varying thickness and different alloys, to make a hollowpoint, or to leave more or less lead exposed at the tip to facilitate expansion. Other variations on the same basic theme include jackets that taper, or get thinner, at the nose or that use cores made of different hardness, or that have grooves at the point to help initiate expansion. This is what I mean by "conventional" bullet construction. What they all lack is a reliable method of preventing bullet cores from separating from their jackets because of the stresses of hitting game, and reliability of expansion at typical hunting ranges.

To work as intended, such bullets have to hit their target within a specific, and fairly narrow, range of velocities. If velocity was too low, or resistance too light, the bullet might not expand and would act like a solid. This means it would punch a caliber-sized hole through the animal without expanding as it was intended to. This behavior tends to produce a relatively small wound, and animals are frequently able to run off a considerable distance and are lost by hunters.

But if the bullet was fired at a higher velocity than it was designed for, or if it hit bone, the bullet jacket would rupture and separate from the lead core. At that point, effective penetration stopped. Such performance typically produces large but shallow wounds, and sometimes produces spectacular "instant" kills, but also results in a disconcerting number of failures because of a lack of penetration.

The basic idea behind the Nosler Partition bullet was to use two cores separated by a strong partition or wall. The front portion was engineered to expand readily over a wide range of velocities, and it even broke off at the partition on occasion. But the rear portion behind the partition remained intact and continued to penetrate. In this regard it resembled the H-Mantle. This design principle is still very much in use today as new designs incorporate it along with newer developments in bullet technology.

It was about twenty years later that the next great leap forward in bullet building took place: a bullet with a bonded core. The Bitterroot Bullet Company, founded by Bill Steigers, developed a way to bond the jacket, which was made of pure copper, I believe, to the lead core. (I'm not sure the Bitterroot was the first bonded-core design, but I think it was among the earliest.) The result was a bullet that regularly retained more than 90 percent of its weight (which was unprecedented) and seemed never to come apart, no matter what it hit. Because of this feature, these bullets penetrated well, expanded reliably, and, by all accounts I'm aware of, performed very well on game. Unfortunately, the company was never able to keep up with the demand for its products, even though the bullet was still listed in the 1995 *Handloader's Digest*. Later on other companies used the same idea to make great game bullets. Core bonding is probably the most popular technology in use today for making superior game bullets.

In terms of bullet construction, probably the most significant and radical development since core bonding has been the homogeneous expanding projectile, as exemplified by the Barnes X-Bullet, introduced in 1989. This bullet is solid copper with a hollow at the tip to initiate expansion and form a mushroom. Naturally, since it does not have a core or a jacket, these two elements can't separate. Although it always surprises me, the small hollowpoint used on this bullet seems to be very reliable, and I can't recall ever hearing a complaint that the bullet did not open up when it hit game. The bullet solves both of the problems that have always plagued conventional softpoint bullets: the jacket and core separation resulting in inadequate penetration, and the failure to expand. Other premium bullets (aptly named, since a person pays a premium for them) have incorporated a variety of these features in different combinations to give us the finest selection of bullets ever made.

In summary, since the use of jacketed bullets began in the late nineteenth century, the three most significant technological developments in structural features of game bullets have been partitions, core bonding, and homogeneous bullets. Their development has largely solved the problems of penetration and expansion.

All of these developments in bullet making were designed to solve the problems that resulted in failure in the past, and the developments appear to have succeeded. Using any of the types mentioned, a hunter is not likely to experience the kinds of failure that plagued early hunters, or even hunters thirty years ago. There is room for improvement in accuracy and fouling, problems that occur with some bullets, but progress is being made in that area as well.

Experienced sport hunters as well as professional hunters are increasingly recommending the use of these premium bullets in preference to those of conventional design for African game. When specific brands are mentioned, I've most often seen the Nosler Partition, Barnes X, Swift A-Frame, Woodleigh Weldcore, and Trophy Bonded Bullets recommended among softpoints. Lately, the new Winchester Fail Safe bullet has received excellent reviews.

Several of these premium bullet companies also make solids, which are designed for maximum penetration. The new generation of solids appears to resist deformation very well. The question of whether all are equally proficient in maintaining penetration in a straight line in game is not as well resolved. Some of these solids resist deformation by being made of stronger, sometimes homogeneous, materials like bronze. Some companies employ core bonding with their solids like they do with their expanding bullets. All seem to work better than conventional solids that vary primarily in jacket thickness or alloy.

To increase penetration for a given bullet design, most PHs today appear to recommend using "heavy-for-caliber" bullets for African game. In a given caliber, for a given design, these heavier bullets should penetrate better than lighter ones. The term "heavy-for-caliber" has no clear definition, but I think you can approximate the idea by selecting bullets with sectional densities in the range of .280 to .325. Examples of bullets in this range include 150 to 160 grain in .270, 160 to 175 grain in 7mm, 180 to 220 grain in .30-06, and 225 to 250 grain in .338.

I had a bullet problem that may be worth relating to illustrate some of the pitfalls one can still encounter, particularly with conventional bullets that are designed for a specific range of velocities, and often for particular cartridges.

Prior to my African hunt, I'd taken two animals, a deer and a caribou, with the wildcat .375-06—a .375 bullet in a .30-06 case. I'd used the same bullet for both, the 235-grain Speer semispitzer softpoint designed for the .375 H&H. This is a conventional softpoint, which is relatively light for its caliber. It has been, I believe, a standard weight since H&H introduced the .375. Apparently the bullet was introduced for use on animals like plains game when the heavier bullets recommended for large or dangerous game weren't needed. I'd used it because I feared heavier bullets, presumably meant for larger game in the H&H, would not expand at the velocities possible in my wildcat .375-06. Unfortunately, I did not test this hypothesis before my safari. While I had excellent results on both animals taken with this bullet, I wanted something heavier for use on zebra and eland.

CHOICE OF BULLETS

After firing hundreds of rounds in load development, I settled on two bullets as the best choices for the range of game I was to hunt. One was the 270-grain Hornady Spire-Point, and the other was the new Nosler Partition 300-grain spitzer.

My testing showed the 270-grain Hornady to be very accurate as well as sufficiently flat shooting, and was my first choice. It is of conventional construction, with no core bonding or partitions. The bullet has been around a long time, and I assumed it would expand and give adequate penetration from my .375-06. I thought it had given good results in more powerful .375s, though I had no field data to support this view. I chose it in part because I believed it was designed for soft-skinned game and would open up on the wide range of antelope I would be hunting, and it did. Virtually all the ammo I took was loaded with it to a muzzle velocity of just over 2,500 feet per second. This is 200 to 300 feet per second slower than the same bullet can be driven in the .375 H&H, for which it was arguably designed, so I expected it would expand less and give more penetration in my rifle.

The Nosler 300-grain partition in spitzer form had only been on the market a short time, and I knew little about its field performance. I feared that, at the somewhat reduced velocities I was getting compared to the H&H, it might not expand sufficiently. I suspected the bullet was designed to open up on Cape buffalo and other large beasts. My concern proved groundless. Still, I was curious and took along about ten rounds loaded with that bullet at about 2,400 feet per second. I also took along the same number of rounds loaded with the superbly accurate 300-grain Hornady solid just in case of an emergency encounter with the local rhino or elephant.

After I'd taken three animals, including a zebra, with the 270-grain Hornady, I became concerned about its lack of penetration. It had zipped right through both shoulders of a warthog, but stopped in an impala and did not give enough penetration to suit me on the zebra. The only bullet I recovered was from the impala. It had penetrated a portion of the paunch and one lung, and I found it—a picture-perfect mushroom—bulging the skin on the off side near the shoulder. It had stayed together, but was expanded nearly all the way to the bullet base.

At that point I switched to the 300-grain Nosler with results more to my liking. With four of those ten rounds, I took a bushbuck, (one shot), a kudu (two shots, one to finish a bull whose neck I'd broken with the first shot), and an eland (one shot). My PH in South Africa fired the remaining six shots just to see how my rifle handled.

In all but one case, the 300-grain Nosler bullet opened quickly, making a large wound as it entered the animal, gave complete penetration, and exited. It performed that way on the hundred-pound bushbuck and the thousand-pound eland. The exception was a finishing shot on the kudu, purposely fired into its chest at a range of about three feet at an angle so it would traverse the entire length of the animal. That was the only bullet I recovered. It held together and behaved like all the other Nosler Partitions I'd used previously, even at muzzle velocity.

From this experience I concluded that, while the 300-grain Nosler *appeared* to be far too heavy for most of the game I hunted, of the two bullets I had with me it alone gave the penetration I wanted on all game from bushbuck to eland. The sectional density of the 300-grain bullet in .375 caliber is .305, or heavy for its caliber. With a sectional density of .274, the 270-grain Hornady was at the lower end of this range as I have defined it. The extra weight of the Nosler and its superior construction seemed to provide better penetration at the velocities my rifle gave it.

If I had done some penetration testing before selecting bullets for this trip, these differences might have showed up. I certainly would have preferred to do this before the trip, but I did not, as it would have been somewhat awkward to do so at the public range where I did my shooting.

If there is a moral to this little story, perhaps it is this: The premium bullets we have today—which incorporate one or more of the three key technologies of partitioning, core bonding, and homogeneous materials—have solved most of the serious problems experienced with game bullets for the last one hundred fifty years. Bullets of conventional design, which by definition lack these features, are subject to failures that the premium bullets are not. Although conventional bullets will continue to have many applications, for hunting large game, at least, I believe the premium bullets discussed here will give superior results and should be chosen instead of conventional designs.

If you use a relatively heavy bullet for your caliber, and use one of the premium designs mentioned, you will be using the best available and should have no difficulties related to bullet performance. If you use something else, I wish you luck.

BULLET PLACEMENT

Placement of the bullet in a vital area is the sine qua non of humane kills. About this there is, practically speaking, no disagreement among experienced hunters, whether professional or recreational. While there have been anomalies reported, such as "unexplained" deaths of animals shot in the leg or some other nonvital area, these are rare and in no way predictable. Although the importance of bullet placement has long been recognized, there is a related issue that has not received the attention it deserves. This is the matter of first-shot placement.

Anyone who reads the literature on African hunting will recognize that one of the common themes is that some animals demonstrate an unbelievable ability to absorb shot after shot, even in the vital areas, and still manage to charge or run off. And these are not necessarily the animals most noted for their toughness. Jim Carmichael provided some interesting examples in his book *The Modern Rifle.* These included a warthog that ran off and was lost after being shot in the chest at close range with a .458 Winchester, and a deer that took two hits in the chest cavity from a .338 magnum and appeared not to notice that it should be dead.

Perhaps the gold medal for tenacity when wounded would go to the Cape buffalo, whose ability to absorb numerous bullets "in the right place" is legendary. It is not unheard-of for a wounded buffalo to be shot ten or more times with big-bore rifles at close range and stay on its feet until a shot to the brain or spine finally brings it down.

How can that be? The explanation lies in the resistance that develops once the animal's arousal system is in high gear. Without getting into the specific physiology involved, this state is sometimes referred to as the "fight-or-flight" mode. Once an animal is alerted, and particularly if it is wounded, a series of physiological and psychological changes take place that render the animal much less susceptible to the effect of subsequent wounds. In effect, the hunter is dealing with a different animal after the first shot.

It has often been said that under those conditions, the only shot that will stop a charging buffalo is one that enters the central nervous system, such as the brain or spinal cord. The lungs, the heart, and other vital organs can be seriously damaged, even virtually destroyed, but the animal can live long enough to stomp you or some unsuspecting native who happens across it later on. This same resistance to the effects of a wound is also common among humans during wartime or other catastrophic events, and probably for the same reasons.

Perhaps the best rule you can follow to stay out of this particular jackpot is to be as certain as possible that your *first* shot goes into a vital area. When you do that, it appears less likely the animal will survive long enough to enter that fight-or-flight state of greatest resistance. The necessity of making a good first shot should be thought through before a hunter shoots at running but unwounded game or game that is far away.

It should be remembered that, similar to making a first impression, it is *impossible* to make up for a bad first shot with subsequent shots. After a bad first shot, you will be shooting at a physiologically and psychologically different animal seconds after it is wounded. Although it seems paradoxical, a wounded animal is typically much harder to kill than one that is not.

One aspect of bullet placement I found troublesome is worth mentioning. This is the *angle* of any shot you take. By the angle I mean the way the position of the animal influences the path of your bullet. This is a crucial matter in shot placement and doesn't receive the attention it deserves. Numerous sources give illustrations showing where bullets should be placed depending on an animal's position. Broadside, straight-on or rear-end shots cause little difficulty, but I found quartering shots particularly troublesome.

I confess I have a tendency to rush my shots and don't always take enough time to assess the way a bullet will travel in a quartering animal. I know some hunters have the opposite difficulty, taking so long to get off their shot that the animal may move and may even put some sort of barrier, including another animal, between the hunter and itself. Neither of these extremes is desirable. Timing is important.

To minimize the need to follow up a wounded animal, one must simply take the time to assess the effect of the animal's position in relation to the hunter, but not take so long that the opportunity for a shot is missed altogether. This strategy is undoubtedly easier said than done for many of us.

Your PH should be able to help you with bullet placement. It would not be out of line to ask him to remind you, just before you shoot, where to place your bullet, just in case you get excited and forget those neat diagrams with the bull's-eyes you've studied. An example of a helpful hint at such a time might be something like this: "He's quartering away. Put your bullet at the back of the ribs directed toward the off shoulder." To avoid giving offense, many PHs probably won't offer such advice on the spot unless asked. But unless you are a *very* experienced big-game hunter who does not have problems doping out these angles, I recommend you ask your PH for a little reminder before you shoot. And it wouldn't hurt to also ask him to give you his estimate of the range to your target.

Another subject about which there is wide, if not complete, agreement is on exactly where to place your bullet relative to the animal's anatomy. There are two areas recommended for nondangerous game: the shoulder and the heart-lung area. Even if your Uncle Mort always dropped his deer with a neck shot, the target usually recommended is the heart-lungs or the shoulder. No matter which angle your game is facing, the idea is to direct your shot to this area.

An animal shot in the lungs is typically dead by the time a hunter can walk up to it, often after an animal makes a short, fast run of thirty to one hundred yards. The shoulder shot is frequently recommended for African game, but I believe it is highly overrated as a general strategy. Most ungulates, such as antelope and zebra, can go a long way with a shoulder wound, even if it's broken. If the bullet has enough muscle, after penetrating and breaking the shoulder, it will continue on to damage the lungs. Then you have a lung-shot animal with a broken shoulder, a much better deal. It's the damage to the lungs, not the shoulder, that ultimately kills the animal. The broken limb may well aid in tracking, but this is a poor substitute for a fatal shot to the lungs or heart from which the animal dies in a few seconds.

For dangerous game, or when it's necessary to prevent an animal from running off, a high shoulder shot has some advantages. This can be tricky because of the variation in body structure of different animals. But a shot that breaks the shoulder high will often transmit enough shock to the spine that the animal will be anchored on the spot. The animal will usually require a finishing shot because the spinal injury, while immediately immobilizing, is not itself always immediately fatal. I have seen animals from duiker to caribou and kudu dropped in their tracks with a high-shoulder shot and still require a finishing shot. If the caliber and bullet you are using have the muscle to break both shoulders of an animal, the shot is likely to drop it in its tracks, or at least prevent it from moving far after it has been hit. In many cases such a shot will damage either the spine or lungs, or both. Kevin Robertson's *The Perfect Shot* shows shot placement on African game in great detail.

HANDLOADS VERSUS FACTORY LOADS

Since increased velocity, increased accuracy, and premium bullets are probably the three main reasons one would want to use handloaded ammunition instead of factory ammunition on a safari, it seems to me that the advantages to be gained by using handloads today are not so clear. Though it pains me to say it, as a passionate handloader for over thirty years, today I think it is probably not a good idea for the average reloader to bring handloads for his safari.

There was a time when handloading was the only way to get ammunition loaded with the finest game bullets, but this is no longer the case. Several of the best bullets available are now offered in factory loads by various companies, some of which are listed in appendix D. A brief review of what's available from factories today will illustrate how the situation differs from what shooters had to choose from in the past.

I think that Weatherby was the first major U.S. brand to offer premium bullets, as I have defined them here, in their ammunition. For years they have provided their magnum calibers with the option of Nosler Partition bullets, probably the first widely available premium bullet in the States. Weatherby still offers its ammunition with Nosler Partitions but now has added both the Barnes X and Swift A-Frame bullets to the lineup.

Today, the clear leader for offering premium bullets is Federal. According to its 1998 catalog, this company offers no less than sixty-four different premium bullet loads in a multiplicity of calibers ranging from the .22-250 to the .470 Nitro Express! There are even premium bullet loads for the .30-30 and the ancient .300 H&H Magnum. Federal's premium and safari lines are available with bullets from three companies: Trophy Bonded Bullets, Nosler, and Woodleigh. I seriously doubt there has ever been a broader selection of premium hunting loads of comparable quality than the current offerings by Federal.

Remington also offers a line of premium bullet loads using the Swift A-Frame, which shares some features of both the partition and bonded-core designs. Lately, Winchester has started offering a premium line of ammunition featuring its Fail Safe bullet, which seems to be a blend of some characteristics of partition bullets and the Barnes X. PMC also offers its ammunition with premium bullets.

These premium bullets will not necessarily result in quicker kills than conventionally constructed softpoints, which often go to pieces violently even on soft lung tissue, but they are regarded as more reliable killers. That's because they don't disintegrate, they retain a high percentage of their original weight, and they give relatively deep penetration, which helps to ensure that the bullet reaches the vital areas or exits to leave a blood trail to aid in tracking if necessary.

The price one pays for this "conservative" performance is that the animal may run off a few more yards than it would if hit with a fast-opening soft- or hollowpoint, but it is also more likely to leave a blood trail from an exit wound. And it is more likely to be wounded in a vital area because of greater penetration. If the hunter places any of the premium bullets mentioned, or something similar, into the heart-lung area of any of the plains-game species at a sufficiently high velocity that the bullet will expand, his game won't go far, and he won't have occasion to be dazzled by the prowess of his native trackers.

So I could avoid problems related to Africa's heat, when I was working up loads for my safaris and had found one that I thought was suitable, I placed a few rounds so loaded along with my rifle in the bed of my pickup in the sun for up to two hours so they would get good and hot. I then fired and chronographed them. There was never a sign of high pressure, so I figured all was OK. I would have rejected a load that showed *any* sign of excessive pressures, including cratered primers, hard extraction, or excessive case expansion. Even unexpectedly high velocities raise a red flag since I know they frequently result from higher pressures.

After my hunt in South Africa, my PH asked to shoot my .375-06, so we walked to a small range facility he'd constructed on his farm. I had a few rounds left over from an earlier hunt that were loaded with 300-grain Nosler Partition bullets, which had been driven into the case by my foolishly leaving them in the magazine during a sequence of one-shot kills. I'd left these rounds in the magazine and loaded a fresh one in the chamber when we went hunting. Even though the loads were already compressed, the hammering they took in the magazine drove bullets still farther down into the powder space, so that they were now supercompressed. There was every reason to believe pressures would be higher in the 90-degree heat of South Africa than when I developed the loads in Alaska when temperatures were in the 70s. Yet all fired perfectly with no signs whatever of excess pressure.

I did use only handloads on two safaris and had no problems related to my ammunition, per se. But neither the wildcat .375-06 rifle nor my ammunition alone would have been of use to anyone else. It's possible there was not another .375-06 in all of Africa at the time, and my .270 digested loads somewhat in excess of most recommended maximums. It would not have surprised me if they were excessive in another .270, and if so, no one else could use them safely in their rifle.

Handloading will often produce more accurate ammunition for a given rifle than factory ammunition. But, for the most part, hunting African game does not require the level of accuracy that handloading makes possible. Though I continue to hear stories about hunters shooting kudu at three hundred yards, I'll bet the majority are taken within one hundred fifty. Certainly all the bush species are typically shot at short-to-moderate ranges in southern Africa. I suspect that if a person tried a number of brands of factory ammunition using premium bullets available in the States today in his rifle, he would find at least one that would produce groups of two inches or so at one hundred yards. I think that's good enough for just about any shooting you're likely to do in southern Africa.

No one with an ounce of sense would take a long shot at a dangerous game animal unless it was wounded and escaping. Your PH will probably not let you take such a shot, preferring to get you to within one hundred yards to make sure you hit the animal right the first shot. Minute of angle is simply not required for this kind of hunting, and minute of Cape buffalo is not that hard to achieve, particularly at one hundred yards or less. What is important on all dangerous game is bullet placement and bullet performance.

Among the other benefits of using factory ammunition is that the companies that produce it test regularly to be sure it is safe under a variety of conditions, such as high temperatures, for example. It is also tested enough that getting a whole box of duds is not likely. Unless you are an experienced and careful handloader, it is quite possible to trash all the primers in a particular box by using careless loading techniques or make a mistake in resizing that causes excess headspace or a round that won't chamber.

My point is that high temperatures and improper techniques *can* cause serious problems if you are careless in assembling your ammunition. It has often been said that one of the reasons the old British big bores had such big cases was to allow them to be loaded to sufficiently high-performance levels without resorting to high pressures. They did this to avoid pressure problems in the tropics when temperatures were high. This example illustrates how ammo companies can look out for the hunter in ways he may never appreciate.

It's probably worth noting that most professional hunters in Africa use factory ammunition exclusively, for one reason or another, and always have.

ARE AFRICAN ANIMALS TOUGHER?

It seems appropriate at this point to briefly consider the claim that African game is harder to kill than, say, North American game of similar size and type. I have not shot enough game in the two places to have an expert opinion based on my own experience alone. However, I have noted over many years that there are equally experienced hunters on both sides of the issue.

One side, represented by Elmer Keith and Peter Capstick, claims that African game is *much* harder to kill than North American game of similar size. They would argue, I suspect, that a kudu is harder to kill than an elk, an eland tougher than a moose, an impala more difficult than a white-tailed deer of similar size.

This alleged toughness of African game is almost invariably attributed to the evolution of the African species amid an abundance of predators. American game, it is argued, are soft by comparison, as they have had to escape fewer predators over the course of their evolution and don't have the same will to live as their African counterparts.

This argument, of course, is largely speculation since I doubt, for example, if anyone knows enough about the predator-prey relationships of mule deer compared to those of the Grant gazelle over the course of these species' evolution to make such a judgment. Still the idea seems to have great appeal to some people.

On the other side of the issue, perhaps the most famous advocate of using your deer or elk rifle on safari for the taking of similar game is the late, very influential, Jack O'Connor. On his several safaris he used a variety of popular "North American" calibers, including the 7x57mm, .30-06, and .300 magnum. But he also selected a .450 Watts for use on buffalo, I believe, and used the .375 H&H on occasion. Clearly, he respected bore diameter and bullet weight in situations that he thought called for them.

It is evident from his voluminous writing that O'Connor placed little stock in the idea that African game is harder to kill than similar game elsewhere. He would dismiss, I think, the idea that an impala is more difficult to kill than, say, a white-tailed deer of comparable size and under similar circumstances.

Finn Aagaard, in his recollections of hunting in his native Kenya, is another experienced African hunter whose objectivity and attention to detail should be prized by anyone serious about learning what really works on African game. He is among those who discount the idea that African game of comparable size and temperament is harder to kill than game found elsewhere. Aagaard has considerable experience as both a hunter and guide in North America as well as in Africa.

Even the great John Taylor, in his book *African Rifles and Cartridges,* advocated calibers for use on elephant that some American "experts" would frown upon, insisting the calibers weren't adequate for elk. This difference of opinion is not an exaggeration, as anyone familiar with the hunting literature of the last one hundred years or so will recognize. It is my impression that the current crop of gunwriters, who have far more African hunting experience than gunwriters of the past, also tend to reject the argument that African game is harder to kill in general than game in North America or elsewhere.

Of course, there are not always animals of similar size and temperament to compare on the two continents. It follows that there may be no comparable animals in the hunting experience of the average first-time safari hunter. What, for example, among North American game compares to an elephant, or even a zebra? Or how about an antelope like the eland, which can weigh a ton? And just because animals are of similar weight does not make a moose (the largest member of the deer family) necessarily comparable to an eland (the largest member of the antelope family). For these reasons the client should take seriously the recommendations of professional and experienced hunters, including his own African professional hunter, while recognizing that there are extremists in both camps.

Another reason for the client to pay serious attention to his own PH's views on the matter is that it may be important for the PH to have confidence in his client and his weapon. By having this confidence, the PH will feel comfortable giving his best effort to find the game sought. A PH with a client who cannot shoot his new .458 well enough to make a killing shot on buffalo may be inclined to immediately follow up any of the client's shots with some of his own to avoid losing the animal, or worse, robbing said client of taking the animal on his own. It is probably for this reason that a hunter is usually guided to nondangerous game first by his PH so the latter can assess the hunter's shooting skill and evaluate the risk to him and his staff when dangerous game is on the menu.

In conclusion regarding the toughness of African game and its implications for your choice of rifles and loads, I think this much can be said on the subject, supported by a vast body of experience of professional and sport hunters: If a particular rifle-ammunition combination is adequate for a given North

American animal, the same combination would be adequate for a comparable African game animal under similar conditions. I believe there is clear consensus on this matter. It may be that a *wounded* animal in Africa is tougher to bring down, but a combination that is generally adequate for one will also do for the other.

It is also true that a poor or marginally effective shot is just that, no matter what the animal is or what it's shot with. An animal that is shot in the paunch or has a broken leg is likely to present some difficulties before it can be hung on the meat pole. There are other variables, such as species-specific vigor (to the extent this exists) and an animal's physiological state when shot, which are likely to play a larger role in the ultimate outcome than what continent the animal lives on.

Finally, the hunting literature surely suggests that some animals of a given species, like people, are just tougher than others. Some individual deer, antelope, elk, or whatever animal seem tougher to put down, even when not alarmed or wounded, than the average of the species. There appears to be some individual variation in vitality that can't be explained any other way.

There is no way to tell *before* you shoot which particular animal will show this trait, so the hunter is well advised to assume that any animal he shoots at is one of these tough characters and to place his shot correctly every time. For the most part, even these relatively tough animals will not long survive a properly placed bullet that does what it is supposed to do. The tough ones just take longer to recognize that they are dead.

But if you really want to see how tough African game can be, here are a few pointers. Shoot offhand or at running animals whenever possible. Take long shots, meaning those at the limit of your own skill, instead of trying to get closer. Take lots of frontal shots on tough animals. And less obvious perhaps, make it a point to shoot your game through one lung rather than two. If you follow these guidelines, I can almost guarantee that you will become a member of the "ironclad African game" fraternity with lots of stories to tell about how animals shot in vital areas still managed to escape, or were brought to bag after long and difficult trailing. If you engage in these particular practices, you are likely to find most game "incredibly difficult to kill," in the words of one noted scribe. If you don't do any of these things, and place a premium bullet in a vital area on the first shot, you are likely going to wind up in the other camp on this issue.

SELECTION OF RIFLES AND CALIBERS

It is possible to be grossly "undergunned" or "overgunned" even following "expert advice" and neither is desirable. We can select rifles that are inadequate in power for what we expect of them, or we can try to compensate for poor shooting by taking rifles whose recoil prevents us from shooting them well. We novices must rely on our own, usually limited, experience and that of *competent* authority to select reasonable safari rifles.

Most of what has been written about selecting rifles for African hunting is concerned with dangerous game, namely the Big Five. There is probably good reason for this. The consequences of making a poor choice in this area can be embarrassing, possibly even fatal. And I would not discount the element of bravado and presumed manliness (my apologies to Osa Johnson and other accomplished female hunters) that has always been associated with the pursuit of dangerous game.

There is little doubt that hunting animals that can kill or maim you adds spice to the enterprise, which the hunting of more docile species lacks. Shooting the large-caliber, hard-kicking rifles typically recommended for big game bestows a certain status on the shooter that the use of a smaller caliber does not.

But due in part to the expense involved, the average American going on safari, for whom this book is written, is much more likely to concentrate on plains and bush game than this elite group of animals that can claw, bite, and stomp you. Indeed, many, probably most, safaris today in southern Africa focus *exclusively* on plains- or bush-dwelling animals, mostly various pigs and antelope, virtually none of which are dangerous except under somewhat special circumstances, such as being wounded and cornered. This has a large effect on the choice of weapons, as well as the costs, for a safari today. Such hunts may lack the element of danger, if not entirely, of hunting the Big Five, but otherwise provide all the excitement and satisfaction of being on an African safari.

There are at least four sources of information on the subject of selecting rifles for African game. One is the opinion of resident hunters in the country where you will be hunting. They live there and hunt the same game and should know what works, at least for them. Another is the opinion of professional hunting guides, including the one you ultimately book a hunt with. These fellows see more game shot in a few seasons than most safari clients will in a lifetime. A third is the experience of other hunters of your acquaintance or those who write about their experiences, like professional gunwriters. Finally, there is your own experience. None of these is necessarily the best source or the last word on the subject. A person's preferences are often determined by their peer group, their own particular experiences, or simply prejudice, as well as other factors too numerous to mention.

One must start the search for useful information with the knowledge that recognized experts with equal experience—

professionals and sport hunters alike—sometimes have irreconcilable disagreements on which rifles and calibers are appropriate for which species and under which circumstances. There are several reasons for this, it seems to me, but one cannot avoid the reality of these differences of opinion. That's why it's important to seek out a variety of sources and make some judgments about who the careful observers and unbiased reporters might be.

Now let's take a look at what we know about the preferences for African plains game of the people we might look to for guidance in making our own selection.

PREFERENCES OF GUNWRITERS

Several fine books are available that address in considerable detail the specific choices one might make in a rifle type or caliber for Africa. One of the best recent discussions is found in Craig Boddington's *Safari Rifles,* a comprehensive work based in part on his survey of African professional hunters. Some of those he cites were commercial ivory hunters and explorers in the days of muzzleloaders. Others hunted during a period when muzzleloaders and smokeless powder cartridges overlapped. He also describes the recommendations for clients of today's professional hunters as expressed in his survey, as well as the preferences of gunwriters themselves.

Another work that should be on the "must read" list of the safari-bound is Finn Aagaard's *Hunting Rifles and Cartridges,* which reflects his own wide experience as a professional hunter and sportsman in Africa and North America. Then there is John Taylor's classic, *African Rifles and Cartridges,* which I highly recommend.

The books by Boddington and Aagaard were written by men with extensive experience. In reading both books, I detected very little bias toward one ballistic gospel or another. Both authors usually say so when they have an opinion that they know reflects a personal preference, and they don't parade their opinion as revealed truth. It is for these reasons that I highly recommend both. Taylor's book is also a valuable resource written by a man of extensive experience and with a thoughtful, analytic disposition.

PREFERENCES OF THE PROFESSIONALS

It is clear that neither the number of animals bagged nor the years of experience alone make a PH a reliable source about the selection of rifles. Several of the professional hunters who responded to Boddington's survey in *Safari Rifles* reported using rifles for *their own hunting* that many would consider much too light for the game specified. These choices often were quite different from the recommendations they made for their clients, or the rifles they used when backing up clients. Since these PHs are still with us, I think we have to acknowledge that they know what they are doing, and that what they use works for them.

A noteworthy finding from Boddington's survey was the familiarity of the calibers that the pros used themselves and the calibers that they recommended to clients for plains game. Most were in common use in the USA for deer, antelope, and elk. Rather than a lot of exotic "African" calibers, these men frequently mentioned the .243 and .270 Winchester, 7mm Remington Magnum, .30-06, and .300 magnum. When eland were on the menu, the .375 H&H was popular too, and it seemed to be regarded as the best all-round caliber for all African game.

On weapon preferences of PHs and other experienced hunters, Boddington said that of those who were living shortly after the introduction of smokeless powder, many preferred small 6.5mm-caliber rifles, probably Mannlichers and Mausers, for all game up to and including elephant! Many today would consider this calibers marginal for mule deer, and the bullets were simply primitive by comparison with those we have today.

Another example of the small-bore aficionado is the manager of a large, southern Zimbabwe ranch where I had hunted. A native of the country, he told me he'd bagged all the different types of plains game in the area, including eland, with a .22 Hornet! This is like sending a seventh grader to play professional football!

Finn Aagaard, a vastly experienced native of Kenya, writes in *Aagaard's Africa* of a chum who slew not only duiker and bushbuck, but also leopard, waterbuck, zebra, and Cape buffalo with the Hornet. And not just one or two, but scores of some of the toughest. Aagaard himself reports using the Hornet on game up to the size of impala, which would be considered by many an act worthy only of the reckless and naive. Aagaard is neither; he is a very experienced hunter and he got away with it.

It is also instructive to recall that the .22 Savage Hi-Power, introduced in 1912, which fired a diminutive 70-grain bullet at the then astounding velocity of 2,800 feet per second, created quite a stir among the hunting brethren when it came along. There are many accounts of it being used successfully on tigers and other large, sometimes dangerous, game.

Taylor recounts that the .22 Hi-Power was used by resident hunters on some tough critters, including zebra. John Burger reports that he used the rifle with satisfaction on animals up to five hundred pounds, and says his acquaintances, "the cream of African hunters," used it on eland without difficulty. The caliber is still loaded in Europe today, where it's known as the 5.6x52Rmm, and is popular for combination guns. Today most would consider it inadequate even for our North American deer, and somewhat light even for rock chucks. There are also reliable accounts of the successful use of the .220 Swift on elk, and not just a few elk either.

In Zimbabwe there were two professional hunters using the camp while I was there. One was an experienced older man, the other relatively inexperienced as a PH. The older man, who had for years hunted for market in Zimbabwe, had two rifles in camp. One was a Brno Mauser in 7x57mm. This was a typical European-style rifle with a flat-bolt handle as I recall, double-set triggers, and a thin comb with excessive drop. I used the rifle myself to shoot impala and bushbuck and found it accurate, though a little awkward since I like a high, thick comb. His other rifle was a Whitworth Express in .375 H&H on a Mark X (Model 98) Mauser action.

The client of this older pro, whom I will call William, was a young American working in Europe who did not bring his own rifle. He used both the 7x57mm and .375 to take some bush game and one of the rifles (I'm not sure which) to take a leopard. I noted with interest that this client appeared to use the two rifles interchangeably when after leopard, and the PH clearly thought both were adequate under the conditions. I don't recall what ammunition was used in the .375. The game I shot, resulting in three one-shot kills, I took with his 7x57mm loaded with what I think were 170-grain H-Mantle bullets.

My PH, the younger of the two, was more modestly equipped. His primary weapon was an SMLE (Short Magazine Lee-Enfield) rebarreled to .308 Winchester, referred to there as the "NATO" round. His choice of this rifle appeared to be based on three factors: availability of the action, availability of ammunition, and availability of FMJ bullets.

Since Zimbabwe, formerly Southern Rhodesia, had British colonial roots, it's likely the SMLE actions were fairly common. Both sides in the recently ended civil war had used automatic weapons chambering the NATO 7.62mm (.308 Winchester) so that ammunition was likewise relatively plentiful. The FMJ ammo was seen as particularly useful for dangerous game like elephant as well as for culling excess grass-eaters, usually impala, in that area.

This culling activity is worth some elaboration. Impala thrive in the dry, thornbush country of the low veld of southern Zimbabwe and are present in great numbers. These beautiful antelope weigh around a hundred pounds. Because they are so numerous, they compete with the domestic cattle as well as with some of the more valuable game species like zebra and kudu.

As a result it was a common practice to kill large numbers of impala to keep their numbers at desired levels. This was typically done at night by riding around in a Land Rover with a spotlight until a herd of impala was located by their remarkably bright eyes reflecting the light. The culling then commenced with several animals killed in each group before the survivors ran off. My PH reported killing around 15,000 impala in this manner, mostly with a Ruger .223, using head shots. I understand that many of the carcasses were sold to local crocodile farms.

PREFERENCES OF RESIDENT AFRICANS

Both John Taylor and Finn Aagaard say that the 9.3x62mm Mauser was the most popular all-round rifle used by residents in Kenya until it was eventually supplanted by the .375 H&H. The 9.3x62mm is much like the .338-06, .35 Whelen, and similar medium-bore cartridges based on the .30-06 case. The Mauser uses a slightly larger bullet of .366-inch diameter in a case virtually identical to the .30-06 except that the neck is shorter, giving the cartridge a small advantage in case capacity over those formed by simply necking up the Springfield case. As a result, the 9.3x62mm gives about 4,000 foot-pounds of muzzle energy—about like the old .375 H&H Flanged Magnum, introduced along with the familiar belted version in 1912—compared to 3,700–3,900 foot-pounds produced by the other mediums noted from .338 to .358 caliber. Incidentally, my .375-06 produces nearly identical ballistics to the .375 Flanged.

For my second safari I went to South Africa, where I hunted with a personable young Afrikaner named Johan, who was also relatively new to the business of professional hunting, though a native of that country. The scarcity of guns and ammunition I'd seen in Zimbabwe did not appear to be a factor in South Africa. Here the government, unlike most other African countries, allowed at least some of the population to own a variety of weapons, and they could also reload.

Johan had recently acquired a South African-built Musgrave rifle, a Mauser-type bolt-action in 8x68Smm caliber, a magnum 8mm of European design. He also had a .243 Winchester that he liked a lot. He expected to hunt professionally in Botswana and Zimbabwe as I recall, and I believe his choice of the 8x68Smm was because of his anticipation of hunting dangerous game, often referred to as "big game" there. He expected to hunt buffalo, I believe, and later he developed a specialty in leopard hunting.

Since all my hunting with him was for plains game, I never saw him carry the big rifle. On one occasion he packed a 12-gauge autoloader filled with slugs when we hunted gemsbok. Another time, during a daylight hunt on foot for a bushpig, he carried a 7x57mm Mauser. He said it was to protect against accidentally running into a leopard in the thick and thorny Limpopo River bush. His father, a lifetime hunter and native of South Africa, used a .30-06 as his primary weapon.

In the case of Johan and his father, availability was not a determining factor in the calibers they chose, nor was the expense in their choice of weapons. The family was well-off and could have had about anything they wanted. I believe their choices reflected their ideas of what was adequate for the game of southern Africa.

I suspect that most of the resident hunters you will meet during your travels in Africa are likely to be carrying rifles in the same calibers you'd encounter in a deer or elk camp in Montana, with the occasional .303 British, 7x57mm or 8x68Smm thrown in for good measure because of their cultural heritage.

PREFERENCES OF FIREARMS

There is a risk that the hunter new to Africa will succumb to the temptation to buy some cannon he or she thinks is necessary for hunting African game. To paraphrase Robert Ruark, who wrote a book admonishing hunters to "use enough gun," it is also possible, and I suspect more common, to use "too much gun," at least too much for the shooter to handle effectively. This can lead to considerable disappointment or worse. But first, let's consider the opposite problem, that of being undergunned.

One of the facts that tend to confound the discussion about adequate calibers is that under the right circumstances some very large animals can be killed with very small calibers. A contemporary gunwriter, Ross Seyfried, calls this general phenomenon as taking a rifle "out of its class." It appears that there has always been a fascination with taking game with what appears to be an inadequate caliber, like being able to brag you killed a buffalo with a big stick, I suppose.

There is a huge difference between what may be accomplished by a "local" hunter or professional cropping officer—similarly undergunned, but not on a tight schedule—and a safari client. The resident hunter is likely to be familiar with the country and the game, and can walk away if a suitable shot is not presented. He is also likely to have much more hunting experience.

In contrast, the typical safari client is paying from $350 to $1,500 per day, plus a trophy fee that can be $1,500 or more, for some antelope, even if it's wounded and lost. He has limited time and normally only a few opportunities to bag his game. He has probably never before laid eyes on the animals he's hunting before he shoots one, and may never again after his safari. This guy will be reluctant to pass up *any* decent shot.

It is for this reason that many will decide to bring a rifle considerably more powerful than they are used to in hopes that the extra power will compensate for poor shooting, or that they can make that "long shot" if necessary. This mind-set can result in disappointing marksmanship as well as wounded and lost game—not to mention the embarrassment when our hopeful Nimrod realizes what his PH and everyone else in camp knows: He can't shoot his shiny new cannon worth a hoot.

I can appreciate as well as the next guy the beauty and utility of a fine Holland & Holland side-by-side double-chambered for a cartridge the size of a carrot. But Africa-bound hunters emphatically do not have to take out a second mortgage or abandon the goal of sending their kids to college to buy one so they can hunt in Africa.

Rather than rushing out to buy a new .470 Tyrannosaurus, a .577 Bellowing Behemoth, or some other teeth-rattling juggernaut capable of one-shot kills on Mount Rushmore, the hunter can get by just fine using a rather pedestrian cartridge suitable for the deer, elk, and antelope-sized game of his home country. Examples of these are the .30-06, 7mm Remington Magnum, or some variation of the .300 magnum. The super magnums, like the .378 Weatherby, are about as unnecessary, and surely as undesirable, as an extra two hundred pounds on your favorite fashion model.

The average hunter is more likely to own, and would be better served by, a Winchester Model 70, a Remington 700, a Weatherby Mark V, a Ruger 77, or a custom-built Model 98 Mauser bolt-action chambered for a familiar "all-round" cartridge suitable for North American game.

One piece of good advice I chose to ignore was that I bring just one load for each rifle. I fully agree that it is generally best to use one load for one rifle so that one may avoid misses, caused by not knowing the trajectory of the bullet loaded, or other adverse outcomes. Then there is the possibility of experiencing some other unpleasantness because of an unintentional, and unfortunate, substitution of a soft for a solid at an inopportune time. My situation was such that I decided on a different course, but taking one load is still good advice.

AMMUNITION AVAILABILITY

Why the caliber and type of rifle you take might be worth a second thought can be illustrated by my own experience. Consider my situation when I arrived in Zimbabwe, but my gear and rifles did not. Fortunately they showed up later, but the situation provided considerable food for thought.

While in the hotel in Harare, Zimbabwe's capital city, waiting to be contacted by my outfitter, I called out of curiosity the one or two stores listed in the phone book that appeared to handle guns and ammunition to see what was available. I learned that there was a double-barrel 12-gauge and a Lee Enfield in

.303 for sale, and some .22 rimfire ammunition. That was it. There were apparently no rifles available to rent of any kind.

On my two safaris to southern Africa I took two rifles. One was a wildcat .375-06, the other a garden-variety .270 Winchester. The rifles and my baggage showed up on the fifth day of my ten-day hunt in Zimbabwe. From what I have heard from other hunters traveling to Africa, this is not an unusual occurrence. It was only through the efforts of my safari outfitter, a native of Zimbabwe with many contacts, that my rifles and bags were recovered in time for me to use them on my hunt. If my ammo had not shown up, the .375-06 would have been useful as a walnut club and for little else. I could probably have found some ammo for the .270 though.

An acquaintance of mine went on a safari to Namibia with his son. This guy had considerable experience hunting in Kenya and Alaska. To minimize ammunition and potential parts problems, both brought rifles in the same caliber, 7x57mm Mauser. They had developed handloads that worked well in either rifle. I think this was a very savvy approach. Since this is a popular caliber in southern Africa, if they'd needed to, they could surely have purchased or scrounged some ammunition locally.

The possibility of not having your ammunition make it to Africa with you, while your guns do should not be discounted entirely. Of course, the reverse is also possible: your ammo arriving, but your guns being routed to some village in the Congo or to some Bedouin camp in the Sahara Desert. In the former case, using a caliber common in the hunting area, or one that can be safely used with ammunition that is, seems like a good idea and may allow you to at least use your own guns. If, for example, one brings a .223, .243 Winchester, .270 Winchester, 7x57mm, 7mm Remington Magnum, .308 Winchester, .30-06, .300 H&H, .300

Weatherby, .300 Winchester, .375 H&H, or .458 Winchester, it's likely some ammunition could be located if need be.

In the second case where your ammo arrives packed with your clothing and other gear, but your rifles don't show up, at least if you have commonly used ammo, you might use it to barter the use of a good rifle. Your handloaded ammo for your wildcat .379 Grass Burner Express probably won't buy you much of a loaner rifle and would be useless to anyone else.

My bringing a wildcat .375-06 clearly violated this principle, as would any wildcat cartridge except "improved" versions of popular calibers. In a pinch, .300 H&H ammunition can be fired in the .300 Weatherby, which is an improved .300 H&H, though not conversely. There are no problems firing .458 ammo in .458 Lott or .450 Watts, and the .458 is probably the most commonly used big bore in Africa today. The possibility for such substitutions is limited but still merits some thought. Even if a substitute caliber would not work in your rifle, it might be convenient to bring a rifle chambered in a popular caliber.

I learned that many PHs in Zimbabwe have a small cache of ammunition left behind by visiting hunters that could be tapped in emergencies, such as the loss of a client's baggage containing his ammunition. These professional hunters, of course, also have a supply of ammunition for their own use. Inevitably this treasure would reflect the popularity of calibers among both resident hunters and their foreign clients.

People like me who insist on bringing rifles chambered for wildcat cartridges, other than the "improved" variety, would simply be out of luck and forced to borrow a rifle for which ammunition was available, if theirs was lost somehow. This may not be a problem for some, but for me would have been a severe disappointment. It would have lessened my safari experience substantially if I'd had to use a borrowed rifle for the whole trip.

Before my own rifles caught up with me, and without any assurance that they ever would, I actually did borrow a rifle for a while. My young PH generously offered to loan me his SMLE in .308 and a supply of military-ball ammunition. I believe I could have shot the rifle well enough to kill some game, but it would have been a challenge. The rifle had a poor trigger and the stock was a nightmare. Fortunately I was able to borrow the 7x57mm described earlier from the other PH and hunted with it until my rifles and gear, thankfully, showed up. Traveling to Harare from the low veld to retrieve them cost me a day's hunting, but it was well worth it to be able to use my own stuff.

SCOPES

In the last two or three decades the variable scope has largely replaced the fixed-power variety, at least in the States. It is pointless to argue whether the versatility they provide is really necessary since most people use them anyway.

When I have seen recommendations on scopes, which are less often mentioned by safari companies than bullets or calibers, they are usually for a fixed power of 2.5 to 4. All scopes I saw on professionals' and residents' rifles in Zimbabwe and South Africa were fixed power and 4X, I believe. My rifles wore 3X9 Leupolds, and I don't recall using more than 4X for any shot at game. I made no shots that could not have been made equally well with a 2.5X scope.

One thing that surprised me about residents' scopes was that they were generally cheap ones, considerably below the quality any American would be likely to use on an important hunt even in North America.

I noted with interest that Peter Capstick used a rather common-variety Bushnell variable scope with the "command post" feature mounted on his custom-built .375 H&H for his videotaped hunt for Cape buffalo. I suspect that if he thought it was necessary to have a ponderous German scope, which cost ten times as much and was as bulky as a large possum, he could have had one. But he obviously didn't.

The quality of scopes undoubtedly reflects the cost of such equipment in southern Africa, as well as the dry weather there during the hunting season, which is less demanding as to waterproofing than, say, hunting on the Alaska Peninsula might be. This matter should also suggest that a fine gift for a PH after a successful safari would be a high-quality American scope. As a gratuity after my safari was over, I gave my PH in South Africa a 3–9X Leupold, brought along as a spare, with which he was clearly delighted.

For plains game I think a variable of 1–4X would be about right, and I would use the same power range for larger game, too. If you plan to hunt leopard, which are typically shot in near darkness, a scope with a larger objective might be appropriate. I saw nothing in Africa that suggested more magnification than 4X was required, though some situations might make more power useful.

SPARE PARTS AND ACCESSORIES

Another issue that deserves some attention is the possibility of a mechanical breakage of some kind. Although the odds are strongly against this happening during a brief safari, it's always possible for a firing pin or some other crucial part to fail. In my case it was my quality compact binocular that failed almost simultaneously with my arrival in my safari camp. If one is using a Model 98 Mauser, I think it would be easier to locate a part for it in Zimbabwe or another southern African country than if one was using a proprietary gee-whiz express rifle of a rare type. Still, I believe it's a good idea to bring along a few critical spare parts, including an extra scope, and maybe even a spare binocular if you have the space for it.

A smart hunter will do some research and consult experienced gunsmiths regarding parts likely to fail on their particular rifles, such as firing pins, ejectors, and extractors. Fortunately these parts are small and inexpensive. I thought having them would provide some peace of mind, so I brought them along. Also, both my rifles were Model 70 Winchesters, which I knew had been popular in Africa for decades, and hoped this would be helpful if a repair needed to be made. I even brought a small quantity of epoxy in the event of a cracked stock.

One other item of equipment you might consider taking along is a broken-shell extractor. This inexpensive little gizmo, available from Brownells, is designed to extract the forward portion of a case cut off by a head separation. This condition, which may be caused by greatly excessive pressure or a weak case, results in the extractor pulling out only the head and a small portion of the brass case, leaving the rest firmly stuck in the chamber. If you are unlucky enough to experience this problem on your hunt, it can really slow things down. I have found it very difficult to get the stuck portion out without damaging the chamber. One of these devices in your kit will put you back in business without the necessity of locating a gunsmith. This is a cheap form of trip insurance.

SIGHTING IN

Let me say a few words about the ranges at which game is taken in this region and the implications I think this has for how to sight in your rifle for plains game.

So far I've hunted in two African countries for a variety of plains and bush game. I took most of the species generally available in these areas except sable and wildebeest and some of the smaller antelope. Many of these animals inhabit fairly dense thornbush, some open mopane forest and brushy riverine areas, while others live in very open grasslands.

Altogether in seventeen days of hunting on these two safaris, I took eighteen animals, which is typical for the area. The longest shot I took at an *unwounded* animal was at a gemsbok, which I estimated at two hundred yards. The absolute longest was at a *wounded* kudu that may have been near three hundred (my first shot was at about one hundred fifty yards). All the other animals were taken within two hundred yards, and most within one hundred.

If I or my PH had wanted to shoot these animals at long range for some reason, we could probably have found a way to do it. But we preferred to stalk close enough for a certain kill whenever possible. The terrain was such that we could nearly always get within one hundred fifty yards or so, often much closer. One exception was the evening when we set up to watch for klipspringer about two hundred yards from a large kopje situated in a flat grassy area that looked like a golf course. It reminded me of hunting rock chucks in eastern Oregon. There was no cover closer to the rock pile that we could use.

My African experience was similar to my experience in North America. I've often read how caribou are typically shot at long range over tundra "plains" and require very flat-shooting rifles. I have no doubt some are shot this way. But I have taken two nice bulls, on unguided hunts, and both were shot at about one hundred fifty yards. I had to make a stalk to get that close, but this wasn't difficult in the rolling hills where I hunted.

Pronghorn antelope and caribou are probably the only true plains animals in North America. Pronghorns are another species said to be a long-range proposition, and I'm sure they can be. Of the two I've had a chance to shoot, both were within one hundred fifty yards. I had to crawl on my belly a considerable distance to get into position for a shot on both occasions. I killed one but missed the other, but not because it was too far away.

All of these experiences illustrate, I believe, my personal hunting style as much as anything else, and I don't mean to suggest otherwise.

My point is that it appears to rarely be *necessary* to shoot at game at ranges over 200 yards, or for that matter any self-imposed limit, in the countries where I've hunted. An exception, from what I have seen, is lechwe in Zambia, which I have not hunted. These animals inhabit open grasslands and appear difficult to approach. I nearly always pick rifles that are capable of taking the game I'm hunting at three hundred yards or more, though I have rarely needed to take such a long shot. The more experience I have, it seems, the closer I want to get before I shoot.

There are some implications worth mentioning, based on these experiences, for how to sight in your rifles for plains game. When I was growing up and learning the ropes of hunting and shooting, it was something of an article of faith that a rifle firing a typical high-velocity cartridge should be sighted in to hit three inches high at one hundred yards. This idea was promoted heavily by the man I considered my mentor, at least in the early years, Jack O'Connor.

Jack grew up in the Southwest and cut his hunting teeth on the small deer of the desert country there and in northern Mexico, or so I gather from his writings. The principle he articulated was this: "You should sight in for the longest range that does not cause midrange misses." The idea is to sight in so that one does not have to worry about holding over or under out to the rifle's "point-blank range". In the case of his favorite .270 with a scope, this was about three hundred yards. You just hold where you want to hit out to the point-blank range of your rifle, ignoring trajectory. Since he appears to have done lots of shooting at running game, this undoubtedly helped him concentrate on lead and angles as his quarry bounced through the cactus and rocks.

After moving to Idaho, Jack wrote a lot about hunting in the Rockies, in the States and Canada, and his passion always appeared to be sheep hunting. It was always clear that he was no brush buster, but preferred to hunt open country and took his game at fairly long range. I have no doubt this sighting arrangement worked well for him considering his preferred way of hunting, and the game he hunted.

There is really nothing sacred about the three-inch number, in my opinion. On an animal the size of a moose, one could well sight in to hit four inches or even eight inches high at one hundred yards using the same principle. The bullet could probably drop at least a foot at longer ranges and still stay within the vital zone of a moose. Whether your rifle has the muscle to kill the animal at maximum range is another matter. If you are hunting woodchucks, on the other hand, three inches high or low is probably too much.

I have nearly always used this three-inch rule and did not have any reason to question it, as I generally hunted deer in open country, too, and frequently with a .270. Then I encountered the duiker and the steenbok. These little guys do not have the ten- or twelve-inch heart-lung area I generally shoot at when deer hunting, or the thirty-inch diameter vital area of a caribou or elk. It's a lot closer to three inches. A hold on one of these tiny fellows in the center of this area at one hundred yards is likely to go right over its back if you are sighted in to hit three inches high at that range. I suspect it wouldn't be too hard to shoot right over a leopard or springbok either. I don't expect everyone will agree with me on this, but considering the ranges at which the great majority of African plains game is shot, at least in southern Africa, the plus-two-inch rule makes more sense to me.

Using cartridges in the velocity class most people use today, you can sight in to be on at two hundred yards, and your bullet will be about two inches high at one hundred yards, and around nine inches low at three hundred. I call this the "209 rule," and it works well for a wide range of cartridges. If you compare your rifle's trajectory when sighted in for two hundred yards versus being sighted three inches high at one hundred, you'll find the trajectory at all ranges is easier to remember.

I think you should give plenty of thought to those three-hundred-yard shots anyway. It should not be too much of an inconvenience to hold the horizontal cross hair on the back line of the animal for such long shots, which I will assume is standing still, while you settle into your solid rest. This way of sighting in is discussed in more detail in appendix C.

As a final note on knowing where your rifle hits at various ranges, I suggest you conduct some first-shot drills. I have emphasized that the first shot you get at an animal is your best one for getting a clean, quick kill. It follows that you need to know where that first shot is going to go.

"What's the problem?" you may ask at this point. "I always sight in my rifles before a trip and check them after arriving in safari camp." This, of course, should be done. The mistake many hunters make, including me for most of my big-game hunting career, is not knowing where that first shot from a cold, oiled barrel is going to go relative to where the rifle ordinarily groups at the range. I wish I could say I came up with this insight myself, but when another outdoor writer mentioned it, I immediately saw the wisdom of his words and applied the principle to my own shooting.

I found that some of my rifles placed their first shot from a cold, clean barrel in the same group fired with a hot and fouled barrel, but most did not. A favorite rifle of mine would put the first bullet several inches out of the group before it settled down. This particular rifle, a Model 99 Savage in .358 Winchester, has a twenty-four-inch, lightweight barrel. I found that running a dry patch through the bore of this rifle before shooting helped somewhat.

PRACTICE, PRACTICE, PRACTICE

Since shot placement is so critical to the success of a hunt, it follows that one's skill in using whatever rifle he or she brings is every bit as important, probably more important, than the selection of a rifle and load. It is no surprise, therefore, that another bit of advice many agents and PHs will give prospective clients is to *practice, practice, practice.*

Prior to my own safari, which I had to arrange on relatively short notice, I fired several hundred rounds at the range from the rifles I was taking. This was in addition to the several hundred rounds of big-bore calibers that I normally fired each month while working on one project or another. At the time, I was able to do far more shooting than the average hunter.

The majority of my shooting was done from a bench, as much of it involved load development. But I also fired a few hundred rounds from various field positions. Before my next hunt I'll do much more of the latter. I plan to shoot a minimum of forty rounds per week from each of the rifles I'm taking, at least half from field positions once the guns are sighted in. Ten to twenty might be enough for a heavy like a .458, just to help keep your teeth in place and avoid feeling like a crash dummy.

While actually on safari I fired a few shots offhand (a position I practiced a lot, with a corresponding increase in humility), two or three kneeling, none from prone. I did not shoot any from the cute little tripods made of sticks used by some PHs, as mine didn't use them. The majority of my shots were from what I would call the "lean-and-grab" position. This involved leaning into a tree or bush, either of which was almost certain to be covered with nasty thorns, and grabbing hold of a branch to use as a rest. Sometimes I did this in a kneeling position, at other times from a standing position. To minimize injury from thorns, I wore a tough but flexible elk-hide leather glove, on my left hand only, so I could grab hold of the thorny local flora and not interfere with the trigger finger of my right hand. This worked great for me.

I'm convinced that the use of a rest of virtually any sort in the field will do more to ensure hits than any other shooting technique I know of. In my opinion, one should *never* take a shot without a rest if one is available, including the shoulder of your long-suffering (and partially deaf) PH.

Once, while lining up on my nyala in Zululand, I practically lay down on a large thorny bush growing out of the hillside that I was on, assuming a sort of leaning prone position for the shot at a partially obscured animal. It was a little like lying on a pincushion. The bullet hit exactly where I wanted it to, and resulted in an instant kill. The nyala bull just fell over backward, all four of its legs fanning the air. It was dead long before we climbed down to where it lay.

Here's a final thought on preparing and maintaining your rifles on safari. Certainly all screws, including those holding the scope and the barreled action to the stock, should be checked for tightness regularly with well-fitting screwdrivers, which you will have brought along for just that purpose. With all the travel over rough, dusty roads, things can easily work loose. The bore should be checked for obstructions regularly and before it's loaded for each day's hunt. Failure to take these simple precautions could cost you a fine trophy, or worse.

Before you leave home, whether you are using factory ammunition or handloads, *every single round you'll be taking should be run from the magazine through the chamber and ejected* to be sure there isn't an oversized cartridge that will lock up your action. I think it's also an excellent idea to fill your magazine while at the range or wherever you shoot at home, and fire at least five shots by single loading, leaving the rounds in the magazine as you do. This procedure may reveal a weak magazine catch or some feeding problem that would not be evident otherwise. It may also reveal problems such as inadequate grip of the case mouth on the bullet, which will cause the bullets in the rounds in the magazine to be driven deeper into the cases from recoil. This may change the ballistics or feeding characteristics of the bullet.

THE FUN FACTOR

Whatever else it may be, a safari should be fun for the participants. The particular rifles you decide to take could well affect how much you enjoy the hunt.

I've often thought it would be great fun to hunt plains game with my Savage Model 99 in .358 Winchester, a favorite of mine. It has a gorgeous custom stock and is slick as glass from years of use, and it has been a lucky elk rifle for me. I'd probably use the Nosler Partition 225-grain or a similar premium bullet and would expect excellent results on everything, including eland, within that cartridge's range limitations. Since most of the game I shot in Africa was at moderate ranges, this would not have been a problem. Though I have never seen such a rifle recommended for African plains game, I think it would be both adequate and fun to use one, at least for me.

Another idea I've had for a second or third safari would be to target the smaller antelope, from dik-dik to impala and bushbuck, and use a high-velocity, small-bore number like my gorgeous custom Sako in .222 Remington Magnum, a .22-250, or a .243, or something similar. Bullet selection would be critical, as most of these animals are well beyond the woodchuck class and require some penetration to kill adequately. But with the right choice of bullets carefully placed, these would do the job. Although these are not generally thought of as calibers for African game, all have proven very useful there in the hands of a good shot.

When hunting with such light rifles in Africa, though, one has to be sufficiently disciplined to pass up any shots at larger game should they present themselves. Alternatively, see to it that a rifle adequate for the largest game you're after is readily available while in the field.

Because the size of the animals you encounter on a safari will vary widely, even for safaris focused exclusively on plains or bush game, the usual strategy is to have in the safari vehicle a rifle big enough to handle the largest game that you are seeking. Most of the time you can probably have a light rifle along, too. This may not work out if you are on foot some distance from the hunting vehicle with your light rifle, say a .22-250, while after duiker and are confronted by a trophy eland or sable. It would probably be a good idea to have the PH or an assistant carry your heavy rifle if he's willing.

I have read about people who went on safaris armed with iron-sighted Model 94s in .30-30 or Model 99s in .300 Savage, and even black-powder-era numbers like the .45-70, presumably because they enjoyed hunting with them and had confidence in them. In my experience, any of these would do the job for at least the range of game from duiker to kudu if the hunter puts a good bullet in the right place on the first shot.

Others derive the greatest pleasure from hunting with "classic" rifles and calibers such as a side-by-side double rifle chambered for the .500-450, like President Roosevelt used on his famous safari in 1909 with his son Kermit. Or perhaps you have located a .318 Westley Richards Mauser in great condition that you'd like to try out. If you are a lever-action fan, maybe that .405 Winchester Model 95 would be your ticket to Valhalla.

Within a broad range of calibers, if a hunter is conscientious in his choice of shots and puts an excellent bullet in a vital area the first shot, I believe he should use a rifle he enjoys hunting with, shoots well, and has confidence in. All these factors appear to be more important to success than the particular caliber choice he makes.

SOME CONCLUSIONS

Even though a fascinating debate has gone on for at least a century and a half, I believe it's possible to draw some conclusions from the hunting literature, and from my own observations, regarding the adequacy of certain calibers for certain African species. I have read dozens of brochures and have spoken with several safari outfitters, agents, bullet and ammunition makers, and PHs about caliber and bullet choices for Africa. In spite of my earlier remarks relating to opinions about the controversy over calibers suitable for African game, I believe there is far more agreement on the basic issues than one might surmise considering the length and vigor of the debate on the matter.

By taking into account a broad range of views, you can base your decisions on the average experience of many hunters rather than on the advice of a single "expert" who religiously advocates just one position. Remember, I am here concerned primarily with plains-bush game.

Big-game guides the world over have similar views on what rifles their clients should bring on a hunt, subject to some legal limitations on minimum calibers. This seems to be true whether the hunt is for elk, brown bear, kudu, or Cape buffalo.

It appears that guides would much prefer that a client bring a rifle he can shoot well if it is legal for the game hunted, even if marginally powerful. They appreciate how important it is for the first shot to go where it should. It seems to me most would prefer this to the client bringing a more powerful rifle that he does not shoot as well, and which may cause him to flub a shot at a fine game animal.

I recall reading an article in *Rifle Magazine* a few years back about the effectiveness of different calibers on guided hunts for North America's largest carnivore, the Alaskan brown bear.* These critters can weigh as much as an eland and are said to be a whole lot nastier when provoked. In general, when it comes to selecting rifles and loads, these great bears are placed in a category all their own, and may be the one area where the heavy rifle has a legitimate role in North American hunting, at least as a backup.

This same article reported that fewer shots were required, on average, to bag a bear with rifles of .30 caliber or less (4.0 shots) than with larger calibers (4.9 shots). The calibers requiring

*See Layne Simpson, "What 63 Dead Brown Bears Can Tell Us," *Rifle Magazine* (July/August 1989), 124–125.

the least number of shots (3.7 per bear) were the group including the .264 Winchester, .270 Winchester, .30-06 and 7mm magnum, which collectively accounted for 6 bears. The next best showing included a couple of the popular .300 magnums and the .375 H&H (each with an average of 3.9 shots), which accounted for 39 bears. The big .33s, the .338 Winchester and .340 Weatherby, averaged 6.2 shots for the 14 bears taken with them. Even a couple of medium- and big-bore sluggers like the .378 Weatherby and the .458 Winchester required an average of 8.5 shots for the 4 bears they felled. These results were based on a data set consisting of detailed records kept by the outfitter.

Thus, with the exception of the .375 H&H, which was used by most of the guides and which also gave the most one-shot kills—small bores proved more effective than either medium or large bores in this sample. The only explanation for these results that I can think of is superior shot placement by those using the lighter calibers, since every other factor related to killing effect, except perhaps velocity, favored the larger calibers. Better a .300 Savage bullet through the lungs of a kudu than a .300 magnum in the guts. Better a .375 in the chest of a buffalo than a .458 bullet through an ear or which breaks a leg.

As always, the conditions under which an animal is hunted can modify the usual recommendations considerably. For example, because of the terrain they prefer, it appears that the vaal rhebok and mountain reedbuck, which weigh one hundred pounds or less, must be shot at long range in open country. A .30-30 adequate for our white-tailed deer, a woods-dwelling critter about the same size, may not be the best choice under these conditions because of its curved trajectory.

It's possible to make a case that, all things considered, *everyone* going on a safari—even if one or more of the Big

Five are on the menu—should take a .30-06 and a .375 H&H and be done with it. By the same logic, we could probably get along well enough with only vanilla ice cream, and make due with Honda Civics as our only means of motor transportation. We could probably muddle through with only Phillips screwdrivers, claw hammers, and regular gas. We could probably get by, but who wants to?

Fortunately, we don't have to limit ourselves to such a restricted range of choices in these matters or in our hunting rifles. There is a great variety of calibers and mechanical types that will get the job done, if we do our part in the shot-placement and bullet-selection department.

Do you need to buy a special rifle to hunt African plains game? It depends on what rifle you already have. If you have a rifle and load that you have used successfully on North American deer or pronghorn antelope, you should feel confident that the same rifle and load would be equally effective on plains game of about the same size and weight that is available in southern Africa.

For the sake of argument, suppose you have successfully hunted the animals mentioned above with a .243 Winchester. Not everyone will agree with the use of a .243 on kudu, and I would not insist on that one, even though resident hunters appear to routinely use the caliber very successfully on these animals in South Africa. But I believe a .243 would certainly be adequate for at least the many small critters such as the dik-dik, duiker, bushbuck, impala, mountain reedbuck, common reedbuck, vaal rhebok, warthog, steenbok, grysbok, klipspringer, baboon, jackal, common nyala, all the small cats, springbok, and puku. For this large group of animals, a .243 Winchester, a .257 Roberts, or the 6.5x55mm should suffice, assuming the shot is well-placed and that you are using premium bullets.

Similarly, if you have a rifle you have used successfully on elk, caribou, or moose, the same weapon should be entirely adequate for eland, kudu, gemsbok, zebra, wildebeest, hartebeest, sable, roan, and others of similar size and weight. This might include anything from the .300 Savage to the .375 H&H. It would certainly include the .30-06 and .300 magnums. I believe many experienced hunters would add the various 6.5s, the .270, the .280 Remington, and the 7x57mm.

I would be surprised if you found many professional hunters who would *not* agree that the old reliable .30-06, if properly loaded and shot, is perfectly adequate for all the antelope in southern Africa with the possible exception of eland. Similarly, I would be surprised if any PH objected to a hunter bringing a .375 H&H that he shot well for all game, including the Big Five, or which included the larger plains game like sable, roan, and eland.

However, if a hunter suggested bringing a .243 as his light rifle for game up to and including kudu, sable, and eland, unless the hunter's skills were impeccable and known to the PH, I would expect there to be some raised eyebrows at minimum, even though it's not likely that local hunters' use of the same caliber would be seriously questioned. But I suspect that any rifle chambering a cartridge ranging from the 7x57mm to the .338 magnums and the mediums based on the .30-06 case would be met with approval as long as the client could shoot it well and used premium bullets.

Craig Boddington summarized the situation this way: "There may never be a consensus on calibers, but the professionals agree on this: Whatever rifles and cartridges work best for you, give you confidence, and perform consistently because you shoot them well, those are the ones to use on Africa's game" (*Safari Rifles*, p. 387).

THINGS TO DO

1. Take a rifle or rifles that you know well in terms of their mechanical functioning and ballistics.
2. Sight in so that the bullet hits not more than 2 inches high at 100 yards, is zeroed at 200 yards, and know where it hits at 50 and 300 yards.
3. Run all loaded ammunition through the chamber and magazine of your rifles before you leave home, whether you are using handloads or factory loads.
4. Learn where the *first* shot from a *cold* barrel goes from all your rifles at ranges from 100 to 300 yards. Placement of this shot is *the* most critical element in achieving clean kills. If you blow it, you can never catch up with subsequent shots.
5. Use a caliber that is reasonably common so that you can scrounge up some ammo for it in Africa if you need to. You wildcat lovers probably won't, and you have my sympathies.
6. Whether you handload or use factory ammunition, use premium bullets if at all possible.
7. Practice, practice, practice, with half or more of your shooting from field positions, including offhand, and do lots of dry firing, too.
8. Practice shooting from improvised rests, and always use one in the field, even if you have to change position to get to it.

TAXIDERMY AND TROPHY CARE

TAXIDERMY

Prior to my Africa trip, it was no big deal to have my exceptional trophies mounted. Usually, this was one animal every few years, so the cost was not much of a problem. Only later did it dawn on me that having over a dozen heads mounted, several of which were as large as a bull elk, and finding a place to put them, was going to be a challenge.

One acquaintance of mine had a simple solution to the problem. He'd hunted extensively in Kenya when that was still possible and had recently returned from a plains-game hunt in Namibia. He expressed little desire to have a bunch of stuffed heads in his modest home. He opted to have each skull prepared European style. In this method the skullcap with horns attached is cleaned, bleached white, and may be mounted on a plaque for display. This method is vastly more economical than a shoulder mount. This guy didn't even have a plaque attached to the horn or hang it on the wall, preferring instead to simply lean it against the wall of his gun room. He seemed perfectly happy with this solution.

Another acquaintance, who never seemed short of money, bought a house with very high ceilings in order to have room to display his several forty-inch-plus Dall sheep heads and his full-size brown bear mount. Since he had anticipated his African hunt, there was plenty of room for his full-body lion mount and various antelope. Another guy I knew built an addition on his house to hang his large collection of trophies. But I am an average Joe; I did not have a palatial trophy room to display my trophy heads, and I could not afford to build one.

My solution involved a multiphased process. Since all skins and capes are typically delivered to a taxidermist in the country where they are taken for processing and shipping to the client's home country, there is an opportunity to leave some or all of one's trophies with him for mounting and shipment to the states. I had never realized this was an option before my trip, but it is in some areas, and I discovered it has some real advantages.

At the end of my hunt in South Africa, and prior to departing with my PH for a tour of the great Kruger National Park, I accompanied him to the taxidermist who would prepare my trophies for shipment. After examining his work and his fees, I decided to give that option a try. I left my nyala and gemsbok heads with him to be mounted and shipped to me in finished condition. All other capes, skins, and horns were to be prepared only for international shipment, which includes treating for pests. I was assured that, even with the shipping costs included, this approach would be cheaper, and much faster, than having my capes and horns returned to me in the States in raw form and given to a taxidermist there.

This turned out to be the case. I received the shoulder mounts and other capes and horns from South Africa within four months and was well satisfied with the quality of the work. This was much faster than I could have had the capes *tanned* at home. The estimates I had on time for taxidermy to be completed were a year or more. They were not as well done as the work I had seen by the best U.S. taxidermists, but the cost was considerably less, and I received the mounted heads in perhaps one-fourth the time it would have taken in the States. I would do this again, particularly since the only additional weight would be the lightweight foam forms used for shoulder mounts.

While doing research for this book, I came across several postings on the Internet that indicated other hunters' experiences with taxidermists. The consensus was that it was cheaper to have the raw trophies shipped to the States and have the taxidermy done locally. I would investigate both options before leaving home. Also, don't forget to include the cost of tanning, in both time and money. In some cases I suspect this will take longer than the taxidermy itself.

I was fortunate to have an acquaintance who was not only a skilled big-game hunter, but also an accomplished amateur taxidermist. He advised me of an excellent tanning facility, so I sent my capes there. During the time it took to get them back ready to be mounted, this fellow went on a safari of his own and returned with several antelope heads. He let me look over his shoulder while he mounted a couple so that I could get an idea of the basic techniques.

With this information, and a promise of his assistance should I need it, I purchased several books on taxidermy, subscribed to a magazine on the subject, and proceeded to mount several of my trophies. Once the capes were tanned, they could sit for some months before being processed into mounted heads. I had the time and space for the undertaking and went ahead with the project.

I confess it would not be difficult for anyone familiar with *good* taxidermy to pick mine out as the work of a novice. The heads I did ranged from duiker to waterbuck and required far more skill than I had at that point. When the animals were finished, I felt they looked, in general, like the animal they were supposed to represent, but the details were crude. Still, I rank this as a major accomplishment, and I certainly have a better appreciation for the hours of labor and the artistic skills required in this craft. In the final analysis, my work was good enough that I could enjoy having the trophies around, while knowing all the mistakes I'd made. The cost of materials to mount these animals was a tiny fraction of the cost of professional taxidermy.

The cost of having all my trophies professionally mounted would have funded another safari. If you doubt this, I suggest you get a price list from an established taxidermist. Never mind the full-body mount of your bongo or lion, just figure out how much it would cost to have shoulder mounts done of, say, five large antelope, five small antelope, and your warthog, and to have zebra skin done. I am sure it would be possible to find a seven-to-ten-day, plains-game safari for a comparable price. Given that choice, I'd go on another hunt and leave the capes in storage.

Because of the time and effort involved in doing the taxidermy, it is not something I'd recommend to everyone. But for those up to the challenge, it can provide considerable satisfaction. I also learned a great deal about the animals by researching and studying the shapes of their faces, their expressions, the location and shape of scent glands, and other minutia I probably would never have noticed had I not undertaken the work. In addition, it is possible that in the process you could find a whole new way of relating to the game you take, and an interesting hobby.

SHIPMENT OF TROPHIES

To give the reader the range of possibilities that are available for preparation and shipment of trophies, I'll relate how this task was accomplished in South Africa and Zimbabwe and the costs associated with each. Keep in mind that my safaris were in 1991, so the cost might be higher today.

SHIPMENT FROM ZIMBABWE

At the cattle ranch where I'd hunted in Zimbabwe, they did their own preparation for international shipment right at the ranch headquarters. On my safari, there was an excellent skinning facility and a trained skinner who caped and skinned the animals. He was also responsible for boiling the skulls and fleshing and drying the skins and capes in preparation for shipment. The work was done in a special salting facility right at the safari camp and was considered "field preparation."

I am not sure where the "dipping" and other treatments for pests were done, since that occurred after I had left the premises. After preparation for shipment, all my trophies were enclosed in a heavy-duty cardboard box and placed in the hands of a suitable international freight company by the safari company. I was charged just $300 for all these services, the field preparation being included in the daily rate, which I'd known about beforehand and which I thought was very reasonable. Everything arrived in excellent condition.

The only problems I had were a missing hide and inadequate documentation on treatment of the warthog. The full hide of one of the bushbuck I had taken was missing. Instead of a whole skin, only a back skin (the part of the hide that's left after removing the forward cape for a shoulder mount) was included. Working through my agent and the safari company, I was able to resolve this matter to my satisfaction without difficulty. Another hunter brought the hide to the States, and I paid the cost.

For whatever reason, when the crate arrived at the U.S. port of entry, the documentation of the special treatment required for swine products was either missing altogether or was somehow inadequate. This required that a local taxidermist provide the treatment before the crate containing the warthog could be forwarded to me. This treatment was accomplished for a nominal fee.

The cost to ship the box to me in Juneau, Alaska, from Zimbabwe was $780. This was more than I'd expected, but I was unable to obtain information from anyone prior to my trip regarding the cost of this service. Total cost for preparation and shipment: $1,080.

SHIPMENT FROM SOUTH AFRICA

In South Africa, trophies were handled differently. This was a bargain-priced hunt arranged through a fairly new agent and equally new PH. My PH did practically all the field skinning and caping himself. As I described earlier, after the hunt all my capes and horns were taken to a taxidermist who was to prepare them for shipment.

Apart from the cost of the two shoulder mounts, my bill from this taxidermist for *preparation for shipping* was $1,175. This was for disinfecting and preparation for shipment only.

Packing my trophies in a plywood box cost an additional $391. Before my stuff left South Africa, then, the cost was $1,566.

Everything arrived in excellent condition. The bill for *shipping* the trophies came to $2,300, not including the taxidermy for the shoulder mounts.

The cost to get my trophies home was about $5,000, a substantial sum in relation to the cost of the safaris themselves. Remember, the shipping cost was for two safaris and not one. Nevertheless, the cost of getting my trophies home from South Africa was higher than from Zimbabwe.

For the Zimbabwe hunt, preparation and shipping amounted to about 21 percent of the safari cost, including both daily and trophy fees, and transfers. On the safari in South Africa, the total for dipping and shipping came to over 80 percent of the cost of the safari, including all hunting-related costs such as daily fees, trophy fees, and transfers.

Shipping trophies costs about the same as a budget, seven-day plains-game safari at today's prices. Since the time of my safari, there have been new entrants into the international trophy-shipping business, providing competition and perhaps also lowering shipping prices. Hunters recently returning from hunts in southern Africa told me the cost of their trophy preparation and freight to the States, and it was comparable to what I paid in 1991.

PART II
MY SAFARI IN ZIMBABWE

I MEET SOME AFRICANS

THE WA-BENZI

My first stop after leaving America was Frankfurt Airport in Germany. I had a layover of several hours before my flight to Jan Smuts Airport in South Africa. Killing time, I wandered among the shops, shocked by the high prices for German optical equipment on sale, and had a disgusting lunch at the only cafeteria in the airport. This place was shabby and expensive compared to a similar facility at any American airport of even a medium-sized city. Seattle would put it completely to shame. We Americans often fail to realize how rich our choices in everyday living are compared to the rest of the world. Eventually I worked my way to the terminal area from which my plane was to leave.

While seated there, I observed a portly, black man in a dark business suit with lots of miles on it. He was of muscular build, and I guessed he was in his fifties and about five feet, ten inches tall. He was struggling to drag a large suitcase, about three feet square and held together with a leather strap, onto a baggage cart. Its contents were threatening to burst the bag's seams at any moment. The suitcase looked like it had as many miles on it as his suit and had a large banner stuck to it, apparently placed there by the airline staff, which read: "heavy." Considering the effort required to move it, I thought this banner appropriate. The man disposed of the bag and settled in to wait for the same flight I was taking.

I didn't see the black gentleman again until after I boarded the Air Zimbabwe jet for my flight to Harare, that country's capital, where I was to meet my safari contact. The man, whose name I later learned was John, sat next to me on the plane, which left from Johannesburg at 10 P.M. I was pretty tired and grouchy, and my mood wasn't improved by learning that my guns had not yet arrived in Johannesburg. I did not feel very sociable.

Both John and I have broad shoulders, and as we tried to eat our airline dinners, we couldn't help rubbing elbows. Soon the situation became comical, and when I made a comment about this, we started talking. Eventually I told him of my safari plans and lost luggage. When I asked about his reason for traveling to Europe, John explained that he was "trying to become a business man" and was returning from Austria, where he was exploring the possibility of importing parts for refrigeration compressors for assembly and sale in Zimbabwe. The "heavy" bag was apparently filled with parts for compressors.

I learned later that international sanctions against Zimbabwe, formerly Southern Rhodesia, had fostered a strong sense of economic independence among the residents, who did their best to get along without imported goods. The resulting shortages produced some surprising changes in the value of things. For example, I learned that the people of Zimbabwe and of South Africa, similarly denied many imports because of sanctions, placed an extraordinary value on things like batteries, duct tape, and many small items we in the States and in Europe take for granted.

In addition to his business aspirations, John also described himself as a farmer. He said that his son Paul, who had just graduated from college, was to pick him up at the airport, and he offered to give me a ride to my hotel. This turned out to be very helpful, since my hotel was several miles from the airport, and we'd arrived close to midnight. He also helped me get to the correct customs window to declare the amount and kind of money I was carrying. Keeping track of the country's currency and foreign exchange was very important to the government of Zimbabwe at the time.

John's son picked us up, driving a new Mercedes Benz sedan, which I learned had been a gift from his father on the occasion of his graduation. He was accompanied by a distinguished older man, George, who appeared to be an official in John's company. Paul and George were clearly pleased by John's return, and all were in high spirits.

The three men were jovial, laughing and joking all the way on the twenty-minute drive to the Harare Holliday Inn, where I had a reservation. I found it remarkable how comfortable I felt with this group, and they seemed equally comfortable with me. They alternated speaking in English and in the Shona (John's tribe) language, and I believe they spoke English mainly to keep me from feeling left out.

When they dropped me off at the hotel, John said I should regard them as family and call them if there was any way they could help. I was deeply moved by this expression of friendship, which clearly came from John's generosity, as I had done nothing to merit such kindness. This was my first contact with African residents, and it felt great. I seriously considered staying with them and canceling the hunt entirely because I was quite upset about my baggage. I'm sure my stay with them would have been interesting. John even offered to have Paul drive me around Harare, and to let me stay at the farm if my safari plans were delayed. As it happened, I was able to get in touch with the safari operator and decided to proceed with my trip the next day.

I managed to pick up a few words in the native languages. One thing I learned was that the term *Wa* or *Kwa* was used to designate ownership or belonging, the former in Zimbabwe and East Africa, and the latter in South Africa. For example, the home territory of the Zulu people is known as *Kwa-Zulu,* meaning "land of the Zulus." In keeping with this usage, I decided that an appropriate "tribal" designation for the obviously well-to-do African "farmers" I'd just met would be the *Wa-Benzi.*

As it turned out, John was indeed a farmer. He owned a large truck farm, several, I believe, and was obviously quite wealthy. The Wa-Benzi were well represented in the country, it seemed, as Mercedes Benz was clearly the prestige car for the wealthy, as well as the government and army.

DEREK AND MARGARET

In spite of all the years of anticipation and months of preparation, my safari almost died at birth. Because of a combination of factors, including the vagaries of international air travel in the age of terrorism, neither my clothing nor my gear and rifles arrived in Zimbabwe. In addition, on the night I arrived at the Harare Holliday Inn, I turned on the TV to learn of the coup attempt against the Russian leader Mikhail Gorbachev, and I wondered if we were on the brink of World War III. This news added to my depressed state.

Now I faced the necessity of making the hunt with a rifle borrowed from the PH or outfitter, a prospect almost as grim as that of a third world war. From what I'd read, these rifles were often less than satisfactory compared to what clients usually brought on safari. This would have been the case were it not for the generosity and taste in firearms of another PH hunting from the same camp.

Though I arrived in Zimbabwe's capital city of Harare, which is in the northern part of the country, my hunt was to take place near its southern border with South Africa in an area of scrub and thornbushes known as the lowveld. It was cheaper to have someone from the ranch pick me up in a vehicle than to charter a plane to fly me from Harare to the ranch, so I took the less expensive option. On the rather primitive road system this was a trip of about five hours. A safari-company representative would have to drive to Harare to pick me up and then return with me to the ranch.

I'd hoped to find a message from my safari outfitter waiting for me at the hotel when I arrived in Zimbabwe, but found none. My world seemed increasingly dismal, and I was feeling pretty discouraged at that point. I began wondering if the whole trip had been a big mistake. I briefly considered calling the whole thing off if I didn't hear from my contact, whose name was Derek, pretty soon.

Next morning, with still no word from Derek, I went to the dining room for breakfast. Here I could choose among many breakfast entrees, including several right out of *Sesame Street*— Big Bird's Boiled Egg was one offering. For dessert you could have a Care Bears Milk Shake, a Garfield's Lazy Sundae, or, if so inclined, a Punky Brewster's ice cream dish.

The many breakfast entrees were roughly grouped as continental—Danish and coffee—or "full English"—Danish and coffee with eggs and ham. The lunch menu included five kinds of burgers, and steak or roast beef was featured on the dinner menu. The selection seemed remarkably familiar. Back at my room, one of the two channels available was CNN! This was my first experience of the way in which elements of American society have been incorporated into the culture of southern Africa.

Fortunately, Derek showed up at the hotel just after I'd finished breakfast. I liked him immediately and felt comfortable with him from the beginning. He had not received my message sent the previous night that my bags had been lost. His reaction when I told him about the situation was a thoroughly British "bloody hell!"

Derek was a tall, lean man who looked like he belonged to the upper class in British Africa, which in effect he did, though he was a native of Zimbabwe. He wore tan hunting clothes, had a friendly smile and a distinctive accent that I soon came to recognize as that of a European raised in Zimbabwe.

He thought he could expedite the recovery of my rifles and gear and took me to a hotel where Lufthansa's Harare office was located. There he introduced me to a woman who worked for Lufthansa and whose husband was a professional hunter he knew. With her assistance we began a computer search for my baggage.

Then we headed downstairs to the hotel restaurant to have lunch. On the way we met Ann Whittall. She was tan, thin, maybe in her late forties, and very pretty. She fit my best-case image of a real frontier woman. We learned her PH husband, whom I knew to be among the best known in Zimbabwe, had just been mauled by a wounded lion while out with a client. His arm had been bitten and the prognosis was unclear at that time for getting the use of the limb back, though he was apparently in no danger of dying. She seemed calm about the situation, as though it was all just part of being the wife of a professional hunter. Later he wrote saying that he'd substantially recovered from his wounds, and his wife said that he was back hunting lions. Hair of the dog, and all that, I suppose.

When Ann learned of my situation, she offered to provide lunch and a place at her house in Harare, where I could take a nap. I was very touched by her hospitality. She later helped me sort out a problem with one of my trophies that would have been difficult without her assistance. Since Derek said that we'd be leaving shortly after lunch for the lowveld, I declined her generous offer. The Whittalls have several hunts each year on their ranch and on government land, and I hope to return to hunt with them.

Derek had some errands to do in Harare to prepare for my hunt, including the acquisition of permits and other items. Once this was completed, we headed out of town in his Datsun pickup truck. He drove the truck like a weapon through crowds of people on the streets. I wondered if this reflected some sentiment left over from the recent civil war. In America, there remain deep and powerful feelings, as well as great differences of opinion, regarding our own Civil War now one hundred thirty years or so behind us. The civil war in Zimbabwe had concluded only some eleven years earlier, and it was reasonable to expect hard feelings on both sides. Most whites left the country after that war, and the few who remained made up only 1 percent of the population.

Finally on the road to the lowveld, we were soon hurtling along at 90 mph on a narrow, two-lane "highway." On occasion, I glanced fearfully at the speedometer to confirm my impression that we were going really fast. I was moderately alarmed. Not long after we left Harare, it got dark. I don't believe I have ever experienced a period of such sustained fear as on that ride to the ranch in the steamy African night in that little Datsun pickup. I again had thoughts about backing out of the trip, but again decided to stick it out, though I really believed my life was in some danger. After it got dark, I began to worry not only about my safety, but also the safety of the hundreds of people who walked along the roadside.

There were people carrying a fascinating variety of objects on their heads that ranged from small pots and groceries to ten-foot-long bundles of grass used for making roofs for their huts. Of course, all these people were black, often visible in the dark only because of their light-colored clothing. There was also an assortment of wheeled conveyances in use by those fortunate enough to own one. These included wheelbarrows, bicycles, and various other carts. The relatively well-to-do people had their carts pulled by a donkey.

Numerous buses traveled the highway, and bus stops were crowded, even late at night. Dozens of goats and cattle, many also black, were feeding along the road, and seemed oblivious to the deadly traffic rushing by in the dark, as they wandered aimlessly onto the road. Years later I learned that, indeed, highway deaths were significant in Zimbabwe, and tourist travel at night was strongly discouraged.

I got a brief respite from road terrors when we stopped for a soft drink in one of the small settlements along the way. Shortly after leaving this location, I saw my first African game animal, a steenbok, one of the intriguing tiny antelope in this area, in the knee-high grass. Just at dusk I even saw a lone zebra. These were the first African animals I'd seen outside a zoo.

Four days later I would travel to Harare from the lowveld to retrieve my rifles and baggage that finally caught up to me, thanks to the efforts of Derek and some of his friends. It was a more enjoyable trip that time, and considerably slower and safer, as it was made entirely in daylight. On that trip I was able to enjoy the African scene in a more relaxed state of mind.

The roads were crowded as before with a steady procession of people carrying things on their heads. This time, though, there were also roadside vendors, usually young boys, holding bunches of baobab pods, which, I was told, were the source of the spice cream of tartar. Others, as I recall, were selling fruit, and occasionally we'd pass a vendor with an assortment of tourist-type memorabilia such as masks and carved figures.

During the five-hour drive from Harare to Devuli Ranch, I learned more about Derek. He was a native of Zimbabwe in his late forties. He was the manager of the ranch where I was to hunt. The total acreage of this ranch was originally around 1 million acres, he said, and had been established around the end of the nineteenth century by one of the white pioneers who later founded the country of Southern Rhodesia under Cecil Rhodes. The ranch was now owned by his heirs. It began as a working cattle ranch but was undergoing a dramatic change like many similar ranches in southern Africa. It was being converted to a game preserve and farm stocked with the animals that had once lived there, but had been killed off to make room for cattle.

Raising cattle in the arid part of southern Africa appears to be a tough go. There is relatively little groundwater or rainfall, yet the animals have to feed off the land, as there is little or no irrigated pasture on which to graze. I assume irrigation is prohibitively expensive there since water is scarce and electricity expensive. Much of the water needed for household use was pumped from rivers to where it was needed by using a remarkable device called a Lister diesel engine.

Periodic droughts are devastating to cattle and game alike in the lowveld. Cattle, even those bred to withstand the rigors of this thornbush country, are subject to a variety of diseases and require dipping in repellant, vaccinations, and various other labor-intensive maintenance so that they can be profitably raised for sale. The prices of beef, I gather, are regulated by the government, which since independence has been communist, making it difficult to profit from raising cattle. Farmers are squeezed from both the bottom-end production costs and by artificially low prices at market.

Because of the difficulties of making a living, many ranchers have restocked their land with native species of wildlife and have phased out cattle, in order to capitalize on the increase in

Elephant can be hunted in seven of the ten countries featured. Their hunting availability in the future depends on population levels and politics.

Today, elephant numbers often exceed the carrying capacity of their remaining range. They have to be reduced by culling to protect habitat for themselves and other species.

Efias, a skinner, begins to cape one of my impalas.

This is a Lister diesel engine, used in place of electricity to power water pumps in rural Zimbabwe.

Guinea fowl is a game bird frequently seen in southern Africa, except in the driest desert regions.

Vervet monkeys are regular bush comedians.

Bullet placement is complicated by the position of the animal. A front-quartering shot (left) is more difficult than a broadside shot (right).

The following are the cartridges recommended by safari companies for plains game. Left to right: .270 Win., 7mm Rem. Mag, .30-06, .300 Winchester Mag, .300 H&H Mag, .300 Weatherby Mag, and .375 H&H Mag.

Two of the most popular calibers for plains game—the .30-06 (left) and the .375 H&H.

Waterbuck are one of the largest antelope. This one was taken in the Transvaal Province of South Africa a few yards from the Limpopo River.

Impala are numerous in southern Africa and make a beautiful trophy.

The distinctive baobab tree, shown here without leaves during winter, at a Zimbabwe ranch.

The Olifants ("elephants" in Afrikaans) Rest Area in Kruger National Park has a unique display of skulls, tusks, and biographical information on some of the park's world famous tuskers, the Magnificent Seven.

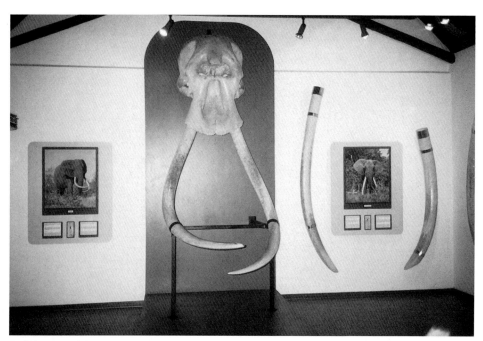

Inside the Olifants.

Kudu are widespread and of record-book quality in several southern African countries.

The shoulder bulge on the impala was caused by a 270-grain bullet that failed to exit. Switching to 300-grain Noslers gave better penetration. The caliber used was .375-06.

Of the Big Five, leopard are the most widely distributed and least expensive to hunt.

Several rivers in Kruger have crocodiles, such as these two crawling onto a sand bar.

Bushpig live in habitat that is damp and thick with vegetation. This one we found dead, apparently killed by a predator.

Bushbuck inhabit all countries featured. This one was taken in Zimbabwe.

This nyala was mounted by a taxidermist in South Africa. Its quality was very good and it was completed much quicker than if done in the United States.

Do-it-yourself taxidermy. A fixture to hold the trophy and an adventurous spirit are key ingredients.

Leopard are hunted over baits practically everywhere in southern and East Africa.

Blesbok are found only in South Africa and Namibia.

Eland is the world's largest antelope. Bulls may weigh a ton. This cow is as big as a very large bull elk.

Nyala, which have a very limited range, are one of the most exotic of African antelopes.

Zebra, Kruger National Park.

At Kruger National Park, animals are the featured attraction, as reflected in this magnificent impala sculpture at Skukuza.

Tourists staying overnight in Kruger are required to bed at one of these well-groomed rondavels.

Of Kruger's large mammals, giraffe are the most visible.

Impala are very numerous in Kruger.

A rondavel for Kruger tourists in Lower Sabi. Game is frequently visible from its windows.

Entry and exit at Kruger is by gates, such as this one at Punda Maria, at the north end of the park.

Gemsbok are a premier antelope trophy. They live in dry habitat such as the Kalahari Desert. This one was taken in the Cape Province of South Africa.

Portrait of a baboon, made possible because the animal was on the hood of my car.

Sunset on the Limpopo River in the Transvaal. The opposite shore is Botswana.

wildlife-related tourism. Native wildlife is relatively resistant to diseases endemic to the region. It remains to be seen whether this enterprise will return sufficient profit to sustain it, but it cannot be doubted that the number of game animals, and certain others with primarily viewing value, have increased dramatically in recent years because of the efforts of these ranchers.

Some ranchers in the area have accepted baby elephants belonging to mothers who were killed to prevent them from destroying crops or their own range in other parts of Zimbabwe. These babies would have been killed along with their mothers had it not been for these ranchers. The baby elephants will be used to establish breeding herds. One evening I watched a truckload of ostrich being delivered to the ranch for release to reestablish a breeding population. The species had been eliminated long before to prevent competition with cattle for scarce feed.

I learned from Derek that several adjoining ranches in the area were planning to create a "conservancy," a kind of private preserve. By eliminating all interior cross fencing so that animals can roam freely over several million acres of bushveld, on ranches belonging to different owners, the ranchers would be aiding in the improvement of wildlife habitat. Some of the mature animals would be taken by trophy hunters, others would become part of a breeding herd for viewing and stocking other properties.

After I returned to America, I learned that the conservancy had been established. I believe the government of Zimbabwe had agreed to relocate some of the few remaining black rhinos in the country, which had dwindled to near extinction under the "protection" of the government, to the conservancy in order to provide better protection.

Without fear that wild "cattle" would spread diseases to the domestic cash cows, once they were phased out, there were even plans afoot to reintroduce Cape buffalo to the conservancy area.

There were some rhino and elephant there when I was, and from time to time we'd cut their tracks while hunting something else.

Derek had grown up in a culture of which hunting was a major part. He said he'd bagged all game in the area, including eland, with a .22 Hornet while still a boy. He had become too busy to do much hunting because his job demanded running the ranch and outfitting safaris, but he had retained a keen interest in wildlife. As I was leaving, he was loading his family into the family car for a drive to a nearby game preserve called Gonarezhou to view some lions that were reported to have wandered in.

Derek's wife, Margaret, was pretty, friendly, and a generous hostess. Derek proved a helpful, businesslike, and generally decent sort, who always went out of his way to see that I got my money's worth on my hunt. He was always ready to assist and accommodate me so that I got what I wanted from my safari at Devuli. He also tolerated my constant questions about the wildlife, people, and politics of the area. If he found me tedious, he didn't let on, and I learned a great deal from him.

MICK AND ALISON

My PH, Mick, was a personable young man, married with two small kids, and built like a rugby player, which he was, I believe. I judged him to be in his early to mid-thirties. He was a native of Zimbabwe and had fought on the side of Southern Rhodesia during the long civil war that had ended only about a dozen years before I arrived. Like me, he had been a soldier and a paratrooper. The insights I gained from the ten days I spent in Zimbabwe with Mick and his family—insights about the war, the culture, and the wildlife— are invaluable treasures that alone would have been worth the trip. I learned to love hearing the British dialect of white Zimbabweans and came to admire their resourcefulness and courage.

Mick and his wife, Alison, also a native of Zimbabwe, lived in a large, ranch-style white house on the Devuli ranch, as part of Mick's compensation. It was a one-story, rambling place made of stone with a covered patio and large garden. Clouds of crimson bougainvillea dominated the vegetation near the house. They heated water, pumped from a considerable distance, with wood. As I recall, their electricity was also produced on the premises.

In many respects their home looked like something from the American frontier, but there were significant differences that reflected both the nature of the recent civil war and the difference in latitude. For one thing, instead of a willow or poplar tree in the yard, at Mick's place there was a huge baobab tree, known as the upside-down tree because of the impression that its roots form the above-ground structure.

All windows were covered with wire mesh to prevent grenades from being thrown or shot through them by the rebel forces during the civil war. There was an underground shelter with a heavy, lockable cover, reminiscent of a bomb shelter. It was the last redoubt where Mick, Alison, and the children were to hide if they were overrun by rebel forces and in danger of annihilation. From there they would use a shortwave radio to contact the army so that they could be rescued. Another difference was that the weapons used by both sides were significantly more lethal than those in use by American settlers and the American Indian. Both sides were armed with automatic weapons, grenades, mines, and the army had aircraft.

Other security measures at the ranch included a wire fence at least eight feet high with a guarded gate at the main entrance. I found this to be typical everywhere I went in rural Zimbabwe and also in South Africa. The white population always lived in some fear of attack by black nationalists or thugs and poachers who operated across national borders throughout the region. The atmosphere was like that of a frontier or a guerrilla war.

Mick had a guard dog, a rottweiler, and a cat. The dog protected the garden from local predators such as the duiker. The cat was just a pet. When I asked about the cat, which I was surprised to see in such a remote area, Mick told me "everyone has them", and he said cats survive better than dogs due to their ability to avoid snakes. The area apparently had a robust population of mambas and cobras, both deadly to people and pets. The mamba has the reputation of being aggressive, too.

Mick related a snake story that will help to illustrate the danger. He and his tracker were riding on the ranch in Mick's Toyota Land Cruiser. It was winter and the weather was cool, so they had the top on, which also has sides, windows, and doors. Apparently they unknowingly ran over a mamba crossing the road. The snake struck at the offending vehicle, its head smashing into the window next to where the tracker was sitting. Had the top not been installed, it appears he would have been bitten by the mamba and died, due to the snake's poison and the great distance to a medical facility.

During the ten days I walked around Devuli Ranch, I often saw the trail of large snakes, some presumably mambas, in the dust. It always created a little adrenaline rush when I did because these snakes can be quite aggressive and difficult to kill with a hunting rifle. A shotgun would have been far more useful, but there was never one available when we were on foot.

Like most of the European-owned property in this part of Zimbabwe, Devuli was a working cattle ranch. There were facilities at Mick's house, which appeared to be the original ranch headquarters, for slaughtering and storage of beef. One of these was a large, concrete pad, which was shaped like a broad, flat funnel that sloped to a drain at the center. There was a water hose at the site, and it was used on occasion to clean game taken by clients.

Turgwe Camp was a drive of an hour or so from Mick's house, so during the long hunting season he didn't see much of his wife and children. When we were hunting in the vicinity, or when he needed facilities not available in camp, we would stop by his house and visit with the family. On these occasions Mick and Alison were wonderful hosts, and I enjoyed the time spent with them as much as I did the hunting. I would not have wanted to miss either.

One of the chores that sometimes required special equipment was maintaining the very well used Toyota Land Cruiser. It had a leaky radiator that required frequent attention in the form of the regular application of duct tape and occasionally bondo to keep it functioning. Another chronic problem with the Toyota was flat tires. Hard as it may be to believe, driving around on the dirt roads of the ranch resulted in a flat tire every day or so. The problem wasn't nails, my usual tire nemesis, but thorns. The most common vegetation in the area consisted of mopane trees and various kinds of acacia bushes. These frequently have thorns that make those on our North American roses or brambles look like the fuzz on a peach by comparison. Some of the thorns were three to four inches long and regularly punctured the tires on the Land Cruiser. After we had spent a day driving around the ranch, the tires were literally covered with these thorns. The tires were rugged but the thorns went through them with apparent ease.

ELIJAH AND EFIAS

The first morning in Turgwe Camp, I met Mick's tracker, Elijah. He was a dark-skinned Zimbabwe native and a member of the dominant Shona tribe. He had a sunny disposition and proved to be not only a fine companion but also a superb tracker even though he was still in training.

Though I had never really thought about it, I suppose I always presumed native trackers learned their craft at an early age from tribal elders. This may well happen, but I learned that the professional hunters association of Zimbabwe provides formal training for student trackers who want to work in the hunting industry. I gathered the training was paid for by the safari operator or professional hunter for whom the tracker worked. Elijah was still in training at the time of my safari.

Every ethical hunter abhors the loss of a wounded animal. For me, the experience is like a festering wound on my own body that never heals. It may fade from daily memory, but never really goes away, nor can it be atoned for. Yet few American hunters have at their disposal the skills of a tracker comparable to those I saw demonstrated by Elijah. Indeed, the only U.S. hunters I have ever seen actually follow a track and then bag the animal have been those hardy fellows who track elk on newly fallen snow. I don't know how often they are successful, but I've heard some consistently are.

But as will be illustrated later on in this book, that kind of tracking is simply child's play compared to what Elijah did for me. It is no exaggeration to say that his skill alone saved me from losing at least one fine trophy and suffering the guilt from doing so, not to mention the suffering of the animal that would have resulted had he not found it.

Efias was from another tribe in Zimbabwe, the Shangans, I believe. Mick asked him to join Elijah and me when we hunted eland, perhaps because he had some special skills for hunting those animals. His usual job was as the skinner and trophy preparer. He did not look like Elijah; Efias was slightly built and had a lighter complexion, but he was just as friendly and a welcome companion.

TURGWE CAMP

When we arrived at the Devuli Ranch headquarters about 11 P.M., Derek's family was awake to welcome us. They included his wife, Margaret, and his daughter, who loaned me her coat (mine was with my lost baggage) for the ride to camp. It was at that time that I first met Mick Wilson, my professional hunter, and boarded his open Toyota Land Cruiser for our trip to Turgwe Camp, about forty-five minutes away.

For those who imagine that Africa is always and everywhere hot like the Sahara Desert, I can assure you it's cold as hell in the winter at night. The trip in the open Toyota would probably have been more enjoyable had I not been so tired and cold. As it was, when we got to camp, I was shown to my quarters and soon went to sleep.

The next morning I surveyed the camp. It was situated on a relatively open, flat area of mopane trees above the Turgwe River, after which the camp was named. The riverbed was sandy and the banks were covered with dense foliage. The locals call this "riverine" habitat. It is the favorite haunt of the bushbuck and various other indigenous animals. Enormous anthills dotted the area, some at least thirty feet wide at the base.

Shortly after my arrival in camp I saw a small bushbuck down in the riverbed a few hundred yards from camp. I discovered later that there were a few remaining pools of drinkable water scattered along the generally dry riverbed that attracted the local fauna, but the whole area was generally quite dry in winter. Across the river was the ranch belonging to Roger and Anne Whittall.

The structure that was to be my abode for the next ten days was a sort of bungalow modeled after the local native architecture, I suppose. It was large enough to accommodate two double beds with a small, free-standing closet for each resident. The lower ten feet or so of the structure was made of locally produced bricks. The rafters, set at an angle to form the frame of the roof, were rough-hewn poles. The roof itself was made of beautifully shaped, thatched yellow grass at least a foot thick, a type of roof I saw all over southern Zimbabwe and in the ritzier parts of South Africa. The front was open except for a covering of chicken wire that helped with ventilation, and presumably would keep out the larger of the local pests like baboons.

In addition to two bungalows like this one for clients' sleeping quarters, the camp contained a permanent eating area, a heated bath facility with flush toilet and shower, and a fire pit surrounded by a concrete pad. There was a large cooking area fenced off from the main camp with bunched grass, which was used in lieu of wood. In this area there were some simple quarters for the camp staff.

Outside my bungalow was a small, green wooden table. Neatly placed on it each morning before dawn was a rubber wash basin, a folded towel, and a bar of soap. A mirror hung from a wire attached to one of the roof beams close to the table. Each morning Moses, the camp attendant, would bring warm water heated over a wood fire and pour it into the wash basin. Usually I was awake by then. If not, he would run his hand or some object over the chicken-wire front of the bungalow, which made a raspy sound, and in his thick native accent say, "Good morning, Sir." He spoke in somewhat halting English and had an infallibly cheerful disposition. The experience of getting up each morning this way was one of the most pleasant aspects of my stay at Turgwe Camp.

Another greeting I heard most mornings was *ha, ha, hadeda,* the distinctive call of the hadeda ibis. These large birds were plentiful along the river as were hamerkop and various species of eagles that were often visible soaring over the bush. My favorite was the ubiquitous yellow-billed hornbill, later featured in the Disney film *The Lion King.* Another sound I heard frequently was the curiously human call of the gray lourie or "go-away bird," so named because its call sounds like *go waaaaay.*

As one of two professional hunters using the camp, Mick had his own quarters. This was a green-canvas safari tent pitched near the guest bungalows. I believe his tracker had his own tent there as well, apart from the quarters of the other camp staff. Trackers are accorded special status, and for good reason, as I learned later on.

Down the hill from the living area of the camp, at the end of a short, steep, dirt road, was a skinning area covered by mosquito netting, complete with running water and a central drain. It was here that all animals shot were brought to be skinned, caped, and butchered. It was arranged so that the safari truck could simply back into it and drop the animals off. *Pretty slick,* I thought.

Another interesting and necessary structure was the salt shed. Salt is applied to capes and skins to draw out the moisture and prevent decay. This is necessary to preserve the skin until it can be treated for mites and other vermin and sent back to the hunter's home country. To accomplish this task, the ranch had a cinder-block building that had coarse salt several inches deep on the floor. Hides could be placed in the salt, periodically scraped and salted again, until the desired condition was obtained. When I was in the shed, there were always a few drying skulls of local animals leaning against the wall, possibly to keep them close to their associated cape skins. Each skin and skull was securely tagged with a number or name identifying the hunter who shot the animal.

RHINO PROTECTION

Mick and I agreed to hold off hunting the more glamorous species until my own rifles could be located and brought to the ranch. While waiting for that to happen, we went to Roger Whittall's ranch across the river. Since Roger was recovering from his encounter with the lion, I did not get an opportunity to meet him, but I did get an interesting short tour of one facility and took the opportunity to photograph some hippos.

The facility we visited was the antipoaching unit devoted to protecting rhinos. I learned that this unit, funded entirely by local ranchers, actively patrolled the thousands of acres of their ranches to protect the remaining rhinos there.

While at this antipoaching facility, I noted that all the windows of the main house, like Mick's, were covered with wire mesh, and there was a high chain-link fence around it. These features, I learned, were common among white dwellings in southern Africa and were reminders of recent, even ongoing, armed conflict in the area. In addition to intertribal wars and politically motivated conflicts, I learned that groups of armed bandits occasionally crossed into Zimbabwe from Mozambique and sometimes attacked local ranchers.

While there we visited with two native men who were part of the antipoaching staff. They showed us a rhino skull left by poachers, and posed proudly with it while I photographed them. I later sent prints for them to Roger along with a thank-you note to his wife and wished him a speedy recovery. He wrote back thanking me for the pictures and said he'd given them to the two men. He mentioned that he had arranged to use the Turgwe Camp for the next hunting season.

Although rhinos had been virtually exterminated from the rest of Zimbabwe by poachers, there were several on the Whittall and adjacent ranches. The rhinos had been killed off in the rest of Zimbabwe in spite of the government's, presumably, best efforts to prevent it. Ultimately the government admitted that the rhinos were better protected by the ranchers and relocated many of those that remained to their property, where they could be more effectively protected.

DAILY ROUTINE

Each day at Turgwe Camp was memorable for one reason or another, and I enjoyed every moment. Each morning before daylight Moses would wake me up as described. After a shower and shave I'd wander down to the cook area for a cup of coffee. The camp cook, Jen, would have coffee ready and would be working on breakfast. She was a sweet, gracious cook and hostess, and the wife of the older PH using the camp at the time. Soon Mick would join us, and we'd discuss the day's hunt plans.

Each morning when we left camp, typically before sunup, we would hunt for a different animal. Particular animals tended to be more plentiful in one area of the ranch than others because of habitat requirements or some other factor. Often these areas were a half-hour or more apart by road. Sometimes we'd take lunch with us, and occasionally we'd plan to eat at Mick's house, depending on our expected location around noon.

Plains game was plentiful, and usually we found what we were looking for, though not always the quality of trophy desired. The only other hunter in camp was focused on leopard and spent virtually every late afternoon and evening trying to catch one on a bait. This required him and his PH to sleep much later in the morning than Mick and me, so we didn't see much of them. Sometimes in late morning or early afternoon they'd hunt for the few plains species that this hunter appeared interested in.

Ordinarily we returned to camp around lunchtime. After eating, I usually caught a short nap. Around mid to late afternoon we'd be off for an afternoon hunt, often for a different animal than we'd hunted in the morning.

Seating in the Land Cruiser was always the same. I sat in the front passenger seat, which is on the left since Zimbabweans drive on the "wrong" side of the road like their British colonial ancestors. Mick drove and Elijah sat or stood in the back. We usually had a small, battered fiberglass cooler with us with some water and soft drinks, and at least a beer apiece if we expected to be out until dark.

It is a tradition among the English settlers in southern Africa to have a drink or "sundowner" to celebrate the end of work for the day, and to relax and contemplate the day's events. Though temperatures often climbed into the seventies and eighties each day, the nights were at least twenty degrees cooler, and it got rapidly colder as the sun went down. I didn't mind too much that the beer was warm by the time we toasted sundown if we were out in the field. Though we had a cooler and the camp was capable of making ice, the safari staff never seemed to put the two together so that we could have cold beer in the field. They seemed well acclimated to warm beer.

Going to and from the camp required crossing a dry riverbed perhaps thirty yards wide, which took a matter of a few seconds in the Land Cruiser. One day as we crossed it, I wanted to show off my African vocabulary and remarked that in East Africa such a dry watercourse was called a *donga*. I asked Mick what it was called locally, and he replied, "In Zimbabwe we call this a dry riverbed. *So much for trying to impress the natives,* I thought.

A SCARE IN THE SHOWER

Turgwe Camp had a surprisingly posh bathing arrangement. It was a small green building containing a flush toilet and a shower with hot water that was heated by a wood furnace made from a metal drum adjacent to the structure. The shower stall had a wooden floor grate so that clients wouldn't have to stand on the bare cement floor. One day I learned that we were not the only ones who benefited from the shower.

The location of the camp was on a riverbank covered with dense vegetation. The slope from camp to river was covered with dense brush. It was perfect habitat for many birds, animals, and reptiles, particularly snakes. Their tracks were often in the dust of the surrounding bush. Traveling in the open Land Cruiser was dusty business as the area was very dry. By the time we returned from our morning hunt we were usually tired, hungry, and dirty. Consequently, when time permitted I took a shower and caught a nap before the afternoon hunt.

On one such occasion I was standing in the shower on the wooden grate when I became aware that a reptilian head was protruding from beneath the slats. Fear shot through me as I imagined being trapped in the shower with a deadly mamba, as whatever was attached to the head was between the door and me. A few moments of growing apprehension passed before I could identify the creature. It was a large frog.

Underneath the planks it was dark and damp, far more frog-friendly than the dry riverbed nearby. What a relief!

TO TAKE A DRINK

Among the high points of wildlife observation on my trip to Zimbabwe was watching impala and warthog at water holes. On one occasion we were watching a water hole just to see what might show up. This was a pool only a few yards wide and perhaps fifty feet long in the bed of the Turgwe River. It was the rainless, winter season, and the river was generally bone dry in the area near camp. We'd staked out one of the few remaining pools of drinkable water.

After we waited a few minutes, a group of five or six impala ewes approached the water with extreme caution. They'd get within a few feet, obviously fearful of approaching the water, and then they would wheel around 180 degrees on their hind legs like a cutting horse, obviously in a panic, and run away a few yards, as though a lion had charged them from the water. This approach and withdrawal was repeated over and over for probably fifteen minutes, with each approach getting closer and each retreat shorter.

After their repeated withdrawals, the group managed to get their collective noses into the water just far enough to take a drink. With necks stretched to the absolute limit, ears on maximum alert, legs splayed, poised for flight, they sucked in a drink of cool water for a few thirst-quenching seconds. The entire episode was painful to watch but comical at the same time.

This is hot, dry country with few water sources, so it would be natural for predators to ambush their prey at water holes. I wondered if the leader had been charged by a croc or a leopard some time in her life, making her extra cautious, as she appeared really frightened approaching the water. After they left, when it was nearly dark, I shot a nice bushbuck as he worked his way along the brushy bank.

On another occasion we were waiting for an eland to come to a raised metal water tank provided for cattle when we observed three young warthogs approaching. We were maybe fifty yards away, but well hidden so they were unaware of our presence. Unlike the impala, the three piglets approached the tank with little apparent concern. When they were at the tank, which was perhaps two feet high, each reared up on its hind legs, hooked its front legs over the rim, and began drinking.

The three little pigs were nearly the same size and were about evenly spaced along the tank, their shoulders practically touching as they drank. Although it is difficult to do justice to the comical nature of this scene in print, it was indeed a funny sight at the time. This incident, and that with the impala, were two occasions I wished I'd been holding a camcorder instead of a rifle. No eland ever showed up, but the time was certainly well spent.

THE CAMP CAT

About the fifth or sixth night in camp while dozing off to sleep, I noticed that a troop of baboons a few hundred yards from my bungalow were making a lot of noise and were clearly alarmed about something. I'd read enough about Africa to know that one likely reason for this would be the presence of their chief predator, the leopard. The alarm conveyed by what sounded like at least a dozen baboons was quite convincing, and I was quickly wide awake.

Gradually the clamor of the baboons subsided, and I began to doze a little. But before I could drop off to sleep, I heard a deep, throaty, coughing growl that could only have been a leopard. The growl sounded like it was coming from the direction of the recent ruckus among the baboons, but much closer. I reached for my rifle, which was leaning against the wall of the bungalow.

As you may recall, the front of my quarters was covered with fragile chicken wire, which also "protected" the area above the brick walls to nearly the top of the rafters. While this would keep out large snakes and baboons, I doubted it would pose a serious barrier to a determined leopard. I felt quite vulnerable.

These cats, which rarely weigh as much as 150 pounds, as far as I can determine, are nevertheless able to climb straight up the side of a tree trunk while holding in their jaws an antelope that weighs as much as they do. Furthermore, they will on occasion attack people, and some in India have killed hundreds of humans before they were tracked down and shot. From what I'd read about these man-eaters, dragging their victims from their huts at night seemed to be their preferred method of hunting. Such stories raced through my mind as I sat in my bed, white-knuckled, loaded rifle at port arms, back to the wall, awaiting developments.

The location of the camp made it a perfect setting for a leopard walk-through. It was situated in riverine habitat that is a favorite of many of its prey. Like most rural residents I've known, the Devuli staff had a rule against shooting animals (except for vermin) near their place of habitation, including safari camps. Not only was this considered unsportsmanlike, but also everyone enjoys seeing game around camp, and shooting tends to scare everything away. As a result, there were abundant prey animals nearby. The surrounding area was positively stiff with impala, duiker, baboon, hares, and other leopard cuisine.

I sat thus, prepared to repel an attack, for what seemed like an hour but was probably more like a half-hour. Still, I was certain there was a leopard about. I'd heard that coughing growl many times on TV wildlife shows and believed it could have been nothing else. I heard this same raspy growl several times over the next few minutes, and once I thought I heard a soft tread outside my bungalow, which really got the fine hairs on my neck standing at attention. Eventually, not hearing any more from the leopard, I was overcome with fatigue and fell asleep.

Next morning I spoke to Mick and the others about the incident, but all denied they had heard anything, not even the baboons. Furthermore, all denied that they knew of a leopard that regularly frequented the camp, though they acknowledged that it is common for a "camp cat" to regularly visit an operation such as ours and hang around. Mick's failure to hear the leopard's cough was all the more puzzling since his tent was closer to where I'd imagined the leopard to be than my bungalow was. I was half convinced everyone was pulling my leg.

In the morning I looked in the dust of the camp for the leopard's tracks but found none. Even so, there is no doubt in my mind what had happened.

SNAKES ALIVE!

That the area was prime snake habitat was illustrated by an incident that I observed only secondhand but seems to me a story worth telling. Mick and I had returned to camp late one afternoon and had downed a cold Zambezi beer or two when some birds began making alarm calls a few hundred feet from camp. They made quite a ruckus. This I was told often bespeaks the presence of a snake, in the same way that baboons and other monkeys announce the presence of their archenemy, the leopard. I hung around a few minutes in hopes that the interloper would appear, but nothing showed up. I decided to take my customary short nap before dinner and went to my bungalow. When I returned an hour or so later, I heard this story.

Half an hour after I left for my nap, Mick, the cook, and another PH were sitting around the campfire when a large snake slithered through camp from the direction of the birds' alarm calls, then disappeared into the dry Turgwe River bed. The snake was a boomslang, a poisonous tree snake that can reach six feet in length. The staff stepped aside and did not interfere with its escape, but concluded this was the cause of the birds' earlier alarm calls.

The group went back to their conversation seated around the fire and had talked for several minutes when they became aware of some rustling sounds right above their heads in the branches of a tree by the fire pit. Ordinarily, the only sound coming from that direction in the evening was the pitiful cry of a bush baby that appeared to live there.

Looking up they observed a pair of boomslangs that appeared either to be fighting or mating, they weren't sure which. No sooner had they identified the pair than the two of them, now intertwined, came crashing to earth right in the midst of the staff. There was apparently a wild scramble to avoid the snakes, and the staff scattered, knocking over some chairs in the process. The snakes apparently took their activity, whatever it was, elsewhere, as they were not seen again.

INSECT SAFARI

Dinner was typically served after sundown since we stayed in the field hunting until dusk most of the time. I usually took a short nap before dinner, making it necessary to walk in the dark the fifty yards from my bungalow to the dining area. One evening as I stepped from the bungalow door for the trek to dinner, I heard William, the other PH in camp, yell, with a hint of alarm in his voice, "Look out for the army ants!" With visions of the *The Naked Jungle* (a film in which Charlton Heston battles an ant invasion) flashing before my eyes, I stopped cold. Retreating to my bungalow, I returned with a flashlight to see what I could on the trail to the dining area.

I saw a stream of large ants coming and going from an inch-wide hole. The other end of the column disappeared into the darkness of the riverbed. Not being knowledgeable about African insects, I can't say what species these were, but the locals referred them to as soldier or army ants. I've also heard them called safari ants. Ants in this area are remarkably industrious and construct immense hills all over the bush country. I have seen some hills that were over eight feet high, and others with bases that were thirty feet wide.

I stepped carefully over the tiny procession and went on to dinner. Next morning they were gone without a trace except for the small hole in the ground. I asked the safari staff, all natives of Zimbabwe, about this disappearance, and they said that it was typical. No one seemed to know much about the ants except that they appear suddenly and mysteriously vanish a short time later.

TRIXIE, THE LION DOG

One of the most entertaining members of the camp staff was a dog belonging to William and Jen, named Trixie. She was the first member of a breed common in southern Africa that I'd ever seen except in some hunting videos I watched before my safari. She was, and I hope still is, a Jack Russell, a kind of terrier.

Her owners, tongue firmly in cheek, touted her as a "lion dog," about which I had considerable doubt. But she had an intense and friendly personality and appeared to simply love going hunting. If I walked through camp and called to her, she'd dash ahead like a pointer, striking an alert pose and peering intently into the bush ahead, presumably looking for a lion. I'm not sure where she spent the night, but I hope it was in a secure facility—dogs are well known to be among leopards' favorite meals.

I'm not sure what Trixie was looking for on these quasi hunts, but I doubted it was a lion. She reminded me of my German shorthaired pointer. When I acted like a bird was nearby, my dog would rush forward to try to get the scent and pointing every few feet. Trixie did the same thing. If it wasn't for the risk of her getting bitten by a snake, she would have been great fun to use for hunting the local francolin and guinea fowl.

THE GAME IN ZIMBABWE

BUSHBUCK

My first African trophy was one of these fine little antelope, the smallest, I believe, of the coveted spiral-horned group.

As is customary, on the first morning in camp we went to check the sighting of our rifles. Since my own rifles were still in transit, I was using a 7x57mm Brno Mauser borrowed from William, the other PH hunting out of Turgwe Camp. Once this was accomplished by shooting at a rough target stuck to a tree, we took off in Mick's Land Cruiser just to see what we could see. We weren't hunting for anything in particular, at least as far as I knew.

We drove slowly along the dirt tracks on the ranch, with me holding the Mauser, and Mick's tracker, Elijah, standing in the back of the truck looking for game. We had not been out long when Elijah signaled for Mick to stop. He quickly communicated to Mick that there was a bushbuck standing a few yards off to the side of the road that we were traveling, and we decided to have a look.

We dismounted and walked slowly back along the road until we could see a shadowy outline of the little buck standing in thick brush perhaps fifty yards away. Mick looked at the animal for a few seconds through his binoculars then nodded to me that I should take him. I could not make out the animal's horns at all but quickly decided to trust Mick's judgment. With the naked eye I could only see a dark outline of the animal, but through the scope I could see well enough to place my shot accurately. Slowly I went to one knee and fired for the buck's left shoulder, as he stood broadside. The little buck had not moved a muscle that I could see since we got into position.

At the shot the bushbuck dropped instantly, but was still able to move his head a little. Mick got to him in seconds with me right behind him. As soon as we came up to the buck, we could see there was a problem. One of his spiral horns was perfect and of good length, but the other had been broken off near the tip, leaving only a rather unsightly rounded stump instead of a sharp, ivory-colored point like they typically have.

I noticed that as soon as he got up to the bushbuck, Mick grabbed the animal by both horns and held on until the animal died, which took a few seconds. My shot had been high in the shoulder, which was broken, had shattered the spine between the shoulders, and exited. I believe the bullet was a 170-grain H-Mantle bullet of Czech manufacture.

While waiting the few seconds it took for the bushbuck to expire completely, I began reflecting on what I had read about this animal. I recalled that they have a reputation for being very courageous and dangerous when wounded. When I mentioned this to Mick, he acknowledged that was why he'd grabbed the buck's horns when he first got to him.

This was the first bushbuck I had ever laid eyes on, and a beautiful little fellow he was. I have described this antelope in some detail elsewhere, but suffice to say the species is often among the favorites of experienced African hunters, and it is easy to see why. They are very beautiful, almost dainty, and have the most unusual markings on their coats, which are matched by few other African antelope for their beauty and complexity. Though this was my first bushbuck, it was not to be my last.

About a week later Mick, Elijah, and I were sitting near a pool of water in an otherwise dry riverbed. Heavy brush lined both banks down to what was usually the water's edge. What was water during the rainy summer season now was just sand and rock. We were sitting on some rocks that placed us perhaps twenty feet above the bottom of the riverbed.

As I recall, we weren't hunting for anything in particular, but just watching to see what might show up. We'd taken up our position late in the afternoon, so there wasn't much over an hour of daylight left. This was the same occasion where the four impala ewes came to drink from the pool near our hide, which I described in some detail earlier.

In this particular area of the lowveld, the possibilities for what might show up were considerable. There were elephant, rhino, leopard, and even an occasional lion in the area, along with most species of antelope and pigs that inhabit this game-rich area.

But on this evening, nothing else showed up after the impala had left until it was almost too dark to see. With barely ten minutes of daylight left we saw a bushbuck across the river from us on the other bank that appeared to be coming out to feed. When we spotted him, he was less than one hundred yards from us and feeding slowly in our direction. It was so dark that it was difficult to judge its horns, and it was moving so slowly that it appeared unlikely to me it would get close enough to evaluate while there was still light enough to shoot.

We had to remain very still, as we had virtually no cover and were in full view of the bushbuck if he raised his head. Fortunately, after taking a few mouthfuls of browse, the little buck picked up his pace as though he'd forgotten an appointment and had to hurry to make it on time. He came from our right, took a left turn at the base of the rock pile on which we sat, and appeared to be heading right for us.

By then Mick had decided the bushbuck was worth taking and motioned for me to shoot. I was carrying my .375-06. The shot was rather steeply downhill at around seventy-five yards. My scope was a bright 3–9X Leupold, so it was easy to see the buck even though it was nearly dark. The bullet hit where I'd intended, through the top of the near shoulder, and exited through the lower body. I was shooting a .300 Nosler Partition bullet at a velocity that made it nearly the equivalent of a .375 H&H, but the little buck still ran twenty yards before it collapsed and died.

This was my best bushbuck trophy, its horns being around thirteen inches and a very good representative of the species. I was delighted with this animal and decided to have a shoulder mount made, and also have the skin of the first one I'd shot, with the broken horn, tanned.

IMPALA

This area of the lowveld was, as the British say, "simply stiff" with impala. It was almost certainly the most numerous of all antelope species in the area and had to be culled regularly to keep them from overgrazing their habitat. Because they are so numerous, it was a rare day when we did not see several bunches of this beautiful antelope, and often a few scattered individual rams. Mick hoped we could locate a particularly good ram that he'd seen before my hunt, but we never did find it.

Trophy-sized impala were fairly common in the area. It did not appear there were many much over twenty inches, but there were plenty between nineteen and twenty-one inches, which is large enough to be both representative of the species and an impressive trophy. A ram in this size range was the second animal I shot in the lowveld.

While hunting with the 7x57mm, we came across a good ram that appeared to be a solitary male. He offered me a broadside shot at one hundred yards, so I shot it just behind the shoulder. Since I was using a rest, which I nearly always did, I was confident I'd made a good shot even though I was not yet comfortable with the Mauser's set triggers. At the shot the ram took off in a low, fast run and went into dense brush where he collapsed forty yards from where I had shot it. It was dead before we could walk over to where it lay.

This was the first opportunity I had to examine one of these striking antelope closely, and he was even more impressive at close range than when I'd seen impala cantering along the road ahead of us, as they often did. Its coat is soft, and all the impala that I shot appeared to be in perfect physical condition.

After my own rifles arrived I took two more impala, one each with the .270 and the .375-06.

The first that I took with the .270 was another standing shot at about one hundred fifty yards. He was at a rather steep angle quartering away from me. The 150-grain Nosler Partition entered the right side and passed through several inches of paunch before damaging both lungs and exiting through the off shoulder. As the first one had done, this ram took off on a fast run for a distance of fifty yards and collapsed. It was dead when we got to it.

The third impala that I took was shot with the .375-06 and a 270-grain Hornady Spire-Point bullet, and it also required a quartering-away shot. I estimated the range at one hundred yards. The bullet took nearly the same course as the 150-grain Nosler described above, but instead of exiting, I found it, perfectly mushroomed, under the hide on the opposite side from where the bullet entered. This ram's reaction was virtually identical to the other two, in that it made a fast run of about forty yards and died.

I don't want to make too much of this particular example, involving only three animals, but I thought it quite remarkable that with such a wide range of bullet weights and power levels, the reaction of all three animals, as well as the final outcome, was practically identical.

KLIPSPRINGER AND THE ACCIDENTAL BUSHBUCK

One evening Mick, Elijah, and I went to a beautiful meadow through which flowed a slow, peaceful little stream. The main attraction was a large kopje that Mick hoped would contain a klipspringer, the curious little antelope that, like the marmot, inhabits rock piles. The kopje sat back perhaps fifty yards from the stream and formed one corner of the meadow, which was perhaps twenty acres. We were on the opposite side of the stream from the kopje, one hundred yards from the stream, hiding behind some boulders. We hoped to get a shot at a klipspringer moving among the rocks. I estimated the range to the top of the kopje to be two hundred yards.

There was another small rocky area to our right front in the meadow just across the creek (the kopje was in front of us). A large marmotlike animal, the first rock dassie I had ever seen, came out to feed on the grass as the sun started its steep decline into night. As the evening wore on, emerald doves flew in pairs or small flocks over the meadow in increasing numbers. It was a thrilling sight to this old dove hunter. How I wished I had a shotgun to take advantage of the situation!

After watching the kopje and the dassie for perhaps thirty minutes, we noticed a small antelope walking slowly from the wooded area to our right front toward the kopje. Mick glassed the animal and assured me it was a duiker. We both watched the animal as it walked across this bare meadow, which resembled a green on a golf course, and eventually it disappeared into the rocks. He had been in full view for perhaps ten minutes, and I could have easily taken him had I chosen to do so. At that time I had not taken a duiker and had never seen one up close. As it turned out later, this was the best chance I had at a klipspringer, which the animal actually was, though misidentified by my PH.

I don't recall whether the tracker, Elijah, ultimately pointed out the error, or if Mick did, but soon we began to examine the kopje closely with our binoculars, hoping to get a shot at the klipspringer should it make its way out among the rocks. Light was waning, and the chances seemed slim of getting a shot. Eventually a klipspringer appeared near the very top of the kopje, but I missed a shot by shooting over its back. I was happy to have the excuse that I was using a borrowed rifle.

I was sure that I had blown my one chance at a klipspringer. But a few minutes later I noticed an animal feeding far to our left at the edge of the meadow. It was a small buck perhaps fifty yards from the kopje and one hundred yards from where we hid among the rocks.

The animal was facing away from us, unaware of, or at least unconcerned with, our presence. I was sure it was the klipspringer that had come out the other side of the kopje to feed while we searched for it among the rocks. Frantically I attempted to signal Mick, who was intently watching the kopje through his binoculars perhaps thirty feet from me. I hissed, waved, and did everything short of shouting, trying not to alarm my intended victim, to get Mick's attention, but to no avail. I simply could not get him to look in my direction.

Finally, in frustration, I decided to take the situation in hand, and I lined up on the little antelope and fired a shot with the 7x57mm Brno. The animal dropped instantly to the shot and never moved.

The noise of the shot had barely died away when Mick, who now realized what had happened, exclaimed, "That's a bushbuck!" What moments before had been elation at my fine shot instantly turned to chagrin and anxiety as I realized my blunder. Elijah's comment that I appeared to be an excellent shot didn't help much at that point.

The going price for bushbuck was about $400, and I was on a fairly tight budget. I had already taken a good one, and paying for another would probably mean I'd have to pass up some other animal I wanted. And this was clearly a very small bushbuck for me, even as a novice, to mistake it for a klipspringer. I was one crestfallen bwana.

Mick ultimately saved the day. As we walked to retrieve it, he asked me if I really wanted this little bushbuck. I explained that I did not, since it was no trophy, but was resigned to paying for it anyway.

About that time one of the hands who lived in small compounds scattered about the ranch came walking toward us around the brow of the hill, apparently attracted by the sound of the shot. Mick presented the little bushbuck to this man, who seemed very grateful to have the meat.

I wish I could report that I eventually shot a trophy klipspringer, but I never got another chance. This was the only opportunity I had on this safari and on the following trip to South Africa. The good news is this gives me a good excuse to include a klipspringer on my next safari!

DUIKER

The common duiker is well named in that it is very widespread and apparently plentiful all over southern Africa. It is probably the most common of the small antelope. There are several species of duiker that are much less common and considered rare prizes. Trophy fees for these special duikers are often several times as much as those for the common or "bush" duiker, as they are sometimes called. Because of their limited range and their preference for dense forest habitat, I expect a special effort is necessary to bag one of these rare types.

The common duiker, however, is so plentiful and widespread that it does not appear necessary to use any special tactics or to make a special effort to find one. The usual procedure is just to keep an eye out for a good trophy and take it when the opportunity presents itself.

Because this antelope is tiny and not terribly shy, no special care need be taken in selecting a special duiker rifle or load. They are just shot with whatever is at hand when a good one comes along. However, it's still necessary to place your shot in a vital area for the sake of the animal and to avoid a protracted search for a wounded one.

Mine happened along when I was holding my .270, so that's what I shot him with. I made another high shoulder shot, which dropped the little guy in his tracks. It was shooting at such small animals that led me to reconsider my usual practice of sighting in three inches high at one hundred yards.

My duiker's horns were typical of the small antelope, being 4½ inches long, sticking straight up from its skull, roughly parallel with the line of the face. I felt it was a representative adult specimen and was quite pleased.

WARTHOG

This curious pig is standard fare for safaris all over southern Africa, from the semideserts of Namibia to the tropics of Zambia and Mozambique. It's hard to imagine a hunt in this area during which one did not see several warthogs, and I suspect nearly everyone takes one. In addition to their value as trophies, the young of the species are often taken for leopard bait or for a camp barbecue.

I found these animals to be the most entertaining of the nonprimates encountered on my safaris. To me their normal behavior is simply comical.

Like the impala and duiker, warthog are widespread and abundant in many hunting areas in the region. I know of no special tactics used to hunt them. Rather, like the common duiker, eventually one runs into a boar with sufficiently long tusks to warrant taking it, and they are shot with whatever weapon is at hand at the moment. They do have the reputation, like most wild swine, of being quite aggressive when wounded or cornered.

My warthog was a lone boar encountered while we were doing one of our daily game drives, just looking for something worth shooting. He gave me a broadside shot at around one hundred yards. I happened to have my .375-06 loaded with the 270-grain Hornady Spire-Point at the time. My shot took him in the shoulder. When I fired the hog seemed to disappear in a cloud of dust as he started a fast run of about thirty yards before dropping. He was dead when we got to him. The bullet had gone through both shoulders and penetrated both lungs. His longest tusk was just over twelve inches, which I think is a good, representative, though not outstanding, size for the area.

All swine trophies appear to require special handling, which must be duly certified by a taxidermist or other authority, before they can be legally shipped to the client's country. I still don't know whether mine was not properly treated or documented, but my entire shipment of trophies from Zimbabwe—which contained a warthog skull, cape, and tusks—was held up until I could arrange to have it properly treated. This was not much of a problem, but I think it could have been avoided had the trophy been correctly treated and the treatment documented before it left Zimbabwe.

ELAND

Eland were scarce on the ranch, and the effort required to find a shootable one was the most physically challenging of all the animals I took. This was the one animal I hunted where tracking proved to be the preferred method. We did spend some time watching a watering spot where Mick thought one might appear, but none ever did.

When we were out after eland, Mick brought Elijah, the chief skinner, along. I was never sure why he thought this was desirable, but Elijah was a pleasant companion and always welcome when we hunted. He may have had some special skills relevant to eland hunting, but if he did, I never learned what they were.

Instead of the usual method of driving around until we spotted the game we wanted, for eland we looked for tracks. On our first attempt we followed up a mixed herd that included eland, impala, and possibly zebra; I was never certain what animals were in the group. We got close enough for a shot once but could never single out a suitable animal. Once they detected us, they took off on one of the long trots eland are noted for. When these huge antelope are not pressed too hard, their preferred gait appears to be what Roosevelt called a "slashing trot," and they can go a long ways at this pace. My party and I had to jog to keep up with them.

In preparation for this hunt I had regularly walked or ridden my bicycle about five miles nearly every day for several weeks. When we hunted eland, temperatures were hot, perhaps 80 degrees. Trying to follow up this herd proved too much for me, and I had to call it off. My young companions had little trouble keeping up, but I began to fear that if I tried to keep up with the eland, they'd be hauling *me* home in the back of the Land Cruiser. Reluctantly, at my request, we abandoned the effort. I recall that when we did I had a rather remarkable heart rate and was sweating profusely.

We'd gone a long way from the vehicle in pursuit of the eland and had to walk about an hour to get back to our starting point. Once mounted up again, we were heading for another area when, for the first time on the safari, we saw a small group of eland ahead of us. Racing forward to where they'd crossed the track we were on, I got out of the truck and looked for a tree to use for a rest as the small bunch headed for the thick bush. As I was doing this, Mick was sizing up the animals, and when one stopped, he told me to take it.

The animal stood broadside at about one hundred yards. I aimed for a lung shot, using a small thornbush for a rest. At the shot, the animal whirled and started running away from us. I did not fire again, certain of my shot. I was not surprised when it dropped after running one hundred yards.

I was carrying my .375-06 loaded with the 300-grain Nosler Partition bullet, in anticipation of encountering eland. After determining the animal was dead, I walked back to the spot where it had been standing when I fired. There was a fan-shaped spray of blood perhaps three feet wide on a bush just behind where the eland had been, indicating that the bullet had exited, and with some force.

Our autopsy was quite revealing. The bullet had expanded immediately upon entering the skin on the left side and made a hole about four inches in diameter through the ribs on that side. The bullet virtually destroyed the left lung, severely damaged the right lung, made a two-inch-diameter hole through the rib cage on the far side, and exited through the far shoulder. There was an excellent blood trail between the spot where I'd hit the animal and where it died. It never made it to thick cover, but if it had, we surely could have followed it easily.

The animal proved to be a cow, though we were specifically looking for a bull. Her horns were over twenty-eight inches long, and she was an incredibly large animal, probably well over 1,000 pounds. I believe in the heat of the moment, Mick had mistaken her for a bull. Nevertheless, I was very happy with this trophy.

This was one animal we did not even consider trying to lift into the Land Cruiser. After doing our initial dressing, we summoned help from the camp to quarter the animal so that it could be brought back to camp for proper caping and butchering.

KUDU

My original plan was to take one kudu bull, and it was my highest priority. Kudu were plentiful in the area, and we saw some practically every time we left camp, though these were mostly cows.

My first opportunity to shoot a bull happened on about day six, after my own rifles and baggage had been retrieved from Harare and brought to Turgwe Camp. We were traveling through an area of relatively open mopane woodland with patches of much denser, vine-draped thornbush. A large, solitary bull, which looked almost blue in the shaded area under the trees, had apparently been feeding and took off when we drove into its vicinity. We bailed out of the Land Cruiser and I took off at a trot, paralleling the direction the bull had taken. I had gone less than one hundred yards when I saw it standing in some shade two hundred yards away.

There was a large tree between the bull and me that I used for cover to get a few yards closer. This tree had a fork at about my chest height, and I could see the bull framed in this fork like it was in the leaf of an express sight. I recall having to stretch to get a shot at the bull through this fork. When I fired the animal dropped in its tracks.

I had held for a shoulder shot, but the bullet went higher than I'd intended. The shot was instantly effective because the bullet broke the near shoulder and shattered the spine. As with all such high-shoulder shots I have made, the animal was still alive when I approached it. The kudu was unable to move, but required another shot to finish it. To avoid damaging the cape, I fired this shot into its chest area, which was directed to damage the heart and lungs. That was the only 300-grain partition bullet I recovered on the trip.

The kudu hunt was another example of my following the instruction of my PH, and taking animals I wasn't initially hunting for. This was, I believe, the first mature, trophy-class kudu bull I had ever seen, but his horn length of around forty-five inches was considerably shorter than I had hoped.

In retrospect, I probably should have just accepted the trophy for what it was, but I was a little greedy. I had convinced myself that it should be fairly easy to get a bull in the fifty-inch range and had planned to settle for nothing less. Since I was sure this goal was clear to my PH, later I asked if I could take another bull closer to what I'd wanted. Mick supported my request and told Derek he'd misjudged the animal, so I was allowed to take another kudu bull later on. As it turned out, I just barely managed to do so in the waning hours of my safari.

However much one would like to deny it, every safari ends sometime, usually much too soon. I awoke late on my last day, and realized I had been allowed to sleep in, never hearing in the predawn darkness Moses' gentle "Good morning, sir." Dressing quickly, I walked to the mess area where I learned, to my considerable surprise and chagrin, that my PH was also sleeping in. Everyone but me seemed to think the safari was over.

I had collected every animal we'd agreed on and was well satisfied with the quality of the animals, and all other aspects of the hunt until then, with one important exception. I had not yet bagged a suitable kudu bull. In fairness, I had taken a nice bull early in the safari, but we had all agreed I could at least try for a bigger one. Apparently this detail had been forgotten by my PH.

We quickly resolved this misunderstanding when I reminded him that Derek had given me permission to take a larger kudu bull. If he thought my reminder unreasonable, he didn't say, and we were soon off to an area where he believed we might find a bull in the midmorning.

The area he had in mind was one the ranch folk called East Africa because it was flatter and more open than most of the surrounding bush. In truth it was quite flat, very dusty, and surrounded by moderately thick bush, which was often draped with vines or tall grass. I thought it would have made wonderful quail habitat. When I considered the location of this area, it also appeared to be excellent snake habitat. Knowing that the dreaded black mamba inhabited the area made each step I took later in the dense bush a little like walking through a minefield.

We proceeded as usual, Elijah standing in the back of the truck, which was topless throughout our hunt, looking for game while Mick maneuvered the vehicle along the dusty, twisting vehicle track that passed for a road. We had not been in the area long when a shout from Elijah told us he'd spotted something. Somehow Mick also got a look at what appeared to be a herd of kudu bulls hiding in some thick bush. I could see nothing. Mick excitedly told me to get out of the vehicle and get ready, as the kudu were going to come out into an open plain that was perhaps one hundred yards in diameter. This I did as quickly as I could, taking up a kneeling position a few yards from the truck. I didn't have long to wait.

In a few seconds a kudu bull exploded from the thick bush like a clay pigeon shot from a trap and raced through an area in front of me as bare as a plowed field. I thought he was about one hundred fifty yards away. The bull quickly gained speed and headed for some distant heavy cover. I could see immediately that he was not a bull suitable to shoot, having only a single twist of horn, a mere youngster.

Just to be sure I didn't make a mistake, Mick shouted, "Not that one!"

Like an amusement park shooting gallery, a few seconds later another kudu bull, virtually identical in size to the first, exploded from the same cover and bounded along the same path as the first had taken. I was intently focused on the spot these bulls were coming from like one watches a bush from which he expects a pheasant to explode from under his dog's nose. I was unaware of being nervous, but I would love to have a picture of my face at that moment.

Mick advised me that there was a good bull in the bunch and that I should wait for him to come out. By then I had seen enough mature kudu bulls that I could tell the small fry from the big ones, so there was no chance I was going to accidentally shoot one of these teenagers. I hung onto my .270 and waited while a third and a fourth kudu, all small bulls, erupted from the bush and charged across the dusty plain along the same path the others had taken as if they were on a radar beam.

Finally, having exhausted his decoys, the big bull charged from the thicket along the same path, his magnificent fifty-inch horns laid along his back, an unforgettable sight as he tore across the dusty plain, gaining speed with every bound. I managed to get into action and fired my first shot just before he disappeared behind a brushy island about midway across the dusty flats. I recall leading him about ½ his length and felt the shot was good, but the big bull gave no sign it was hit.

By then the kudu was screened by the brushy island, but appeared again at about three hundred yards, running flat out. I took another shot, but the bull gave no sign he was hit and entered thick bush.

Mick and Elijah ran ahead, off to the left of the path the kudu had taken, trying to see where he was going. I was following the bull's tracks at a trot, looking for blood spoor and snakes simultaneously, when I chanced to look up and saw him standing about seventy-five yards away, broadside, watching his back trail. This was obviously the answer to a hunter's prayer, and I was determined not to blow it. Though somewhat winded and very excited, I dropped to one knee, held for a lung shot, and fired. At the shot the bull took off and entered the heavy bush on the far side of the plain.

Incredible as it seemed, it looked like I'd missed that bull completely. I was soon able to take some cold comfort in the knowledge that I wasn't the only one who could blow an easy shot, even at a target the size of a kudu, in the excitement of the chase.

Back on his track I became aware that other animals, probably impala, were making alarm calls in the dense brush in front of me where the bull had gone.

What I am about to relate contains a paradox, considering my personal hunting ethic that includes as a primary goal a one-shot kill with the first shot. In my eagerness to get a bigger kudu, I took a shot I believed I could make, with a rifle I was very familiar with, but perhaps of minimal power for kudu.

Many years before I had taken the advice of Jack O'Connor and hunted jackrabbits with my big-game rifles, usually with the same .270 I used on the kudu. The idea was to practice shooting at game at unknown ranges, and often when it was running. I got fairly good at this kind of shooting, though I didn't reduce the jackrabbit population much. But I sure scared hell out of a lot of them by hitting close to them as they ran through the sagebrush. Based on that experience, I had considerable confidence in my ability to hit a running animal, but my skill was badly out-of-date. For many years I had done most of my shooting from a benchrest.

My ethical problem in this situation, aside from taking the shot in the first place, is that the next hour was one of my most exciting experiences on the safari. If the bull had dropped from any of my first three shots, I'd have missed this experience.

Elijah began tracking the kudu where it entered thick bush after I'd missed the broadside shot. We'd found blood even before that point, though not much, so I knew I'd hit the bull but not where I'd hit him. Mick had taken my other rifle, the .375-06, and a few rounds of ammo when he'd left the truck. He left the tracking to Elijah and stayed off to the left several yards, in hopes of seeing the kudu sneaking out ahead of us. Elijah was directly on its trail, and I was off to the right a few yards.

We had not gone far when Elijah slowly pointed into the bush less than twenty-five yards ahead of us. Mick and I moved in on the spot, rifles ready, just like we were walking in on a covey of quail. We'd taken only a few steps when the bull, which was completely hidden in vegetation that did not look like it would hide a duiker, jumped to his feet and bounded away to our left front. Both Mick and I fired, at no more than thirty yards, at an animal the size of a bull elk, and the kudu disappeared into the bush. Incredulous that he had again escaped apparently unharmed, we again took up his track. It began to look like this kudu was bulletproof.

Less than one hundred yards into the bush, which got thicker the farther in we went, the kudu again lurched to its feet and bounded away, catching both Mick and me by surprise.

Neither of us fired a shot. Elijah had signaled that the animal was practically at our feet, but we had not seen his subtle pointing gesture. Frustrated, we continued on the bull's trail with only an occasional spot of blood to confirm we were following the right track.

To appreciate the skill of this young tracker, the reader should realize that the area we were traversing, from the time we initially took up the bull's tracks, was literally covered with game tracks of all kinds as well as those of cattle. It is no exaggeration to say it was like trying to track *one* of several dozen sheep across a crowded barnyard on ground that was extremely dry and covered with an inch or two of dust or sand. Once we entered the heavy bush, we were walking on grass, which would make no impression of the kudu's hooves. Elijah tracked the animal by relying on his knowledge of wounded game. It was the most remarkable feat of tracking I ever saw.

We jumped that bull three times after we entered the thick bush, and both Mick and I fired at close range on one of those occasions. In the final round, I was paralleling Elijah about ten yards to its right when we came upon the bull for the last time. It was lying down, well screened from the tracker and Mick, in a relatively open area. I saw it struggling to its feet. I shot it in the neck at fifteen yards, ending the matter.

It was a fine bull, measuring 51 inches, made all the more memorable by Elijah's brilliant tracking. In spite of my mediocre shooting, I have rarely experienced so much satisfaction, and relief, bringing an animal to bag. This I surely could not have done without the services of this fine young man whose tracking skills saved my "face" as a hunter, and reduced the pain and suffering of this fine kudu bull.

Examination of the carcass told the story of my skill, or lack thereof, as a running-game shot. Both my shots hit the bull in the paunch, one about amidships and the other considerably farther back. On seeing this, I congratulated myself, not on my shooting, but on my choice of the 150-grain Nosler Partition bullets. I believe a lesser bullet would not have provided the penetration and resulting wound channel that eventually, thanks to Elijah, wore him down. A mark could be seen where a bullet had grazed his sternum without breaking the skin, which I suspected was my missed broadside. It looked like both Mick and I had missed him completely on the occasion when he flushed from heavy cover and we both fired at him at thirty yards.

ZEBRA

Zebra were not plentiful where I was hunting, and we saw few of them in the course of my ten-day safari. Those we did see were in small herds of around a dozen animals.

The reports one hears about how tough zebras are to kill are highly variable. Some hunters find them easy to kill using a .30-06, others find them incredibly tough when using a .375. I think this paradox can be resolved by looking closely at where the animal was hit with the first shot. I suspect that if you gut-shoot one with anything short of a field-artillery piece, or break a leg with anything at all, you will find them tough indeed. But a good softpoint through both lungs with any reasonable caliber will probably put you in the camp with those who experience no problem at all killing zebra. My own experience can illustrate the importance of first-shot placement.

After driving around in the area where the local zebra live, we came upon a small herd. I bailed out of the Land Cruiser and ran forward a few yards for better visibility. The zebra closest to me was a mature stallion.

The animal faced me at one hundred fifty yards, quartering to my left. Because I knew these animals are tough, I intended to place my shot into its near shoulder, expecting to break it, and expecting the bullet to continue into the lungs. I was shooting my .375-06 loaded with the 270-grain Hornady Spire Point. I hit the animal in the center of the shoulder, but this was not the right place to aim. The zebra was angled more toward me than I thought.

The bullet went into the shoulder, but because of the angle, it missed the bone, went through the left lung and into the paunch. A zebra with one lung and four functional legs can go a long way without showing any sign of being wounded. If the animal had been broadside, my shot placement would have been about perfect; the bullet would have gone through both lungs and broken one, if not both, shoulders.

As a result of this mistake, the animal was not disabled immediately as I had planned, but wheeled around and quickly rejoined the herd. Only after some tracking did we come upon the herd again, and we had to follow the herd for some distance before my zebra got sick enough to separate from the rest so we could identify it and close in for a finishing shot. Fortunately, because the first shot had hit its lungs, blood sprayed from its nose as it ran, helping us follow it through the welter of tracks in the waning light of day. There was no blood trail from the bullet wound itself.

When the animal separated from the herd, obviously in distress, Elijah quickly identified it as the one I had wounded.

This time I had a broadside shot and held for the lungs. At the shot the zebra took off again, but was moving slower than before. It quickly disappeared behind some brush. At the shot, Elijah also took off running in the direction of the zebra, hoping to see where it was going. Seconds before Mick and I arrived, Elijah got to the brush where the animal had disappeared.

The zebra was standing in a clear area not more than twenty-five yards from Elijah, who was gesturing excitedly at the animal, indicating I should shoot again. The animal was literally weaving around on its feet, apparently barely able to stand, and looked as though it was about to fall over. As I was preparing to shoot again, Mick stopped me and offered a plan to save ammunition. As bizarre as it may sound, here is what Mick said: "The zebra is dead on its feet and just doesn't know it. I'll charge it, and the effort required to get away from me will be the last straw, and it will just go down without having to shoot it again." Since he was the professional, I agreed and held my fire.

Mick rushed at the zebra, which, to my dismay, gained new strength immediately and launched into a strong gallop to escape. I decided the plan was not working and quickly fired two more shots into the animal's shoulder area at no more than thirty yards. The zebra went down for good.

Zebras have a well-deserved reputation for being tough, but had I placed the first shot in the chest area, angled to hit the spine, or waited for a broadside shot so both lungs would be hit, the animal would have died shortly thereafter. I had simply misjudged the angle and consequently used the wrong aiming point.

The excitement was not over. By the time we retrieved the Land Cruiser and brought it to where the zebra lay, it was dark. Mick assured me that we would not be able to lift the animal into the truck without help, so he dispatched Elijah with the vehicle to find help among the ranch workers to load it.

Mick, who was not carrying a rifle that day, and I sat next to the zebra and listened to the night sounds. We had been advised earlier that there was at least one lion in the area, and as we sat next to the dead zebra, I couldn't help wondering what would happen if it showed up while we waited for Elijah. We had one rifle between us, and I'm not sure we even had a flashlight.

Eventually Elijah returned with some ranch hands recruited at their compound, and together we managed to load the zebra into the truck. The lion never showed up, which was just as well. It wasn't on our menu anyway—and I didn't want to be on the lion's.

PART III
MY SAFARI IN SOUTH AFRICA

THE GAME IN SOUTH AFRICA

After I met my PH, we headed south toward Zululand. Our quarry was the Zululand nyala, an exotic animal restricted in its range to a small area of southeastern Africa, specifically Zimbabwe, Mozambique, and South Africa.

During my safari in Zimbabwe, we traveled in a Toyota Land Cruiser. On those occasions when we traveled to or from Harare, we used Derek's Datsun pickup. In contrast, on my safari in South Africa, we traveled in an air-conditioned Datsun sedan. The drive took several hours on a modern highway much like our freeways. During the trip I was able to learn more about the animal we were going to hunt and to ply my host with questions about South Africa.

NYALA

We were going to be hunting on a ranch belonging to a Mr. Opperman in Natal Province that overlooked a part of Kwa-Zulu, the homeland of the Zulu people. It was a game ranch that was unfenced except for the typical low wire fences used to keep cattle in or out. Game could freely come and go.

Accommodations on the ranch were quite different than they had been in Zimbabwe. I was told that the facility where we stayed had been a motel, though I thought this description curious as there were no public roads close-by. Instead, it was located on the rancher's undeveloped property at the end of a dirt road. It was a rather plain, one-story structure painted blue with a shape unlike anything I had ever seen. It appeared to have been at one time a round building with a pointed, thatched roof, similar to traditional Zulu dwellings, many of which were visible just across a wide valley from the facility. But a rectangular structure had been added to make a sort of bunkhouse for visiting hunters, and there was a small kitchen where guests could prepare meals. The facility came complete with some comely Zulu girls who cleaned up after the guests periodically.

As a side note, one day we were traveling down an unpaved road just as a local school was getting out. High school students lined both sides of the road as they walked home. Their attire ranged from what resembled uniforms typical of parochial schools to lovely lassies dressed in the traditional attire for Zulu females— which does not include covering for their upper body.

The blue motel was surrounded by an eight-foot-high electrified fence. Since Natal Province has for years been the scene of warfare between Zulus and their native enemies, I could only guess what sort of visitors the fence was designed to exclude. Later I learned it was not unheard of for roving bands to kill whites for one reason or another in the area. While we were there, both my PH and I slept with a loaded rifle close at hand.

The only danger I was specifically warned about was a male ostrich that had already sent one visiting hunter to the hospital. This friendly, but careless, chap apparently became intoxicated and tried to pet the bird. The ostrich, it appears, did not appreciate this public display of affection and proceeded to knock the man to the ground with a swift kick, and in the process gave him a nasty wound with its foot-mounted claw. He had to go to a hospital to get stitched up. I made a mental note not to pet the ostrich.

On one occasion, before I shot my nyala, this large, black male ostrich forced the driver of a pickup I was riding in to stop until the bird could be coaxed out of the road. It apparently was prepared to defend its territory, which included the road we were on. One of the passengers, all of whom were farm hands, volunteered to distract the bird long enough for us to get past.

This fellow took off running in a wide arc generally parallel to our line of travel. The ostrich moved a short distance in his direction, apparently not sure whom he most wanted to attack. While he was thinking it over, we proceeded. After we'd driven a few yards, the decoy jumped back into the truck, and we went on our way. I learned the driver had been afraid the ostrich would seriously damage the truck, which belonged to the ranch owner. The bird had earlier made a sizable dent in another vehicle, which I gather did not please the farmer.

My PH, being rather new to the business, did not have his own staff of trackers and skinners who traveled with him. Instead, he'd arranged to use personnel employed on the ranches where we were to hunt.

The head tracker at this ranch was a tall, muscular Zulu named Kak. He wore a baseball cap on which was printed the name Sutton Place and running shoes labeled Super Flash. He and another man were our guides when we went nyala hunting on the first day in "camp."

The terrain we hunted reminded me of the coastal, chaparral-covered hills in California where as a boy I'd hunted black-tailed deer. The hills weren't very high but quite steep and covered with dense brush. Everyone but me apparently spotted some nyala, though none were worth pursuing.

When we failed to locate a suitable animal on the first morning by glassing, our trackers organized a small drive. There were two or three men out of our sight who would beat a brushy canyon while we waited along a likely exit trail. Kak stayed with us while others did the driving. Once the drive began, I noticed he was keeping in touch with the beaters with a two-way radio. It appeared they were telling him what animals were moving ahead of them. I quickly decided this was not an appropriate procedure and asked my PH to have them stop using it. This took some doing, as Kak did not speak English or Afrikaans, and Johan did not speak Zulu. Finally, using sign language, he communicated my concerns and they stopped using the radio.

No nyala appeared as a result of the drive, but a mountain reedbuck did. My PH said he was good enough to make the record books, but I passed him up. This was more a financial than an ethical decision since I knew nothing about the animal at that time and had not planned to take one. Only later did I learn that Natal Province is one of very few places that one could take this animal.

Next morning Kak, Johan, and I began walking along the heads of brushy canyons using our binoculars to spot a decent nyala. We had not been at this for long when Johan saw one at the bottom of a canyon at a range of around one hundred fifty yards. After a brief glance through his binoculars, he urged me to shoot.

We were standing on top of a ridge above the canyon that the nyala was in. It was feeding and had its head and neck completely obscured by brush. There was nothing but a thorny bush growing out of the hillside at our feet for a rest, so I just lay down on it and tried to locate the nyala in my scope. The bush had enough structure to support my weight, and soon I had the animal in the cross hairs. Its body was obscured by brush right up to the shoulder, so I aimed for its far shoulder, attempting to hit the lungs at a rather steep, downward angle.

At the shot the nyala simply tipped over backward, all four feet in the air, and never moved from the spot. He was apparently dead long before we climbed down to where it lay. The 150-grain Nosler Partition from my .270 hit right where I had intended, damaging both lungs and exiting.

As with most of the animals I shot on this safari, I had never seen a nyala before the one I killed. I was immediately struck by the rather bizarre combination of coloration and long hair, the likes of which I had never seen up until then except in nature documentaries. With its spiral horns and long hair, it looked like a cross between a waterbuck and a bushbuck. It was as though the nyala had inherited its long hair from a waterbuck and its horns and multipatterned coat from a bushbuck. I thought it was the most unusual ungulate I had ever seen, and more exotic-looking than a kudu.

It was a fine trophy, with horns 26½ inches long, good enough to qualify for both Rowland Ward and Safari Club International (SCI) record books. I consider this nyala among the very best of my African trophies, along with my best kudu and my gemsbok.

Once my prize was on the ground, Kak enlisted the help of several of the locals to pack the animal out of the canyon. Judging by their dress, I would say they were recruited from the local tavern, though their performance as game packers left nothing to be desired. They used the time-tested method of tying the animal's feet together and inserting a pole between its front and back legs. In this manner the group packed the animal to a place where we could pick it up with a vehicle.

GEMSBOK

We had a long trip ahead of us for the next hunting area, which was in the Orange Free State, in what Afrikaners call the highveld. This is an area that looked to me more like Nebraska or eastern Colorado than Africa, at least based on the picture I had in my mind of what Africa looked like. Much of the country is open plains covered with yellow grass, with pockets of thornbush and the occasional kopje. It reminded me of eastern Oregon wheat fields bordered by heavy sage and aspen, but considerably flatter. Our objective was two plains game species: gemsbok and springbok.

Although I was pretty vague about the different species of oryx before I started planning my safari, the more I saw of the gemsbok, the more I wanted one. This animal, also called the giant oryx, is the largest of the type in southern Africa, and the only one available outside of East Africa to my knowledge. It is a powerful animal with dramatic and unusual markings, particularly on its face, and has some of the most impressive horns of any antelope. It also has a reputation of being courageous and dangerous if cornered or wounded. By any standard, the gemsbok has to be one of the premier trophies among African antelope.

The plan was for us to stay at a facility on a game ranch and to hunt there and at another farm in the area. The ranch where we were to stay was unusual. The farmer was an Afrikaner with the French-sounding name of duToit. His specialty seemed to be black wildebeest and springbok. There were also several ostriches and some cattle on the property.

After a long drive from Zululand we arrived at duToit's ranch. This was a large ranch, originally devoted to cattle and now being replaced by wildlife. The wildlife were mostly big-game species once native to the region. Such ranches are known locally as game farms. Some allow hunting on their premises in addition to selling animals to other farmers to stock their land. This ranch did both.

I learned that duToit's wife was a gourmet cook and had found a way to use her skills to make money with a sideline to the game farm's primary activity. They had built an attractive outdoor restaurant where they served game dishes to city dwellers in the region. To my surprise, I learned that many people in South

Africa grow up in cities and never eat game meat, except perhaps in fast-food form, which is sold nearly everywhere. Dining on impala steak or springbok chops was as unique for them as it was for me, and the duToits had found a way to capitalize on this.

The restaurant was constructed of locally made brick with a tin roof and an attractive, open-air structure. A low wall, also made of brick, kept out the local game animals, but there was a large gap of several feet between the top of the wall and the roof. With this arrangement, visitors could view in safety and comfort the game moving naturally around the farm. The facility was large enough to accommodate a dozen or more tables in two different rooms, so large parties could be separated. Various antelope trophies decorated the walls, some undoubtedly as unfamiliar to the average city-dwelling person from Johannesburg as they would be to the same kind of person from Chicago.

Mrs. duToit was an accomplished cook and had her ovens specially built to use only coals for cooking. She prepared several meals utilizing the game I shot while I stayed at the ranch. Along with excellent South African wines, food there was wonderful and the duToits were friendly and generous hosts.

Sleeping quarters were built onto the restaurant facility for overnight guests. This was the ranch that had the "pet" genet that lived in the rafters over the restaurant that I have mentioned elsewhere. This handsome little animal to me vaguely resembles a tiny leopard, though more like a large house cat in size, with the head of a small fox or weasel. It is not a true cat like several others in southern Africa, but has its own genus, the *genetta*. Based on its location, I believe it was the species called the small-spotted genet. Every night I heard this little creature scurrying about doing whatever genets do when they aren't sleeping.

Johan's father, Nels, had arranged to meet his son at the duToit ranch to exchange vehicles and to pick up the nyala. His own ranch was about a day's drive away near the town of Alldays in the northern Transvaal. Nels had driven the family's Toyota Land Cruiser and exchanged it for the red Datsun sedan we'd been using. He was to take the nyala back to his ranch and put it in suitable cold storage until we could get there in a day or two to finish the butchering job.

After a pleasant evening with the duToits, we went after gemsbok the next day. Gemsbok were on a nearby farm that had a game fence around the perimeter, which was to keep the farmer's animals in and animals on an adjacent preserve out. The fence was eight to ten feet high and made of woven wire supported by poles.

The terrain on the ranch was mostly rolling, low hills covered with now-dormant yellow grass with patches of thornbush between the slash canyons separating open meadows. Through this bush meandered a few dirt roads. Clearly, cattle had used the area in the past, but I don't recall seeing any while we were there.

We drove around in the Toyota until we spotted a group of oryx, which quickly took off. Johan remarked that they seemed very spooky. We followed them on foot and got close enough for a shot after a short stalk. Since both sexes of this species have horns, it's difficult to distinguish between them. I was advised we were only allowed to shoot a bull, so it was clear we had to be careful about what we were shooting at. I had never seen a live gemsbok before and could not make a gender distinction. Johan suggested I look for a penis sheath, a good indication the animal was indeed a bull.

The group stopped long enough for Johan to get a good look at them, and he saw a good bull in the group. I sat down behind him, resting my .270 over his shoulder. But I was never sure enough of which animal he wanted me to shoot to risk a shot. As the animals milled around, I had no idea which were bulls or cows. Finally, the oryx got impatient and ran off again.

We returned to the Toyota, and Johan drove to an area that he thought they might head for. After leaving the Land Cruiser, we'd gone only a hundred yards or so when we saw two gemsbok in an open area covered with grass that came up to the animals' stomachs. Using brush for cover, we approached to within two hundred yards or so and began to evaluate the two animals that were in plain sight. Johan focused for some time on one animal, trying to decide whether it was a bull or cow, as its horns were good enough to justify shooting it.

There was a stiff wind blowing from left to right. Though I tried, even with 10X binoculars I could not see whether the animal had the right equipment because the grass was just high enough to obscure anything below the belly line. Meanwhile, Johan began intently studying the other animal, trying to decide which of the two to take.

I soon became convinced that the animal was a bull, and Johan said it was good enough to take. The wind was gusting, so the grass waved to and fro, making it difficult to evaluate the animal's gender. Finally I had a good look and decided to shoot. I judged the gemsbok to be about two hundred yards away. From a rest I held for the shoulder and squeezed off a shot. I thought I saw the animal move just as I was finishing my trigger squeeze, and at the shot it launched into a powerful run and quickly disappeared around the brow of a hill.

At that remarkably inconvenient time I was finally forced to attend to some personal business I had been putting off all morning, so I headed for the nearest bush. Johan took off on the trail of the gemsbok, carrying his 12-gauge semiautomatic loaded with slugs. While I was still indisposed, I heard him shoot.

When I caught up with Johan, I heard the story. He had been tracking the gemsbok when he came upon it and got in a shot as it disappeared into the thick bush. We took up the track, but found it tough going. There was little blood to help us, and there were lots of other tracks. We worked on the track for several hours until it was too dark to see any more and then reluctantly returned to the duToit's ranch.

I was depressed by the realization that I had wounded and lost this fine animal. Up until that point I had never lost a wounded animal on an African hunt.

Than evening the duToits had friends over, one of which was an experienced South African hunter named James Coleman, whom Johan described as his mentor. When we told Jim about the gemsbok, he quickly diagnosed the wound as a "belly shot." The gemsbok had been facing into the wind when I fired. The wind had been blowing left to right, probably with sufficient force to drift the 150-grain bullet some distance, but I had not allowed for this drift except to hold on the shoulder. I thought that if wind drift had any effect, it should have pushed the bullet into the lung area.

It also seemed that the gemsbok started to move forward just as I got off the shot. In retrospect, it seemed obvious that the combined effects of wind drift and the animal's movement, together with the range, would have likely resulted in a shot into the paunch area. Everything seemed consistent with this view.

Jim generously volunteered himself and his trackers to help find the gemsbok the next day. He expressed confidence that they would find the animal. But the next morning Johan had scheduled a hunt for blesbok on a neighboring ranch that he did not believe we should miss. We decided Jim and his trackers would take up the track of the wounded gemsbok while we went hunting for the blesbok.

After taking the blesbok, we went to the ranch where the gemsbok was shot and located Jim's vehicle. After a few minutes we came upon him and his trackers standing over the dead oryx.

Jim said that they had jumped the animal close to the spot where we had parked our Land Cruiser the night before. It had apparently moved in a circle and was behind and above us when we quit its track the previous evening. It may have been within one hundred yards of our vehicle when we'd left for the duToit's ranch at dark.

Jim and his men had tracked the animal across some rocky ground, and he finally dropped it as it struggled to its feet. It was a fine bull, with horns a bit over 37 inches. Thanks to the skill of the black trackers, along with the generosity of Johan's friend Jim, I had been saved once again from the sad situation of losing a fine game animal.

BLESBOK

Although it was not in my original hunt plans, Johan suggested that while we were at duToit's farm, we should hunt blesbok on a nearby ranch. I agreed.

The blesbok is one of the animals available only in South Africa and Namibia. At one time it was near extinction, but now is present in substantial numbers, virtually all on privately owned game farms. To me this animal has a rather homely face, not much improved by the wide, white blaze that covers its head from above its eyes to the tip of its nose. Except for its face, it is an otherwise fine-looking animal with heavily ringed horns like those of impala and springbok, but with a distinctive shape. It has the curiously downward-sloping back line similar to a hartebeest but less pronounced, making the animal appear more symmetrical.

The animals we were after were in a herd of twenty that contained several trophy animals. We initially tried to approach the herd by keeping brush between them and us, but the herd panicked and ran off. We then crawled on our bellies until we were close enough for a shot.

As if on cue, a good male trotted out of the herd to get a look at us, eventually stopping broadside at perhaps one hundred fifty yards. I waited until it was clear of the herd before attempting a shot. The 150-grain Nosler from my .270 took the animal in the left shoulder and exited after passing through both lungs. The blesbok dropped immediately, though it required a finishing shot. The horns of the animal scored high enough to qualify for the Safari Club International record book.

SPRINGBOK

This beautiful little gazelle is the national animal of the Republic of South Africa. I think it resembles the East African Thompson gazelle, as it is about the same size and has a dark horizontal body stripe. The springbok's horns, however, are quite different from those of the Tommy.

Springbok were one of the most plentiful animals in South Africa before they were decimated by market hunting and by farmers protecting their grazing lands for their domestic stock. Perhaps the most memorable description of bushbuck numbers was provided in the nineteenth century by Gordon Cumming. Cumming spent years in northern South Africa and southern Botswana, both of which are the springbok's primary range today. He told of seeing "hundreds of thousands" of springbok in a single herd, a sight the local farmers said was not uncommon.

DuToit's ranch consisted of rolling hills covered with short grass with little cover except a few scattered trees and some thornbush in the valleys. When we left our quarters to hunt springbok one morning, it was remarkably cold and was about to rain. Though Johan and I were wearing jackets and were walking vigorously, we were still cold. We headed toward a low ridge four hundred yards from our headquarters, hoping to find a herd of springbok on the far side. Since there was practically no cover to use in stalking an animal in this open country, using the hills for cover was about the only way to approach them in hopes of getting a shot at a reasonable range.

I eventually did get a shot at a good springbok downhill from me. The bullet from my .270 entered between the shoulders and exited through the left lung—an instant kill. It was a fine example of a springbok, though not large enough in the horn to be record-book material.

Because the springbok's skin is so beautiful, I decided to take another animal. Preparation for a shoulder mount inevitably requires cutting off one-third of the front of a hide. After a brief consultation with the rancher I was allowed to take an additional animal: a springbok ram with a deformed face that the rancher wanted culled from the breeding stock.

While we drove around, Johan located the animal, and I made a solo stalk, using one of the few trees on the plains for cover. I got within eighty yards before running out of places to hide. I took the little gazelle with a neck shot for another instant kill.

WATERBUCK

I have always thought this large antelope was one of the most handsome in Africa, and it was one of my priority animals in South Africa. We hunted for them on Dr. Botha's ranch. Botha explained that he had purchased a deserted, overgrown old farm near the Limpopo River to develop a breeding herd of waterbuck.

Dr. Botha was our guide in locating a suitable animal. He was a lean, cheerful, athletic sort who appeared to be in his late thirties. His vehicle was unusual. It had the appearance of a military vehicle, but also resembled a recreational vehicle. Botha told me that it had started out as the latter but had been modified considerably for life in war-torn South Africa. The modifications included welded armor plate covering the undercarriage to protect against land mines, and there were other reinforcements to protect the occupants from small-arms fire. I believe the good doctor was carrying an automatic weapon, too.

With Johan driving the Toyota and Dr. Botha standing in the bed as spotter, we began cruising through the farm area. It was near the river and was mostly riverine habitat, meaning fairly thick brush and trees. After we traveled half a mile, the doctor signaled us to stop. He had spotted a waterbuck bull standing in some thick woods we had passed.

The three of us dismounted and began a stalk through the thick cover about two hundred yards from the bull. Eventually Dr. Botha, who had been in the lead, motioned for Johan to take the point since we were getting close to where he had seen the bull. After a few more yards we spotted the animal standing broadside in some scrubby trees, and Johan motioned me into shooting position. The bull was about seventy-five yards away.

When I fired, it wheeled and ran away from us. I quickly bolted in another round, but Dr. Botha said I shouldn't bother shooting again since the waterbuck had already gone down. The 150-grain Nosler Partition from my .270 had gone through the near shoulder and both lungs and exited. The waterbuck ran about seventy-five yards before it dropped. It was dead when we got to it.

This was a fine waterbuck bull with horns 31 inches long, which appeared good enough to make both the Rowland Ward and Safari Club International record books. The farm we were hunting on was in the Transvaal, where many of the top waterbuck listed in Safari Club's record book have been taken.

The waterbuck was the last animal I had contracted to shoot on my South African safari. Once it was loaded into Johan's Land Cruiser, we headed for Johan's ranch outside of Alldays near the Limpopo River. We had a day or two before leaving for the taxidermist and our three-day tour of Kruger National Park.

NELS AND ANKE'S KUDU BUFFET

Johan's parents, Nels and Anke, lived on a large game ranch, which they had developed. Nels was a retired engineer who had worked several years for Kruger National Park. His game stock on his ranch was relatively young, so we had not planned to take any trophies while there. My stay at the ranch was one of the most memorable experiences of my entire trip.

Like many game ranches, Nels's place was surrounded by a high wire "game fence" to keep his valuable stock from escaping. While a four-foot-high wire or wood fence will generally contain livestock, many species of African antelope regard such obstacles as little more than a minor inconvenience. Even the gigantic eland is commonly believed to be capable of clearing an eight- to ten-foot-high fence from a standing start with ease.

In addition to the perimeter fence, the main house and shop were also enclosed by an eight- to ten-foot-high fence with barbed wire at the top to further discourage entry. This second fence was supposed to keep the numerous animals out—including leopard, which were plentiful—and to discourage attacks by bandits or revolutionaries. The family kept in regular contact with a network of neighbors and self-defense organizations through scheduled two-way-radio check-ins. These defensive measures had been in place for years and did not appear to be associated with a sense of imminent danger. The region is more peaceful today, now that black-majority rule is in place.

Because seasons are reversed in the Southern Hemisphere, it was winter in South Africa though the calendar said August. In winter there is less moisture, so water can be a problem for game animals, and the grass and shrubs on which they prefer to feed are scarce or nonexistent.

For this reason Nels had developed a feeding schedule for the lean winter months for some of the more valuable animals like greater kudu. This consisted of feeding the animals alfalfa, fruit, or something else suitable by scattering it on his driveway just in front of the gate into the home compound. The quantities he put out weren't enough to sustain the animals, but represented something more like a snack. To one side of the gate he had constructed a small, covered observation area consisting of a chair and a small tarp over a frame to conceal the occupant from kudu on the other side of the fence. From this hide I was able to obtain photographs of a herd of mature kudu bulls at close range, truly a rare occurrence. I also joined Nels and Johan along with their rambunctious Alsatian, what we call a German shepherd in the United States, in lounge chairs on their lawn to watch the kudu feed.

First the polished ivory tips of spiraling horns would appear on the far side of some wooden corrals just outside the fence. Then kudu bulls would jump over the corral rails, one after the other, like Olympic hurdlers, heading for the food. The bulls cleared these rails, which I'd guess were five to six feet high, with remarkable ease. After one had fed awhile, other horn tips would appear and one by one several magnificent bulls would join the party until there were a dozen or more. I believe the most I saw at one time was thirteen, all bulls. All were mature bulls except for one youngster who looked to be a two-year-old, with no more than a single spiral in its little horns. It must have been a cheeky youngster to eat in this company, but it seemed to know its place and moved when it was necessary to avoid a confrontation with an elder.

Since there was no particular schedule to follow until we had to leave for Kruger National Park, my time at Johan's home was stress free. Anke provided ample and tasty ranch-style meals, often featuring game. In the evening we'd all sit in their small den and watch television. My first evening there I was introduced to the second genet I met on the trip, this one a real pet. Nels had obtained the animal when it was fairly young, and around him and his family it behaved much like a domestic cat, though somewhat more active and less docile. With me there, it was nervous. In the darkened room it would hide underneath our chairs, afraid to show itself. Still, Nels could catch it easily. I later learned that this nocturnal creature spent its days sleeping in a wire cage covered with a tarp in the fork of the tree in the front yard. It could sleep there and not be bothered by the local birds.

As I fell asleep each night, I could hear the coyote of South Africa, the black-backed jackal, making its strange yodeling call a few yards outside the fence.

During my stay, we made two attempts to add to my collection of African trophies. One animal I wanted was a bushpig. Johan and I made a brief hunt hoping to find one during daylight. On another occasion we went to a neighboring ranch, hoping to see a large impala Johan had spotted earlier. Although both efforts were unsuccessful, we nevertheless had great fun. This was one of the few times I was able to hunt on foot, catch-as-catch-can, on the two safaris I made. I'd like to hunt a lot more that way.

ON THE KOPJE

Of all the treasured experiences of my safari in South Africa, the most memorable occurred when Johan and I went to a neighboring ranch in search of a record-book impala he'd seen there. We were in the northern Transvaal, not far from the Botswana border, just across the Limpopo River. It was late afternoon, and he thought the animal might come out of the bush before it got dark for a drink from a watering trough set out for cattle.

Johan parked the Toyota at the foot of a medium-sized kopje, maybe one hundred feet high, consisting of large boulders with many shrubs and small trees growing among the rocks. He quickly bounded to the top, leaping from rock to rock like a klipspringer. I labored after him, feeling more like an elderly, arthritic sloth. Once on top I could see the watering trough, maybe one hundred fifty yards away on the plain below.

I caught my breath and began to appreciate the sights, sounds, and smells of the evening. The experience I had over the next hour is difficult to describe, and I know that only a few who read this will understand. Language, after all, has its limits.

It was near dusk on a clear, cool evening. The magnificent, impossibly huge orange African sun was sinking toward the horizon. I never could capture the African sunset, in a photo or in words, in a way that would do it justice. Like many of the best things in life, it can only be experienced. I looked at the sun through my binoculars and it engulfed me in its enormity, as though I were being submerged in an immense red sea. In *Star Wars*, when Luke Skywalker is contemplating his future, one sees two moons in the sky. The viewer knows immediately that this is not Earth. Watching the African sunset often gave me that same otherworldly feeling.

Thornbush stretched several miles to the horizon, and the thorn trees, mostly acacias, spread unevenly across the veld, punctuated by kopjes of varying sizes. From where I sat high on the kopje, the terrain looked less like a forest than a scale model of one, giving the scene a surreal quality. The view certainly qualified as what a British colonist might have called MMBA—Miles and Miles of Bloody Africa.

After a few minutes I noticed some birds, perhaps two hundred yards away, that were making an enormous racket. Some were perched in the branches of a tree while others milled around underneath. Shortly thereafter I noticed near the water trough a leafless tree full of much smaller birds. There was a great deal of activity and vocalizing going on among them. Suddenly the birds, twenty to one hundred in each flock, began leaving the tree and heading in our direction. They were red-billed finches, and they began to fly past as we sat on the rocks. Nels had characterized this species as the scourge of the bushveld because they existed in great numbers and ate a large quantity of foliage that was needed by game and cattle. When the birds passed us, they made a *whissssh*, like wind through the leaves of a tree.

I became aware of other birds that were equally noisy. They were guinea fowl, preparing to roost in thorn trees for the night. Every few seconds one of the birds would call, sounding like metal being torn from the side of a barn, or a car being cranked in the distance. It seems impossible that such a noise could come from any living thing, much less a bird. Since the guinea fowl's call is an alarm call, ranchers in South Africa keep guinea fowl as sentries; the birds' alarm simply cannot be ignored or mistaken for anything else. When I asked Johan what the birds were alarmed about, he said, "Us." They had apparently seen our silhouettes on the kopje.

The crevices in the kopje were large enough to hide a leopard, and it was that time of day when leopard began to hunt. The crevices were also a great refuge for snakes like cobra and mamba. Needless to say, I was not entirely comfortable.

But instead of a leopard or snake, a different creature emerged. It sat down a few feet from me and began to survey the area. It was a strange-looking, rodentlike animal the size of a fat gerbil. It had a long, highly mobile snout. Its pink, nearly translucent ears looked much too large for its body, making the animal appear like a caricature of a country rube. With its membranous and pink ears and long twitching nose, it seemed this animal should be called elephant mouse. I later learned it was an elephant shrew.

The whole experience was a feast for my heart and mind. I choked back a sob, but tears began streaming down my face. I couldn't help it. It took all my strength not to sob out loud. I was embarrassed that Johan, seated a few feet away, would hear me crying and think I was a sissy, or something equally ridiculous. But I couldn't stop. I cried as quietly as I could for several minutes before regaining my composure.

At first I was confused by this outburst of tears, identifying it as something akin to sadness. I thought it might be because my African experience was drawing to a close. Certainly there was no sadness for anything that had happened to me in Africa, and I still had three days in Kruger National Park to look forward to. No, it was something else. I had longed to experience Africa. And now I had—at the deepest level.

The glorious African sunset on the bushveld, the awareness of my being perched on a kopje holding my favorite rifle, expecting any moment to see a leopard slipping quietly through the thorn trees below: At that moment, even though I had my rifle, hunting was the furthest thing from my mind. I wouldn't have spoiled the magic with a gunshot for any trophy. I had waited fifty years and had come nearly halfway around the world, but not for horns, hides, or adventure. It was ultimately for THAT experience.

I didn't know if Johan knew at the time what I was experiencing. Later I told him about it. He seemed, in his stoic Afrikaner way, to understand. He told me that he always took his clients to this or a similar spot during their safari, and apparently the experience always was a hit in one way or another. The way he put it was, "I always do this for my clients."

That moment watching the sunset from the kopje overshadowed all the hunting I'd done or anything else I'd seen in Africa.

APPENDIX A   DAILY RATES

COUNTRY	Botswana	Cameroon	CAR	Ethiopia	Mozambique	Namibia	So. Africa	Tanzania	Zambia	Zimbabwe
One of Big Five Only										
Elephant	$1,480 (14)			$1,500 (21)		$1,390 (10)	$1,000	$1,480 (21)		$900 (1)
Rhino						$600 (8)				
Buffalo	$1,100 (10)				$650 (7)	$860 (7)	$800	$600 (7)	$940 (7)	$830 (5)
Lion	$1,200 (18)				$940 (14)	$630 (12)	$800	$1,490 (16)		$900 (15)
Leopard					$940 (14)	$475 (10)	$475	$1,420 (16)		$700 (15)
Plains Game / One of Big Five (Combo Hunt)										
Elephant	$1,630 (12)	$1,670 (12)	$1680 (14)			$1,390 (10)		$1,420 (21)		$1,000 (18)
Rhino						$600 (8)				
Buffalo	$1,100 (10)	$1,670 (12)	$1,680 (14)		$760 (7)	$860 (7)	$600 (7)	$1,020 (7)	$940 (7)	$820 (5)
Lion		$1,670 (12)	$1,290 (21)		$1020 (16)	$630 (12)	$950 (16)	$1,420 (16)	$1,300 (14)	$950 (15)
Leopard	$770 (10)		$1,680 (14)		$1,020 (16)	$475 (10)	$550 (14)	$1,230 (21)	$1,000(10)	$750 (10)
Plains Game Only	$490 (7)	$1,520 (12)	$1,680(14)	$850 (15)	$830 (10)	$390 (5)	$410 (7)	$1,230 (21)	$1,020 (7)	$370 (7)

Numbers in parentheses ( ) are the shortest hunt lengths allowed for that particular species.

COUNTRY	Botswana	Cameroon	CAR	Ethiopia	Mozambique	Namibia	RSA	Tanzania	Zambia	Zimbabwe
blesbok						$500	$360			
bongo		$2,300	$2,100							
buffalo	$1,780	$950	$600	$1,000	$2,200		$6,750	$780	$1,400	$1,900
bushbuck		$167	$350	$350	$640		$570	$370	$440	$480
bushpig		$240	$250		$300		$270	$200	$260	$190
cheetah						$2,340				$2,250
crocodile	$1,930				$1,850			$960	$1,300	$1,550
dik-dik						$1,500		$190		
duiker	$225	$280	$160	$140		$270	$200	$200	$220	$140
common eland	$1,900	$2,000		$180	$1,500	$1,370	$1,680	$1,030	$1,480	$1,080
giant eland		$2,120	$2,000							
elephant	$9,000*	$2,350		$10,000		$9,000	$15,000	$4,780		$9,700
giant forest hog		$280	$900	$500				$440		
hartebeest	$850	$540	$360	$2,000	$920	$520	$800	$440	$760	
hippo		$1,000		$600	$1,300		$925	$900	$1,330	$1,800
impala	$360				$180	$340	$270	$260	$260	$175
klipspringer		$170		$700		$750	$550	$860	$600	$390
kob			$320							
greater kudu	$1,250		$4,500	$1,340	$650	$800	$940	$1,320	$1,260	$880
lesser kudu				$1,500				$1,570		
lechwe	$990						$1,530		$1,475	
leopard	$3,550		$1,900	$2,300	$3,250	$2,000	$3,300	$2,200	$2,460	$2,800
lion	$5,000	$2,250	$1,600	$2,000	$3,750	$6,000	$10,000	$2,230	$3,380	$3,670
common nyala					$1,130		$1,550			$1,780

*Elephant in Botswana range from $9,000 to $24,000, depending on the measurement of the tusks.

COUNTRY	Botswana	Cameroon	CAR	Ethiopia	Mozambique	Namibia	RSA	Tanzania	Zambia	Zimbabwe
mountain nyala				$5,000						
oribi			$160		$450		$800	$160	$240	$230
oryx	$1,200			$1,000		$590	$930	$930	$580	
puku								$240	$580	
reedbuck	$620	$200	$280	$350	$530		$540	$310	$320	$450
rhino							$20,000			
roan		$1,100	$890			$3,500		$960	$3,300	
sable	$3,000				$2,820		$4,500	$1,320	$2,500	$2,350
sitatunga	$2,670	$1,250	$1,150					$1,140	$2,275	
springbok	$350					$380	$330			
steenbok	$160					$280	$200	$170		$180
sassaby	$850						$1,320		$1,280	$720
warthog	$380		$250	$200	$300	$330	$260	$350	$390	$260
waterbuck		$600	$350	$450	$1,260	$1,100	$1,450	$480	$740	$1,600
black wildebeest						$940	$820			
blue wildebeest	$880					$680	$830	$330	$540	$700
Burchell zebra	$840				$880	$650	$830	$630	$850	$800
mountain zebra*						$750	$700			

*This animal may require special import or site permits.

APPENDIX C   BALLISTIC RULES OF THUMB

CALIBER	BULLET	MV (fps)	100 yards	200 yards	300 yards
.243 Win.	100	3,300	+1.1	0	-6.0
.257 Rob.	100	3,100	+1.4	0	-7.0
.257 Rob.	120	2,900	+1.7	0	-8.0
.25-06 Rem.	100	3,500	+0.9	0	-5.0
.25-06 Rem.	120	3,100	+1.4	0	-6.0
.270 Win.	130	3,100	+1.4	0	-6.0
.270 Win.	150	2,900	+1.6	0	-7.0
7x57mm	140	2,800	+1.8	0	-8.0
7x57mm	175	2,500	+2.5	0	-10.0
7mm Rem. Mag	140	3,300	+1.1	0	-5.0
7mm Rem. Mag	175	3,000	+1.5	0	-6.0
.308 Win.	150	3,000	+1.5	0	-7.0
.308 Win.	200	2,500	+2.5	0	-10.0
.30-06	150	3,000	+1.5	0	-7.0
.30-06	200	2,700	+2.0	0	-9.0
.300 Win. Mag	150	3,400	+1.0	0	-5.0
.300 Win. Mag	200	3,000	+1.5	0	-7.0
.338-06	210	2,700	+2.1	0	-9.0
.338-06	250	2,400	+2.8	0	-11.0
.338 Win. Mag	210	3,000	+1.5	0	-7.0
.338 Win. Mag	250	2,800	+1.8	0	-8.0

APPENDIX C BALLISTIC RULES OF THUMB

I constructed the table on page 280 in the following manner. I used data from Nosler's *Reloading Manual Number 3*. I selected a few popular calibers I know are commonly used for African plains game. Then I selected the lightest bullet I believe has usually been recommended for animals the size of deer in each caliber, and also the heaviest spitzer shown in that catalog for a given caliber. I used the maximum velocity given for the bullets chosen, generally rounding the number off to the nearest 100 fps. I rounded off the drop figures to the nearest inch. I made no correction for barrel length, just using the data as given.

Using the excellent and easy-to-use ballistic tables provided by Nosler, I extracted the trajectory at 100, 200, and 300 yards, always using data for a 200-yard zero.

After years of staring at ballistic tables, I noticed that certain consistencies emerge from one caliber to another, which can be useful in the field. I used to write trajectory information on a three-by-five card, which I taped to my gunstock.

My .270, for instance, sighted in for about 275 yards, as recommended by Jack O'Connor, then hit around 3 inches high at 100 yards and about 4 inches high at 200 yards. At 300 yards it was supposed to hit around 3 inches low. The numbers I needed to remember were +3 inches, +4 inches, and −3 inches.

I tend to use heavy-for-caliber bullets, and I am particularly fond of medium bores like the .338-06 and .35 Whelen. I also like spitzer bullets and rarely use anything else. I discovered that many cartridges that fit that general description, if zeroed at 200 yards, hit about 2 inches high at 100 yards and about 9 inches low at 300. I call this "the 209 rule."

This rule of thumb is not a perfect predictor, but if you allow a little fudge room and think of the rule as "209 (+ or −

1)," it's a lot better. A glance at the table will show that virtually all of these cartridges, which span nearly the entire range typically used on African plains game, hit between 1 and 2 inches high at 100 when zeroed at 200 yards. I think it is possible in nearly any big-game hunting situation to ignore the small departure from these figures. This is not likely to present much of a sighting problem for a shooter after big game, even if it's the size of a tall toy poodle, at ranges somewhat greater than 200 yards. The bigger problem is likely to be at 300 yards when trying to remember how much hold-over may be required. Using the 209 rule, you only have to remember the 300-yard drop, or just one number. On those rare occasions when you need to thread the needle and slip a bullet through some intervening brush, you may have to recall that your sighting will put you up to 2 inches high at 100 yards. I find this easier to remember, and to use in the field, than a + 3 inches at a 100-yard sighting.

From the data in the table it looks like the rule of 209 might actually be better stated as two rules. The fastest of the loads shown, when using the lightest bullets, usually hit closer to 1 inch high at 100 yards than 2 inches. This group also typically strikes about 6 inches low at 300 yards when zeroed at 200 yards. This might be stated as "the rule of 106."

Whichever category your rifle falls into, I think it is a useful simplification to think of it as a "106" caliber or "209" caliber. Using these rules of thumb, you won't be off more than an inch in deciding where to hold on any shot up to 300 yards. Without having to worry about trajectory problems, you can spend your time learning to estimate range, which is the hardest part and biggest source of error anyway.

APPENDIX D FACTORY AMMUNITION

FEDERAL

CALIBER	BULLET	WEIGHT
.22-250	TBB	55
.220 Swift	TBB	55
6mm Rem.	Nosler Partition	100
.257 Rbts.	Nosler Partition	120
.25-06	Nosler Partition	115
.25-06	TBB	115
.257 Wby.	Nosler Partition	115
.257 Wby.	TBB	115
6.5x55mm	TBB	140
.270 Win.	Nosler Partition	150
.270 Win.	TBB	140
.270 Win.	TBB	130
.270 Wby.	Nosler Partition	130
.270 Wby.	TBB	140
7x57mm	Nosler Partition	140
7mm-08	Nosler Partition	140
7x64mm Bren.	Nosler Partition	160
280 Rem.	Nosler Partition	150
280 Rem.	TBB	140
7mm Rem. Mag	Nosler Partition	160
7mm Rem. Mag	Nosler Partition	140
7mm Rem. Mag	TBB	175
7mm Rem. Mag	TBB	160
7mm Rem. Mag	TBB	140
7mm Wby.	Nosler Partition	160
7mm Wby.	TBB	160
7mm STW	TBB	150
.30-30	Nosler Partition	170
.308 Win.	Nosler Partition	180
.308 Win.	Woodleigh	180
.308 Win.	TBB	165
.30-06	Nosler Partition	180
.30-06	Woodleigh	180
.30-06	TBB	165
.30-06	TBB	180

CALIBER	BULLET	WEIGHT
.300 H&H	Nosler Partition	180
.300 Win. Mag	TBB	150
.300 Win. Mag	Nosler Partition	180
.300 Win. Mag	Nosler Partition	200
.300 Win. Mag	TBB	180
.300 Win. Mag	Woodleigh	180
.300 Win. Mag	TBB	200
.300 Wby.	Nosler Partition	180
.300 Wby.	TBB	180
.300 Wby.	TBB	200
.303 British	TBB	180
.338 Win. Mag	Nosler Partition	210
.338 Win. Mag	Nosler Partition	250
.338 Win. Mag	TBB	225
.338 Win. Mag	Woodleigh	250
.340 Wby.	TBB	225
.35 Whelen	TBB	225
.375 H&H	Nosler Partition	300
.375 H&H	TBB	300
.375 H&H	TBB	*300
.416 Rem. Mag	TBB	400
.416 Rigby	Woodleigh	410
.416 Rigby	TBB	400
.416 Rigby	TBB	*400
.458 Win. Mag	TBB	400
.458 Win. Mag	TBB	500
.458 Win. Mag	TBB	*500
.470 Nitro Exp.	Woodleigh	500
.470 Nitro Exp.	Woodleigh	*500
.470 Nitro Exp.	TBB	500
.470 Nitro Exp.	TBB	*500

Data from Federal 1998 catalog.

* solid bullet

WEATHERBY

CALIBER	BULLET	WEIGHT
.240 Wby.	Barnes X	90
.240 Wby.	Nosler Partition	100
.257 Wby.	Barnes X	115
.257 Wby.	Nosler Partition	120
.270 Wby.	Nosler Partition	130
.270 Wby.	Barnes X	140
.270 Wby.	Nosler Partition	150
7mm Wby.	Nosler Partition	140
7mm Wby.	Barnes X	150
7mm Wby.	Nosler Partition	160
.300 Wby.	Nosler Partition	150
.300 Wby.	Barnes X	180
.300 Wby.	Nosler Partition	180
.300 Wby.	Nosler Partition	200
.340 Wby.	Nosler Partition	210
.340 Wby.	Barnes X	225
.340 Wby.	Nosler Partition	250
.30-378 Wby.	Barnes X	180
.30-378 Wby.	Nosler Partition	200
.338-378 Wby.	Barnes X	225
.338-378 Wby.	Nosler Partition	250
.378 Wby.	Barnes X	270
.416 Wby.	Barnes X	350
.416 Wby.	Swift A	400
.416 Wby.	A-Square	400
.460 Wby.	Barnes X	450

Bullets shown are the Barnes X, Swift A-Frame Softpoint, A-Square Monolithic Solid, and Nosler Partition.

Data from the 1998 Weatherby catalog.

REMINGTON

CALIBER	BULLET	WEIGHT
.270 Win.	Swift	140
7mm STW	Swift	140
7mm Rem. Mag	Swift	160
.30-06	Swift	180
.300 Win. Mag	Swift	200
.300 Wby.	Swift	200
8mm Rem. Mag	Swift	200
.338 Win. Mag	Swift	225
.375 H&H	Swift	300
.458 Win. Mag	Swift	450

Bullets shown are Swift A-Frame pointed softpoints.

WINCHESTER

CALIBER	BULLET	WEIGHT
.270 Win.	FS	140
.270 Win.	PG	130
.280 Rem.	FS	140
7mm Rem. Mag	FS	160
7mm Rem. Mag	FS	140
7mm Rem. Mag	PG	160
7mm STW	FS	140
7mm-08	FS	140
.308 Win.	FS	150
.308 Win.	PG	150
.30-06	FS	150
.30-06	FS	165
.30-06	FS	180
.30-06	PG	150
.30-06	PG	180
.300 H&H	FS	180
.300 Win. Mag	FS	150

APPENDIX D   FACTORY AMMUNITION

CALIBER	BULLET	WEIGHT
.300 Win. Mag	FS	165
.300 Win. Mag	FS	180
.300 Win. Mag	PG	180
.338 Win. Mag	FS	230
.338 Win. Mag	PG	250
.375 H&H	FS	270
.375 H&H	FS	300
.45-70	PG	300

Bullets shown are Fail Safe or Partition Gold.
Data from Winchester's Web site.

PMC

CALIBER	BULLET	WEIGHT
.270 Win.	X	130
7mm Rem. Mag	X	140
7mm Rem. Mag	X	160
.308 Win.	X	150
.308 Win.	X	165
.30-06	X	150
.30-06	X	165
.30-06	X	180
.300 Win. Mag	X	150
.300 Win. Mag	X	180
.338 Win. Mag	X	225
.375 H&H	X	270
.375 H&H	X	300

Bullets shown are Barnes X.
Data from PMC Web site.

APPENDIX E EQUIPMENT CHECKLIST

Clothing

Shorts, 2

Long pants, 2

T-shirts, 2

Short-sleeve shirt

Long-sleeve shirt

Belts or suspenders, 2

Heavy jacket

Caps, 2

Cap, knit
  (watch cap or similar)

Light jacket or sweatshirt

Socks, athletic, 4 pairs

Boots or running shoes,
2 pairs

Underwear, 4 pairs

Leather gloves,
  (close-fitting, medium weight)

Hunting Gear

Binoculars
  (compact, rubber coated)

Gun-cleaning kit
  (with jointed rod)

Screwdrivers, fitting gun,
  and scope screws

Spare rifle parts

Spare scope, Scope caps

Light case for each rifle or
shotgun

Broken-shell extractor

Personal Gear

Shaving kit

Medications
  *(such as antidiarrheal, antacids,
  a strong antibiotic, burn lotion,
  and a general pain medicine
  such as ibuprofen)*

Insect repellent

Sunscreen

Cameras
  *(polaroid, 35mm w/telephoto
  lens; 35mm point-and-shoot)*

Film *(40 or more polaroid;
  10–20 rolls, color negative film)*

Bird reference book

Mammal reference book

Small flashlight with extra
batteries

Sunglasses

Writing journal

Microcassette tape recorder
and tapes, batteries

Documents

Passport

Visas *(if required)*

Prescriptions for medications

Custom form listing firearms
and equipment

Documentation of required
shots *(e.g., yellow fever)*

Proof you're booked to hunt with
a safari company *(e.g., a letter)*

Botswana

There are several game parks in Botswana. Among the best known are Chobe National Park and Moremi Game Reserve in the north, and the Kalahari Gemsbok National Park in the southwest that extends into South Africa. There are one or more parks close to most popular hunting areas, so arranging a trip to a park before or after your hunt should be easy.

The northern part of the country is one of the most popular hunting areas, so the parks in that area would be most convenient for a nonshooting tour. This area is also close to Victoria Falls and several game preserves in northwestern Zimbabwe, such as Hwange National Park, so it is possible to visit several areas in both countries with minimal travel. Perhaps the main attraction in the northern game-viewing areas is elephant, but good numbers of lion and plains game are also represented. Northern Botswana also provides one of the few opportunities for safari riding on an African elephant.

Much of the southern part of the country consists of the Kalahari Desert. One of the world's largest game preserves, the Central Kalahari Game Reserve, is located in the center of Botswana. This huge preserve covers 20,000 square miles, or roughly four times the size of the Serengeti National Park in Tanzania. The park is home to all of the desert-adapted animals of the region, including gemsbok, springbok, red hartebeest, eland, wildebeest, cheetah, and lion.

Cameroon

There are a number of parks and reserves in the Cameroon. In the north there is Waza National Park, which is 378,400 acres.

It contains plains game, elephant, lion, leopard, and cheetah. There are three parks in the southern savanna country—Bubanjida, Benou, and Faro. These parks all contain giant eland, elephant, buffalo, leopard and some black rhino. The extreme south of Cameroon is dense rain forest. There are two areas there where animals are protected, namely Dja and Lac Lobec, both of which contain forest buffalo, elephant, leopard, bongo, sitatunga, and duiker as well as gorillas and chimpanzees. For the energetic, it is possible to climb Mount Cameroon, which at over 13,000 feet is the tallest mountain in West Africa.

Central African Republic (CAR)

The Dzanga-Sangha National Park, called by one source a "primeval rain forest," is located in southwestern CAR. The condition of the park has deteriorated due to neglect and travel, much of it a result of civil war. Other parks are Bamingui-Bangoran National Park in the northern-central part of CAR, and St. Floris National Park in northern CAR.

Ethiopia

Ethiopia has fourteen major national parks and wildlife reserves. The two mainly devoted to wildlife viewing are Mago and Omo National Parks, which are in the southern part of the country near a popular plains-game hunting area. Other parks of interest are the Rift Valley Lakes National Park and the Stephanie Wildlife Reserve, both located in southwestern Ethiopia.

APPENDIX F PARKS AND PRESERVES

Mozambique

Mozambique has several national parks. Maputo Elephant Park is south of the capital city, Maputo, at the extreme southern end of the country. Other notable parks are the Marromeu National Park, located at the mouth of the Zambezi River, and the Gorongosa National Park in central Mozambique. Information about these and other parks in the country is relatively hard to obtain, perhaps because of continuing concerns about tourist safety.

Namibia

Namibia is home to one of the largest wildlife reserves in Africa, and one of the most famous in the world, Etosha National Park, located in the northern part of the country. This park covers over 8,500 square miles and is known for its large elephant population and abundant plains game. National Geographic Society made a superb documentary called *African Wildlife* that featured this park. Another notable park is the Kalahari Gemsbok National Park, located in southeast Namibia.

Farther to the northwest, on the Atlantic Ocean, is the Kaokoveld, home to a herd of desert-adapted elephants. This is a curious environment in which to find such water-loving animals. The area is part of the Namib Desert, a western coastal region that is arid because of the cold Atlantic Ocean currents, which sharply decrease rainfall to the area. It is described as "a world of sand, gravel, plains, and dust" in Bossman and Hall-Martin's *Elephants of Africa*. Besides elephant, the Namib Desert is also home to the gemsbok and springbok.

The Caprivi Strip, a finger of land extending from the extreme northeast of the country along its borders with Angola, Zambia, and Botswana, stands in stark contrast to the rest of

Namibia, which is mostly desert or dry savanna and bushland. The uniqueness of the Caprivi Strip is caused by rivers flowing into the region from neighboring Angola. The great Zambezi River forms a large part of its border with Zambia, resulting in a much wetter environment and the existence of species typical of the lush areas of Zambia and Botswana. In the Caprivi one finds elephant, hippo, buffalo, waterbuck, bushbuck, and sitatunga.

South Africa

South Africa contains some of the finest, and the oldest, national parks and game preserves in Africa. One source lists no fewer than nineteen. The most famous is Kruger National Park.

Johan, my PH on my South African safari, and I visited Kruger National Park at the conclusion of the safari. The park is located in the extreme northeast corner of South Africa and was established by an act of Parliament in 1926. It is the largest of South Africa's parks, covering over 7,500 square miles, making it approximately the size of Massachusetts and slightly larger than the country Israel.

From Johannesburg, you can make the trip to Kruger either by rented car (which is a five-hour drive) or fly there for a round-trip cost of $128. You could also take a bus for about $60 round trip. Johan drove me to Kruger, and we used his vehicle for transportation in the park. Johan and I spent two nights and two and a half days at Kruger, with cost, including gas for Johan's vehicle, lodging, and meals, being about $160 per day. Adult admission is $4. Campsites are $8 per couple per night. Huts are $16-a-night, and the more roomy thatched bungalows are $65. For more information, contact the South African Tourism Board. The phone number is 800-782-9772; fax is 310-641-5812.

APPENDIX F PARKS AND PRESERVES

Kruger has numerous rest areas that are clean and accommodating. Of the rest areas I visited, I found Olifants the most interesting because of its remarkable display. The skull and tusks of six large bulls, known as the Magnificent Seven, that lived and died in the park over the last half century can be seen there. The Magnificent Seven have become world famous because of the number of international visitors to the park and the public's interest in elephants. Since most elephants in the park have been able to live full and natural lives, scientists who have studied them have been able to learn much about the life span and behavior of elephants.

The animals Johan and I saw at Kruger were elephant (my favorite), lion, Cape buffalo, and most of the common antelope, including roan. We were not fortunate enough to see sable or rhino.

In the eastern portion of South Africa are Mkuzi and Hluhluwe Game Preserves, where both black and white rhino can be observed. Also in eastern South Africa are St. Lucia Game Preserve and Umfolozi Game Reserve, both of which are said to be the oldest officially proclaimed wildlife sanctuaries on the African continent. Near the southern tip of South Africa are Bontebok, Karoo, and Mountain Zebra National Parks.

Tanzania

Tanzania has approximately twenty national parks and preserves, including one of the highest percentages of land dedicated to the preservation of wildlife of any country in the world. It also has the highest mountain in Africa (Kilimanjaro) and the largest lake (Victoria).

Some of the world's best known wildlife preserves are located in Tanzania. The Serengeti National Park, possibly the best known of Africa's game preserves, is located in the northwestern part of the country near Lake Victoria. Serengeti National Park extends into Kenya, where it is known as the Masai Mara National Reserve. The Ngorongoro Crater, contiguous to the Serengeti, is a unique game preserve set in the caldera of a volcano. There are several other historically important and scenic parks or preserves in northern Tanzania, such as the Selous Game Reserve, named for the famous hunter and author. It is located in the southeastern part of the country and is the largest of its type in Africa. The Selous is available for both hunting and photography safaris.

Zambia

Nearly one-third of Zambia is set aside as game preserves. There are nineteen national parks and thirty-four game-management areas in the country. The three primary areas for game viewing are North and South Luangwa National Parks, Kafue National Park, and Lower Zambezi National Park.

The South Luangwa National Park, named for the river that flows through it, is located in eastern Zambia. The park would be convenient for hunters to visit since it is near popular hunting areas.

Located in the southwestern part of the country, Kafue National Park is home to the Kafue lechwe, unique to the area. Zambezi National Park is located across the Zambezi River from Mana Pools National Park in Zimbabwe. Canoe trips are available on the Zambezi River.

APPENDIX F PARKS AND PRESERVES

Zimbabwe

Zimbabwe has several parks and preserves and also has world-famous Victoria Falls, near the borders with Zambia and Botswana in the western corner of the country.

Other parks particularly good for game viewing, all located in the north near the border with Zambia, are Hwange National Park (near Victoria Falls) and Mana Pools and Matusadona National Parks. Mana and Matusadona parks are in the valley of the great Zambezi River and offer many opportunities for game viewing, including "walking safaris" and canoe trips. In these areas it is possible to camp out with the game. Hwange, Zimbabwe's largest national park, is particularly well known for its elephants and sable antelope and about the size of Connecticut, covering over 5,500 square miles. Matusadona National Park, near the southern shore of Lake Kariba, covers over 500 square miles. It features many of the area's most sought-after game animals, including elephant, rhino, leopard, sable, lion, buffalo, kudu, roan, and waterbuck. Mana Pools National Park, also in the Zambezi Valley, is known for its large herds of elephant and buffalo. Canoe trips to view game along the river are available, providing a unique glimpse at the game. Parts of the park are designated wilderness and only travel on foot or by canoe is allowed. All of these northern parks are near hunting areas.

Great Zimbabwe and Gonarezhou National Parks are two of the attractions in the southern part of the country. Great Zimbabwe is the site of ruins of an ancient civilization. Gonarezhou is relatively unknown and has not been visited by tourists until recently. It is located in the lowveld on the border with Mozambique. It is the second largest park in Zimbabwe and covers nearly 2,000 square miles. Gonarezhou is noted for its elephant, lion, buffalo, and various plains-game species, including common nyala.

Safari Companies and Agents

There are hundreds of PHs in southern Africa and dozens of safari companies and booking agents. Below is a small sample of companies and agents offering a variety of hunts in countries in southern Africa. Since I have used the services of only one company (Safaris Africa), I am not in a position to make recommendations regarding the other companies and agents. I do recommend, however, that you obtain and contact references and check independent sources like Safari Club International and the *Hunting Report.*

I have also included a list of the members of the American Association of International Professional Hunting and Fishing Consultants (AAPHFC). To become a member of this organization, a company needs to show that their employees meet a certain level of experience (a minimum of five full-time years), outdoor knowledge, and education.

African Hunters' Network

(Bruce Nethersole Safaris, Ltd.)
Phone (Zimbabwe): 263-13-3396
Fax: 263-13-3397
E-mail:
  john@huntingsafaris.com, or
  bruce@huntingsafaris.com
Web site:
  www.huntingsafaris.com

Tony da Costa's Safari
  Headquarters
PO Box 416
Hendersonville, NC 28793-0416
Phone: 828-692-4859
E-mail:
  safarihq@worldnet.att.net
Web site:www.tonydacosta.com

Premier Safaris
PO Box 651
Apopka, FL 32704
Phone: 407-889-9778
Fax: 407-889-3119

Safari Marketers
Phone and fax: 2711-462-6960
E-mail: smsafari@iafrica.com
Web site:
  www.safarimarketers.co.za

APPENDIX G USEFUL CONTACTS

Safari Outfitters
410 West Yellowstone Ave.
Copy, WY 82414
Phone: 307-587-5596
Fax: 307-587-2265
E-mail:
  hunt@safari1.com

Safaris Africa (Len Pivar)
165 Thornbury Lane
Powell, OH 43065
Phone: 614-848-8449
Fax: 614-848-8509

AAPHFC Members:

Ameri-Cana Expeditions
(Pat Frederick)
4707 106-A Ave.
Edmonton, Alberta
Canada T6A TJ3
Phone: 308-254-3658
Fax: 308-254-3658
E-mail:
  americana@sport4u.com
Web pages:
  www.ameri-cana.com

Cabela's
One Cabela Drive
Sidney, NE 69160
Phone: 800-237-4444
Fax: 308-254-3658
Web site:
  www.cabelas.com

Fair Chase LTD
(Col. Bill Williamson)
PO Box 27679
Austin, TX 78755
Phone: 512-345-4891
Fax: 512-343-8215
E-mail:
  billww@fairchaseltd.com
Web site:
  www.fairchaseltd.com

Fred Mau's Outdoor
  Adventures (Fred Mau)
PO Box 2846
Cheyenne, WY 82003
Phone: 800-470-5511
Fax: 307-778-7173
E-mail: fmoa@fmoa.com
Web site: www.fmoa.com

Grand Adventures
  International (Bruce Grant)
9815 Twenty-fifth St. E.
Parrish, FL 34219
Phone: 941-776-3029
Fax: 941-776-1092

Jack Atcheson and Sons (Jack
  Jr. and Keith Anderson)
3210 Ottawa St.
Butte, MT 59701
Phone: 406-782-2382
Fax: 406-723-3318
E-mail: atcheson@in-tch.com
Web site: www.atcheson.com

APPENDIX G USEFUL CONTACTS

Jim McCarthy Adventures
  and Safaris (Jim McCarthy)
4906 Creek Drive
Harrisburg, PA 17112
Phone: 717-652-4374
Fax: 717-652-5888
E-mail:
  jmccarthy@epix.net
Web site:
  www.mccarthyadventures.com

J/B Adventures and Safaris
(Beverly Wunderlich)
2275 E. Arapahoe Rd.,
Suite 109
Littleton, CO 80122
Phone: (303) 794-4485
Fax: (303) 794-4486
E-mail: beverly@jbsafari.com
Web site: www.jbsafaris.com

Mitchell's Adventures
(Darrel Mitchell)
170 Quarry Rd.
W. Springfield, MA 01089
Phone: 413-737-7026
Fax: 413-737-5276

Outdoor Destinations
(formerly Outdoor Adventures)
(Dan Turner)
PO Box 202
Linn, TX 78563
Phone: 800-375-4868
Fax: 956-380-3723
E-mail: info@oaww.com
Web site:
  www.oaww.com

Sporting International Inc.
(Tommy Morrison)
15608 South Brentwood
Channelview, TX 77530-4018
Phone: 281-452-6223
Fax: 281-457-5412
E-mail:
  sport@sportinternational.com

World Trek Travel Inc.
(Georgia Walker)
7170 Turkey Creek Ranch
Pueblo, CO 81007
Phone: 719-547-9777

For more information on the
AAIPHFC, contact Beverly
Wunderlich, 2275 E. Arapahoe
Rd., Suite 109, Littleton, CO
80122. Phone: 303-794-4485.

Health

Centers for Disease Control
  and Prevention (CDCP):
"Travelers' International
  Health Advisory"
Phone: 888-232-3228
Web site on travel:
  www.cdc.gov/travel
Web site on immunizations:
  www.cdc.gov/travel/yellowbk

General information on foreign
  travel, U.S. State Department.
Web site:
  www.travel.state.gov

APPENDIX G   USEFUL CONTACTS

Airlines

British Airways
Phone: 800-247-9297
Web site:
   www.british-airways.com

Lufthansa
Phone: 800-645-3880
Web site:
   www.lufthansa-usa.com

South African Airways
Phone: 800-722-9675
Web site: www.saa.co.za

Virgin Atlantic Airways
Phone: 800-862-8621
Web site:
   www.flyvirgin.com

Alitalia
Phone: 800-223-5730
Web site: www.alitalia.com

KLM
Phone: 800-225-2525
Web site:
   www.nederland.klm.com

Equipment Sources

Brownells Inc.
200 So. Front Street,
Montezuma, IA 50171
Phone: 515-623-5401
Web site:
   www.brownells.com

A source for all kinds of gun-
   related equipment, primarily
   for gunsmiths and hobbyists.

Hunting Report
E-mail: mail@huntingreport.com
Web site: www.huntingreport.com
A good source on current
   conditions in safari-
   destination countries as well
   as reports by subscribers on
   hunts with specific safari
   companies and PHs.

Hunting Information Systems
Rt. 2, Box 248A
Huntington TX 75949
Phone: 409-422-4102
Web site:
   www2.huntinginfo.com
E-mail: info@huntinfo.com
The web site of Hunting
   Information Systems has
   many links to related sites,
   including outfitters, guides,
   and a useful message board
   on African hunting.

Safari Club International (SCI).
An organization for and by hunters.
   They often have information on
   selecting safari companies and
   agents. SCI also keeps records of
   largest game taken.
Web site:
   www.outdoorsource.com/
   safari/index.html

Embassies to Contact for Information on Tourism in Certain African Countries

Embassy of Botswana
1605 New Hampshire Ave. NW
Washington, D. C. 20036
Phone: 202-244-4990
Fax: 202-244-4164

Botswana Division of Tourism
Private Bag 0047
Gaborone, Botswana
Phone: 267-353024

Embassy of Cameroon
2349 Massachusetts Ave. NW
Washington, D. C. 20008
Phone: 202-265-8790
Fax: 202-387-3826

Embassy of the Central
  African Republic
1618 Twenty-second Street
NW
Washington, D.C. 20008
Phone: 202-483-7800
Fax: 202-332-9893

Embassy of Ethiopia
2134 Kalorama Road NW,
Suite 1000
Washington, D.C. 20008
Phone: 202-234-2281
Fax: 202-483-8407
E-mail: e thiopia@tidalwave.net
Web site:
  www.ethiopianembassy.org

Embassy of Mozambique
1990 M Street NW, Suite 570
Washington, D.C. 20036
Phone: 202-293-7146

Embassy of Namibia
1605 New Hampshire Ave. NW
Washington, D.C. 20009
Phone: 202-986-0540

Namibia Ministry of
  Environment and Tourism
Private Bag 13346
Windhoek 9000, Namibia
Phone: 61-284-2330
Web site:
  www.iwwn.com.na/namtour

Embassy of South Africa
3051 Massachusetts Ave. NW
Washington, D.C. 20008
Phone: 202-232-4400
Fax: 202-265-1607
E-mail:
  safrica@southafrica.net
Web site: www.southafrica.net

South African Tourism
(SATOUR)
500 Fifth Avenue, Suite 2040
New York, NY 10110
Phone: 212-730-2929;
  800-822-5368

Embassy of Tanzania
2139 R St. NW
Washington, D.C. 20008
Phone: 202-939-6125
Fax: 202-797-7408

Tanzania Tourist Board
P. O. Box 2485
Dar es Salaam, Tanzania
Phone: 51-111-244
E-mail:
    ttb@tanza.net

Embassy of Zambia
2419 Massachusetts Ave. NW
Washington, D.C. 20008
Phone: 202-265-9717

Zambia National Tourist Board
800 Second Ave.
New York, NY 10017
Phone: 212-972-7200
Fax: 212-972-7360
Web site:
    www.africa-insites.com/zambia

Embassy of Zimbabwe
1608 New Hampshire Ave. NW
Washington, D.C. 20009
Phone: 202-332-7100
Fax: 202-483-9326
Web site:
    www.zimweb.com/
    embassy/zimbabwe

Zimbabwe Tourist Office
1270 Avenue of the Americas,
Suite 2315
New York, NY 10020
Phone: 212-332-1090
E-mail:
    ztony@juno.com

Ammunition and Compounds

Huntingtons
P. O. Box 991
Oroville, CA 95965
Phone: 530-534-1210
Fax: 530-534-1212
E-mail: buy@huntingtons.com
Web site:
    www.huntingtons.com
Carries excellent stock of reloading
    supplies and equipment,
    including Woodleigh bullets.

Midway USA
5875 W. Van Horn Tavern Rd.,
Columbia, MO 65203
Phone: 800-243-3220
Fax: 800-992-8312
Web site: www.midwayusa.com

The Old Western Scrounger
12924 Hwy A-12
Montague, CA 96064
Phone: 530-459-5445
Fax: 530-459-3944
Web site:
    www.snowcrest.net/
    oldwest/index
E-mail:
    oldwest@snowcrest.net
Carries several brands of
    premium bullets, new
    ammunition for obsolete
    American, British, and
    European calibers, and
    current metric calibers.

Swift Bullet Company
P. O. Box 27
Quinter, KS 67752

Trophy Bonded Bullets
P. O. Box 262348
Houston, TX 77207
Phone: 713-645-4499;
800-480-3006
Fax: 713-741-6393
Web site:
    www.huntingmall.com

Barnes
P. O. Box 215
American Fork, UT 84003
Phone:
    888-Barnes-x (888-227-6379)
Fax: 801-756-2465
Web site:
    www.barnesbullets.com

Federal Cartridge Company
Web site:
    www.federalcartridge.com

Nosler Bullet Company
Web site:
    www.nosler.com

PMC Ammunition
Web site:
    www.pmcammo.com

Weatherby Inc.
Web site:
    www.weatherby.com

Winchester (ammunition)
Web site:
    www.winchester.com

APPENDIX H STANDARD HUNT COSTS

COUNTRY	Daily Fees	Trophy Fees	Total Cost*
Botswana #	$ 6,860	$6,035	$12,900
Cameroon ###	$21,280	$4,267	$25,550
CAR**	$23,520	$7,410	$30,930
Ethiopia##	$11,900	$5,960	$17,860
Mozambique****	$11,620	$5,520	$17,140
Namibia***	$ 5,460	$4,850	$10,310
South Africa	$ 5,740	$5,880	$11,620
Tanzania	$17,220	$4,120	$21,340
Zambia	$14,280	$5,200	$19,480
Zimbabwe*****	$ 5,180	$5,580	$10,760

* Total cost is the sum of daily fees for 14 days plus trophy fees for standard game package.

** Substituted averages for wildebeest and zebra.
*** Substituted averages for wildebeest and zebra.
**** Substituted averages for duiker and wildebeest.
***** Substituted sassaby for hartebeest.

Substituted reedbuck for bushbuck, lechwe for waterbuck.
Substituted average fees for wildebeest and zebra.
Substituted roan for greater kudu, bushpig for warthog, averages for wildebeest and zebra.

Questions for Your Agent

1. How long have you been booking hunting safaris in Africa?
2. Have you hunted with the outfitters you book for? Have you visited their facilities?
3. What airlines do you book with?
   A. What are their attitudes toward guns and hunters?
   B. How do they handle stopovers en route (if relevant)?
4. Do you have a brochure describing the hunts you offer that include daily rates, trophy fees, and recommended clothing and equipment? Can I speak with the PH I'll be hunting with before the safari?
5. Do the daily rates and trophy fees include all costs associated with the hunt, such as special licenses, taxes and fees? If not, can you supply me with an itemized list of these additional charges?
6. Are transfers from my arrival point to the hunting camp covered by the daily rate, or are there extra charges for this? What options are available for these transfers, and how much does each cost?
7. Does the outfitter offer lower rates for 2x1 hunts? What are they?
8. What does the outfitter charge for nonhunting observers?
9. Can I take my wife and kids on your hunts? What are the safety issues? Age requirements?
10. How long in advance must I book my hunt?
11. How much of a deposit do you require to confirm my hunt?
12. What is your policy on refunds if I have to cancel? What if the safari company cancels?
13. Can you book a dayroom or hotel room for me to recover from the long flight?
14. Do you handle all travel arrangements to the country where I'll be hunting, including air travel?

15. Are there opportunities for visiting game preserves or other tourist attractions I should consider when I arrange this hunt? Do you handle such arrangements?

16. Can you provide names of people you have booked hunts for as references?

17. Do you book the kind of hunt I'm interested in (for example, budget plains game, short buffalo only, elephant, all of the Big Five)?

18. What are the accommodations like in your hunting camp(s)?

19. About how many hunters have you sent to Africa? How many to the outfitter you are recommending for my hunt?

20. Can you recommend an insurance provider for my guns, health, and trip cancellation?

21. Will someone meet me at my arrival point to help me clear customs and get any necessary permits?

22. Do I need a visa? How do I get one?

23. What immunizations are recommended or required?

24. Does the hunt start the day I arrive? When does it end?

Questions for Your Outfitter

1. Are all of your PHs (are you) licensed for the game I want to hunt?

2. How much experience do the PHs have? The one I will be hunting with?

3. What calibers do you recommend for the game I want? Are there minimum legal calibers for the game I plan to hunt?

4. What brand and type of bullets do you recommend for the game I want?

5. How far will I have to shoot?

6. What kind of hunting vehicles do you use?

7. Please tell me a little about the PH I'll be hunting with, like his background and experience. What is he like personally?

8. Are there opportunities to view and photograph animals in addition to hunting during the safari?

9. Is bird hunting or fishing included in your safaris? Is there an additional cost?

10. Is it possible to rent firearms, such as a shotgun for birds or a heavy rifle for buffalo, or do I have to bring my own? How much does this cost?

11. Is shotgun ammunition available there for my [fill in blank] gauge? What does it cost?

12. What camp staff will be available on my hunt (for example, trackers, skinners, cooks, waiters)?

13. What level of physical effort is required on this hunt? What do I have to be able to do (for example, walk 10 miles every day in 80-degree temperature; climb 2,000 feet each morning)?

14. What will the weather be like? What temperatures are encountered on a typical day in the field?

15. Is there anything I can bring you from home (for example, batteries, bulb for a flashlight)?

16. What are your success rates for the animals I'll be hunting? What trophy quality can I expect?

17. Are alcoholic beverages included in the daily rate (if relevant)? If not and they can be provided, what would this cost?

18. Will I have to travel between hunting camps to get all the game I want? How long will each trip take? How much do these transfers cost? What are the alternatives?

19. How and when do I pay for the balance of my safari? What means of payment will you accept (for example, cash in a particular currency (U.S. dollars, French francs), traveler's checks, cashier's checks)?

20. Can you provide names of people who have hunted with you recently as references?
21. How many other hunters will be using the same camp while I am there?
22. What hunting methods do your PHs use to hunt the game I'm after?
23. Will you be in the U.S. in the near future so I can meet you and discuss booking a hunt with you?
24. What do you charge for field preparation of trophies and preparation for international shipment?
25. How many actual days of hunting will I get on my safari?
26. What would you suggest I give as gratuities for my PH and staff after the hunt?

Questions about Packaged Hunts

1. Is the hunt duration strictly fixed or can I add additional days? What is the cost if I do?
2. If I don't shoot some of the animals included in the package, can I take a different animal or two of another one on the list? That is, do I get "credit" for listed animals I don't shoot?
3. Can I add additional animals of a species not included on this hunt? What would the cost be if they were taken during the time specified for the hunt?

APPENDIX J   FURTHER READING

Further Reading Before Your (First) Safari
by Ludo Wurfbain, Publisher, Safari Press

This section is divided into three sections. It advises on the best books to purchase regarding safari hunting.

Basic Package Cost: $119.95

Number one on my list is a field guide. A field guide will serve two important purposes: It will help you identify animals from a mongoose to an elephant, and it will give you immediate information about the animal in question. The book I like is *Field Guide to the Larger Mammals of Africa* by Dorst and Dandelot ($30.00, hardcover). It is small and handy, easy to put in your daypack

The next book selection is universally considered the best up-to-date volume on rifles, calibers, and scopes to take to Africa: *Safari Rifles* by Craig Boddington ($37.50 hardcover and $24.95 softcover, available from Safari Press).

The final book in the basic package is *The Perfect Shot* by Kevin "Doctari" Robertson ($65.00 hardcover, available from Safari Press). It shows anatomically correct drawings of the location of the vital parts of all African game animals found below the Zambesi. Invaluable! It also has hunting methods and natural history of game animals.

Intermediate Package Cost: $200.00

For those of you who can afford to spend a bit more, I recommend the following, in addition to those titles listed in the basic package. The first book is *African Hunter* by James Mellon (available from Safari Press). It has been universally hailed as the best book ever on African hunting. Although dated (first published in 1975), it remains the standard reference text for all who go on safari. Many chapters, such as

"The Element of Danger" and "How to Book a Safari," as well as the discussion on African animals, are as valid today as they were when the book was first published. It is a must-have, and the only reason that I do not include it in the economy package is the cost—$75.00 softcover, $125.00 hardcover.

The second book is *Where Lions Roar* by Craig Boddington ($35.00 hardcover, available from Safari Press). Excellent background reading on all countries below the Zambezi plus Zambia, Tanzania, the CAR, and Ethiopia. Up-to-date, full of tips.

The third book I recommend for the intermediate package is *Horn of the Hunter* by Robert Ruark ($35.00 hardcover, $18.95 softcover, available from Safari Press). This book has absolutely NO VALUE as a reference work, but it is the best story ever written on the traditional East African safari during the Golden Age of African hunting. So it deserves a spot on the list.

Finally, a record book showing trophy measurements is a great reference to take on safari. Unfortunately, record books are enormously heavy, so I would suggest copying the pages of the animals you are hunting. I recommend the *Safari Club International Record Book of Trophy Animals,* tenth edition (softcover for $90.00, hardcover $195.00).

Advanced Package Cost: $250.00

In addition to the basic and the intermediate packages, you could add the following to make it a deluxe package. If you want to go deluxe and if you want to possess that one small tidbit of information your PH just possibly might not know, then I recommend the following books. All the books I will discuss below are available from Safari Press.

First, Rowland Ward's *Records of Big Game* (twenty-fifth edition). While this is an expensive book ($150 hardcover), it does list where the world-record elephant (with 200-pound-plus tusks!) was taken. It also lists when the only 70-inch kudu ever recorded was taken and where 40-inch-plus rhinos were shot in the Dark Continent. It contains trophy measurements dating back to the mid-nineteenth century. A must for the advanced safari hunter! The new edition was printed last year and is available now.

Second, I recommend *Encyclopedia of Big Game Animals* by Pierre Fiorenza ($100 hardcover). A good book full of color photos of all the major game animals of Africa. Includes tracks, some natural history, and some Rowland Ward listings. Please note that this book is now almost sold out at Safari Press. As of spring 2000, they had only a few copies left.

Additional Reading

Some of the books listed in this section will help you a great deal on your African safari. Some others are considered classics in the field of African big-game hunting. They are also very enjoyable to read. All books listed below are currently or will soon be available from Safari Press.

Horned Death by John Burger is considered the bible on hunting the African buffalo. Though out-of-date, it contains the best buffalo stories around! It will be reprinted in fall 2000. $35.00 hardcover.

Death in the Long Grass, Death in Silent Places, and *Death in the Dark Continent* by Peter Capstick. Good books on the feel, adventure, and lore of African big-game hunting. Not needed for your safari but tremendously entertaining. $23.95 each for hardcover.

Trophy Hunter in Africa by Elgin Gates. A classic on the golden days of the safari. Not needed on your safari but gives a great idea of what the old East Africa was like. $40.00 hardcover.

Pondoro by John Taylor, the notorious ivory poacher. Tremendously entertaining and well written. Covers African hunting as it was before World War II. $29.95 hardcover.

View these Safari Press titles and others at **www.safaripress.com**

BIBLIOGRAPHY

Aagaard, Finn. *Aagaard's Africa: A Hunter Remembers,* (National Rifle Association, 1991). Recollections of an experienced professional hunter of his days in Kenya.

Barnes, Frank C. Mike Bussard, ed., *Cartridges of the World,* seventh edition (DBI Books, 1993).

Barrett, Peter, ed. *A Treasury of African Hunting* (Winchester Press [publishing date not given]). A unique collection of first-person accounts of hunting in Africa during the late 1950s and '60s by several of America's leading outdoor writers. Includes rarely described hunts for giant eland, bongo, common nyala, and other glamour plains game. Covers central, east, and southern African countries including Angola, Chad, the Sudan, and Mozambique.

Bell, Bob, ed. *Handloader's Digest 1995,* fourteenth edition, (DBI Books, 1994).

Boddington, Craig. *Safari Rifles* (Safari Press, 1990). A review by one of the most experienced American hunters. Includes information from his survey of African professional hunters.

Bosman, Paul, and Anthony Hall-Martin. *Elephants of Africa* (Safari Press, 1989). Though focused on the African elephant, this is also an excellent reference on wildlife parks and preserves all over west and sub-Saharan Africa. It was put together by a professional wildlife artist, whose illustrations are throughout the text.

Brander, Michael. *Hunting and Shooting: From Earliest Times to the Present Day* (G.P. Putnam's Sons, 1971). Provides a chapter on the history of game shooting in Africa and the birth of the safari hunting industry.

Brown, G. Gordon, F.R.G.S., ed. *The South and East African Year Book and Guide for 1937* (Sampson Low, Marston and Co., 1937).

Brown, Leslie. *Africa, A Natural History* (Random House, 1965). An excellent and authoritative reference on the entire continent. Well illustrated with maps and color photos of birds and

BIBLIOGRAPHY

animals. If you want the big picture of Africa's flora and fauna, as well as its geography, this is an excellent place to start.

Burger, John F. *Horned Death: Hunting the African Buffalo* (Safari Press, 1985). Though not as well known as Selous or Bell, Burger traveled and hunted widely in central and southern Africa and claimed to have taken over one thousand Cape buffalo.

Capstick, Peter Hathaway. *Safari: The Last Adventure* (St. Martins Press, 1984). An introduction to safari hunting for experienced hunters. Available from Safari Press.

Cumming, R. Gordon. *A Hunter's Life in South Africa,* vol. 1, African Hunting Reprint series (Books of Zimbabwe, 1980).

Estes, Richard D. *The Safari Companion: A Guide to Watching African Mammals* (Chelsea Green Publishing Company, 1993). A unique guide to the postures and behavior of common African species, for those who would like a richer experience. Written by one of the world's leading authorities on animal behavior in the wild.

Greener, W. W., *The Gun and Its Development,* ninth edition, (Bonanza Books, 1910).

Hibben, Frank C. *Hunting in Africa,* (Hill and Wang, 1962). A brief account of the history of safari hunting and descriptions of many of the animals of southern and eastern Africa.

Hunter, J. A. *Hunter* (Harper and Brothers, 1952). A professional hunter's experiences in the early years of safari hunting in East Africa. Describes killing large numbers of rhino to facilitate expansion of native populations.

Keith, Elmer. *Safari,* (Safari Publications, 1968). A colorful account of his experiences by the preeminent proponent of large calibers and iron-clad African game. Emphasizes dangerous game.

Lee, Richard B., and Irven DeVore, eds. *Man the Hunter* (Aldine Publishing Company, 1968).

Moss, Cynthia. *Portraits in the Wild: Animal Behavior in East Africa,* second edition, (University of Chicago Press, 1982). A review of scientific data gathered in the field, written by

BIBLIOGRAPHY

a well-known expert on field observations of African wildlife. Particularly good on big cats.

Nolting, Mark W. *Africa's Top Wildlife Countries,* fifth edition (Global Travel Publishers, 1997). A good general reference on countries in eastern and southern Africa. Exceptional bibliography on Africa flora and fauna. Emphasizes times, places, and methods for game viewing.

O'Connor, Jack. *The Best of Jack O'Connor* (The Amwell Press, 1977). The section on Africa is particularly good on lion hunting and contains the best description on hunting in Namibia I've seen. Interesting information on prices.

———. *The Hunting Rifle* (Winchester Press, 1970). O'Connor's views provide a defense for fans of the big bores. Chapter 1 talks about selecting your ballistic expert and hunting advisor.

Ortega y Gasset, José. *Meditations on Hunting,* (Charles Scribner's Sons, 1972).

Paynter, David, and Wilf Nussey. *Kruger: Portrait of a National Park* (Southern Book Publishers, 1986). The first comprehensive book about the entire park. Also an excellent reference with spectacular wildlife photography.

Richards, Westley. *Guns and Rifles: A Century of Gun and Rifle Manufacture, 1812–1912* (Armory Publications, 1988).

Robertson, Kevin. *The Perfect Shot* (Safari Press, 1999).

Roosevelt, Theodore. *African Game Trails: An Account of the African Wanderings of an American Hunter-Naturalist,* 2 vols. (Charles Scribner's Sons, 1920). The record of the safari by the former president   and his son in 1909. First published in 1910.

SCI Record Book of Trophy Animals: Africa Field Edition, seventh edition, vol. 1 (Safari Club International, 1990). A record of trophy animals published by Safari Club International (SCI). Shows rankings of trophies of virtually all plains game and Big Five. Contains very good descriptions, shows distribution, and includes photos of each animal. Too large to be a field guide, but a useful reference.

BIBLIOGRAPHY

Selous, Frederick C. *A Hunter's Wanderings in Africa* (Arno Press, 1967). Experiences of one of the greatest of African hunters at the end of the nineteenth century.

Sinclair, Ian. *Field Guide to the Birds of Southern Africa* (The Stephen Greene Press, 1987). An excellent field guide illustrated with photos and distribution maps for over nine hundred species of birds.

Smithers, Reay H. N. *Land Mammals of Southern Africa: A Field Guide* (Macmillan, 1986). Well illustrated, comprehensive, and small enough to take with you.

Steele, David. *Wildlife of South Africa, South Africa* (Central News Agency, 1991). Beautifully illustrated portrait of the primary game areas of South Africa, Namibia, and Botswana, including some of the best-known game refuges and parks like Kruger and Etosha. Some of the finest wildlife and nature still photography I've seen anywhere.

Taylor, John. *African Rifles and Cartridges,* (Safari Press, 1994). The classic work on the subject.

The Best of Wildlife Photography in Southern Africa (Central News Agency, 1990).

Young, Eddie and Nicki. *African Wildlife and Safari Guide,* (Eddie Young Publishers, 1987). The best reference I know on all aspects of hunting in southern Africa.

VIDEOS

There are many fine videos about Africa and African safari hunting available today. For a listing contact:

Outdoor Visions Phone: 800-424-6652
Fax: 972-235-8377
Web site: www.outdoorvisions.com